ENDORSE

George J. Zemek and J. Todd Murray,
*Love Beyond Degree: The Astounding Grace of God in
the Prophecies of Hosea*

"Hosea is a profound book that presents a multi-faceted vision of our sovereign God. Indeed, both God's terrifying wrath against sin and his grace to sinners are displayed in perfect balance. One might initially think these images of God are contradictory, but in reality they are complementary, as George Zemek and Todd Murray demonstrate in this insightful and readable exposition. The authors have done a superb job of distilling Hosea's message in its original context, deriving enduring theological principles from it, and challenging modern readers to come to grips with those principles. Like Hosea, they focus on the depth of our sinfulness, the necessity of divine justice, and the magnitude of God's grace that forgives sin while satisfying the demands of justice."

Robert B. Chisholm, Jr., Chair and Senior Professor of Old Testament Studies, Dallas Theological Seminary

"Readers know they have a good commentary when they find themselves returning to it again and again with profit. *Love Beyond Degree* is such a commentary. Zemek and Murray provide a superb exegetical analysis of Hosea while also presenting a challenge to examine ourselves in the light of God's Word. Expositors must confront present-day idolatry from a solid foundation of studying Hosea's prophecies. This commentary will help prepare for sound, biblically relevant exposition."

William D. Barrick, Th.D., Professor of Old Testament (retired), The Master's Seminary

"I am grateful that my friends, Dr. Zemek and Todd Murray, have undertaken this work on Hosea. This powerful prophet is universally ignored by the evangelical church and yet its message is the very heart of the gospel of redemption. Every believer should grasp the power of redeeming love contained in this inspired text."

John MacArthur, President, The Master's Seminary and University

"A Puritan preacher was once asked why he was so precise in his handling of God's Word, to which he answered—'because I serve a precise God.' Indeed! And such can be said of this volume because of the great care taken by the authors George Zemek and Todd Murray. Dr. Zemek's exacting exposition of the Hebrew text, and Pastor Murray's penetrating applications lay bare the astonishing, relentless love of God for his people. And because this truth is conveyed in the true story of a marital relationship, it has a way of informing the soul of God's infinite love that exceeds the bare statement of that wondrous truth. Readers of *Love Beyond Degree* will have their love for God charged and recharged, as well as their love for Christ and his bride, the church, and a lost world."

R. Kent Hughes, Senior Pastor Emeritus of College Church in Wheaton and John Boyer Professor of Evangelism and Culture at Westminster Theological Seminary, Philadelphia.

"This is a most unique study of the book of Hosea. Based on an understanding of the Hebrew Text, Zemek provides a fine exposition of each chapter with a theological emphasis. Murray then follows each exposition with exhortations for practical application. Thus the work is very helpful for pastors and other Bible teachers. I highly recommend it."

Dr. Kenneth L. Barker, General Editor, *NIV Study Bible*

Love BEYOND Degree

George J. Zemek

J. Todd Murray

KRESS
BIBLICAL
RESOURCES

Kress Biblical Resources
The Woodlands, Texas
www.kressbiblical.com

ISBN: 978-1-934952-27-6

NASB, ESV, HCSB, and NIV are used as indicated, and the author's own translations when not indicated.

CONTENTS

A NOTE TO THE READER

Although the book of Hosea exhibits some quite awkward chapter breaks in our English versions, we will nevertheless follow suit with them. This will unfortunately lead to some losses of contextual transitions which in turn will produce a few abrupt chapter launchings. So, reader, please see the forthcoming outline and then follow our clarifying comments near the end of one chapter into the beginning of another for logical continuity.

DEDICATIONS

George Zemek to:

The faithful graduates, students, and
pastor-professors of The Expositors Seminary.

May our Lord bless and sustain you as you carry out
the apostle Paul's 2 Timothy 2:2 mandate.

✍

Todd Murray to:

My precious children and grandchildren

May you never doubt the twin truths of Scripture:
That you truly are as sinful as God says you are
and that He truly is as gracious as He says He is.

TABLE OF ABBREVIATIONS

BIBLE BOOKS

Gen	Job	Hab	1 Thess
Exod	Ps	Zeph	2 Thess
Lev	Prov	Hag	1 Tim
Num	Eccl	Zech	2 Tim
Deut	S of Songs	Mal	Titus
Josh	Isa	Matt	Philem
Judg	Jer	Mark	Heb
Ruth	Lam	Luke	James
1 Sam	Ezek	John	1 Peter
2 Sam	Dan	Acts	2 Peter
1 Kgs	Hos	Rom	1 John
2 Kgs	Joel	1 Cor	2 John
1 Chron	Amos	2 Cor	3 John
2 Chron	Obad	Gal	Jude
Ezra	Jon	Eph	Rev
Neh	Mic	Phil	
Esth	Nah	Col	

ENGLISH VERSIONS

ESV	English Standard Version
HCSB	Holman Christian Standard Bible
LXX	Septuagint (ancient Greek translation of the OT)
NASB	New American Standard Bible
NIV	New International Version

OTHER ABBREVIATIONS

ANE	ancient Near East/ancient Near Eastern
MT	Masoretic Text (Hebrew Bible)
NT	New Testament
OT	Old Testament

Preface To The Exposition Sections

People often, wishing to balance or to buffer the communication of difficult announcements, approach their audience with such words as these: "I have good news and bad news; which do you want to hear first?" God, being perfectly balanced in His Being (e.g., in reference to His justice and His mercy), similarly approaches sinners. But He gives them no choice regarding the content of His communications or the order of them. By grace, He reveals to them exactly what they need to hear, not what they want to hear.

This may seem like He employs a one-size-fits-all communications approach. Well, essentially it is. Through the epochs of salvation history the "eternal gospel" (i.e., playing off the angel's proclamation in Rev 14:6) is uniform in its basics. And its most fundamental basics are the realities of sin, total depravity, and inability on the one hand and the sovereign grace of God on the other.

Whenever the magnificent God of the Bible challenges sinners to repent, He begins by emphasizing the condemnable condition of sinful humankind prior to His merciful publishing of an offer of a pardon (cf. Rom 1:18-3:20 to Rom 3:21ff.; Eph 2:1-3 to Eph 2:4ff.; Titus 3:3 to Titus 3:4ff.; *et al.*). This phenomenon pervades biblical revelation from cover to cover. And it comes forth exceedingly clearly in the Old Testament book of Hosea. This story transcends the prophet Hosea's persistent love for his wife of harlotry. Sublimely it is a Gospel story of God's perfect love for His professing people who all too often were spiritual prostitutes.

Consequently, this work will attempt to uncover, through an essentially theological exposition, the richness of this bad news/good news story of sin and salvation, of apostasy and threatened judgment, of the call to repentance and forgiveness. By the way, like the overall development of Ecclesiastes (cf. chs. 1-12:12 with 12:13-14), Hosea does not fully crescendo to the inexplicable grace of God until chapters 11:8ff. and 14:4ff.

George J. Zemek

PREFACE TO THE EXHORTATION SECTIONS

While it is always a joy to study Scripture, it is a particular joy and privilege to explore one of the Bible's lesser-known books like Hosea. To our detriment, few believers are familiar with the Minor Prophets. Yet, this anthology of Hosea's years of prophetic ministry contains some of the sweetest passages in all of the Scriptures, and for many readers they are virtually uncharted waters. There is something wonderful about hearing the message of God's inexplicable love for sinners in the fresh language of lesser-known biblical similes, metaphors, and images. The Gospel comfort offered in this book is like an enormous expanse of virgin territory, waiting to be explored.

However, perseverance is required to arrive at Hosea's massively consoling passages because this is a book of extreme contrasts. In the same way that a jeweler displays a diamond to its fullest advantage by placing it on black velvet under intense light, Hosea contrasts the dazzling beauty of God's indefatigable love on the ugly backdrop of Israel's horrifying, sinful atrocities. Gross sin is fully exposed under the blinding light of God's holy omniscience.

How To Profit from Hosea

Reading the Old Testament in general

As you embark on continued study of this important book, let's remind ourselves of some New Testament passages that help us understand how to profitably read and apply the Old Testament as New Covenant believers. In 1 Corinthians 10, referring to God's displeasure with Israel in time immediately following the exodus from Egypt, the apostle Paul writes,

> Now these things happened to them as an example, and
> were written for our instruction, upon whom the ends of
> the ages has come. Therefore let him who thinks that he
> stands take heed that he does not fall. (1 Cor 10:11-12)

The heart of the apostle's instruction to the Corinthians is the truth that
the Bible's records of the sins of Israel and the consequential discipline
of God should induce spiritual humility. In a very real sense, as you read
Hosea, you should be saying to yourself, "Let him who thinks that He is
not like Gomer or Israel or Judah take heed lest he fall."

In a similar fashion the writer of the book of Hebrews, citing Psalm
95:7ff., warned his audience from Israel's history that unbelief in the
Word of God lies at the heart of disobedience.

> For who provoked Him when they had heard? Indeed,
> did not all those who came out of Egypt led by Moses?
> And with whom was He angry for forty years? Was it not
> with those who sinned, whose bodies fell in the wilder-
> ness? And to whom did He swear that they would not
> enter His rest, but to those who were disobedient? So we
> see that they were not able to enter because of unbelief.
> For indeed we have had good news preached to us just as
> they also; but the word they heard did not profit them,
> because it was not united by faith in those who heard.
> (Heb 3:16-4:2)

New Testament saints are to learn from Israel's past that the preaching of
the good news is only spiritually profitable in those whose hearts unite
what they hear with genuine faith.

Paul, well-educated in the Old Testament Scriptures even before
coming to faith in Jesus Christ, writes to the believers in Rome concerning the purpose of the Old Testament Scriptures:

> For whatever was written in former times was written for
> our instruction, so that thorough perseverance and the
> encouragement of the Scriptures we might have hope.
> (Rom 15:4)

Here, Paul specifically states that the teaching of the Old Testament develops spiritual endurance in our lives even under long-term trying circumstances. Further, such instruction provides us with consolation and comfort while we are bearing up under trials. The end result is that Scripture fills our hearts with hope—a confident, eager expectation in God's promises and provisions for our lives both here and now and in the future glories of eternity. Reading Hosea will produce such faith-filled hope in your heart.

Reading Hosea in particular

Finally, let me offer some thought on how to profit from the book of Hosea in particular. In order to profit from Hosea, you must read with active faith. From the opening chapters of Hosea, you read of God's unbreakable love for His people in spite of their unloveliness, ingratitude, and infidelity. This is dramatically pictured through Gomer's shameless adultery against her husband, the prophet. Because we live in a corrupt and fallen world, you cannot help but relate at some level to the pain experienced by both Hosea and especially the Lord as you recall your own personal experiences with the wincing heartache of unreturned love and relational rejection. For those who know of deep betrayal within their marriage, for grieving parents who weep for a wayward child, for all those who have felt the unsettling diminishment of a once intimate relationship now unexpectedly strained, certainly the Lord's example of longsuffering love will do much to make their hearts resolve to continue loving others in spite of the cost.

However, to read Hosea and primarily identify yourself with Hosea or God as the rejected lover would be to miss the book's weightier, more convicting theme. The primary message that Hosea proclaimed, both in the pageant of his marriage and the passion of his prophecies, was not how Israel ought to demonstrate God-like love toward people who sin against them, but rather how Israel and Judah were guilty of committing gross relational atrocities against God! Hosea's prophecies were not chiefly lessons on how to love others, but rather robust reminders about how to love God. Hosea's severe oracles served as warnings of the coming judgments against God's people who betrayed God's love and behaved like adulterous Gomer, not faithful Hosea. The prophetic warnings were intended to induce humility and repentance, which, sadly, did not come without the predicted judgments designed by God ultimately to bring about such penitence.

As you study this portion of Scripture, if you fail to perceive, confess, and repent of your own spiritual infidelity toward God, you will miss the real "surgery" that the book is intended to do to your heart. As you read you will have to resist the temptation to think to yourself, "I am glad that I am not like the nation of Israel!" Rather, search your heart for your own forms of spiritual unfaithfulness (idolatry) and humbly admit that you are more like Gomer than God and more like rebellious Israel and Judah than the faithful prophet, Hosea! If you will be brutally honest with yourself, you will no doubt find that identifying yourself with the "role" of unfaithful bride is a far too familiar bit of "type-casting" for sinners like you and me! Gomer IS me/us!

Ultimately this admission of the waywardness of your own heart toward God does indeed become the grounds for your own mercy toward others who sin against you. As a matter of fact, the only hope you have to continue to reach out in love to a wayward spouse, prodigal child, an abusive parent, or a hurtful fellow church member is to realize that the sins that you commit against the Lord are infinitely more provoking, offensive, and grievous to a holy God than any offense ever committed against you, a sinful being. Yet, the Lord continues to treat us with undeserved mercy and is moved in love for us to do anything and everything required to bring us to repentance. Recognizing the undeserved nature of God's love for you becomes both the motive and the model of your loving treatment of others, no matter how faithful or unfaithful they are in their relationship with you (Matthew 18:21ff.).

While reading Hosea, one cannot help but notice the frequent reminder of two crucial truths which are deeply imbedded in the book—truths which expose and confront a corresponding pair of dangerous unbeliefs that were not limited to Israel of old but are equally true of people of every age. The first truth that Hosea's messages regularly reiterate is the inestimable wickedness of the human heart. This utter moral corruption is a spiritual fact that men must hear often because self-righteous hearts are slow to believe the Bible's testimony against us. We are loath to admit that we are actually as corrupt as the Scriptures say that we are. The prophet Hosea employs some of the grossest metaphors in all the Bible to document just how horribly sinful God's people can be. Israel's chronic idolatry and unfaithfulness toward God is likened to the treachery of adultery within marriage. The book regularly exposes the nation's reprehensible ingratitude, rebellious law-breaking, unthinkable pride, and its inherent self-deception. The reader must remember that these indictments of relational atrocity were not brought against pagan nations with no knowledge of God, but were made against who those supposedly "knew" the Lord.

Are the hearts of God's people today capable of being as wicked as the nation of Israel in the eighth century BC? Sadly, the answer is, "Yes!"

The second truth, often doubted in men's unbelief, is the shocking attestation of the incomprehensible love of God in the face of hideous and deplorable sin. Such completely undeserved love is so foreign to our own merciless hearts that we can scarcely bring ourselves to believe it could be true! Hosea recalibrates our understanding of God's love, insisting that divine love be defined beyond all weak human definitions. Yet, these prophecies remind us that the Lord's love is not indulgent. His love will not minimize or ignore the unbridled, chronic sin of Israel. Nor will such unbounded love ever cease. Even when Israel utterly spurned compassionate care, the Lord responds with counter-intuitive pathos saying, "How can I give you up? ... How can I surrender you?" (11:8).

Is God's love for His people, even today, really as eternally relentless as Scripture says? Gloriously, the answer is "Yes!"

Learning To See Ourselves As Idolaters

Embarking on a study of Hosea without taking time to examine how we might be guilty of sinning in ways similar to Israel's atrocious pursuit of false gods would obviously be unprofitable. Admittedly, the concept of the formal idolatry seems foreign to most of us today, yet we do often secretly cherish our hidden idols and, in the privacy of our own mind, participate in un-codified false religion. Yet, all the while, we simultaneously profess a singular devotion to Christ. In order to identify specific unworthy, rival deities in your heart, ask yourself the following questions:

> Is there any possession, pleasure, or relationship that I am willing to sin against God in order to obtain or keep as my own?

> Is there any possession, pleasure, or relationship for which I would sin against the Lord if I could not obtain it or keep it as my own?

> When I am afraid, is there anything/anyone, besides the Lord Himself, in whom I place my trust and confidence in order to experience peace or contentment in my heart?

> Under pressure, do I seek relief, comfort, reward, protection, pleasure, joy, or safety in anything/anyone other than my Lord?

> When I experience success or prosperity, do I give thanks or glory to anything/anyone other than God?

Honest answers to these kinds of heart inquiries often reveal the specific things which we tend to deify and turn to in false trust. A false trust in people, possessions, circumstances, pleasures, demands, or entitlements must be forsaken with the vigor and urgency that Hosea's warnings require.

Because my wife and I did not begin thinking about our sin in terms of idolatry until we were adults, we desired to help our children understand sin at a deeper heart level at an early age. As a result, when the children were young and I would hear them disputing over a toy, I would often tell them that they were making an idol out the coveted plaything. While they would vigorously deny the accusation of false worship, they were more than willing to detail, with great intensity, the gross injustices that they regularly endured from their immature sibling. Determined to make my point about what was really going on in their hearts, I would sometimes kneel on the floor, repeatedly bowing down before the contended toy, and chant in my best Middle Eastern accent, "We worship you, Oh Great Toy. You have the power to make us happy! You can give our lives purpose and meaning." No matter how intense the prior conflict between the children, this admittedly over-the-top parenting method inevitably engendered laugher from both offended parties. Even young children recognized that investing an inanimate object with such potential was utterly ridiculous, even laughable.

Indeed, giving glory and praise to any created thing is completely ludicrous, and yet if you are truthful about the nature of your heart and your struggle with sin, you will have to admit to idolatry at some level. How often do you find yourself guilty of godless musings like, "If I could only have _____, that would give my life purpose and meaning"? Or perhaps you hear yourself sighing, "If only _____, then I would be truly happy"? Without humbling your heart under the sad reality of how frequently you participate in idol worship, you will be tempted to stare at Israel in self-righteous disbelief and say, "How could you be so hard-hearted?" The truth is, reading Hosea should lead us all to decry, "Oh, Father, forgive me! I, too, am often guilty of the pursuit of false gods, misplaced gratitude, etc.—and in self-worship, I ultimately forget You!"

So, with these thoughts in mind, let's begin our thoughtful reading of this often overlooked book of Scripture. Pace yourself on the journey! Be prepared for long, painful stretches of road where the view offers nothing but the bleakness of God's people's sin. Other portions of this spiritual trek ascend to frightening encounters with the wrath of our jealous God. But throughout the journey, there are unexpected, glorious U-turns which magnify the Lord's incredibly gracious nature and which uniquely display His unfathomable love.

J. Todd Murray

BACKGROUND AND
INTRODUCTION

According to the English Bible arrangement of the books of the Old Testament Canon, Hosea is included among the seventeen prophetic books which are subdivided into the Major Prophets and the Minor Prophets. It, of course, sits at the head of the so-called twelve "Minor Prophets."

Hosea's audience was primarily but not exclusively Israel, the ten tribes in the north. So to speak, Hosea took God's prophetic baton from the hand of Amos. From the middle of the eighth century BC when the northern tribes had again come to be quite prosperous until their waning and ultimate demise at the hand of Assyria, Hosea functioned as Yahweh's faithful mouthpiece. In the north and in the south kings had come and gone. Yet he continued with his exposures of political and religious apostasy.

Interposed with Hosea's denunciations were calls to repentance. Such calls are strategically placed between his bad news indictments and his references to the availability of a good-news pardon. Among several cycles of exposure of heinous sins, calls to repentance, and surprising indications of the LORD's forbearance and forgiveness, this overarching pattern pulls the whole book together. It begins with curse pronouncements such as "no mercy" and "not My people." Yet with seemingly unpredictable mind-blowing reversals, these cycles move into the realm of the availability of unfathomable blessing. It is hard to imagine a more dramatically profound presentation of the Gospel of God's sovereign grace in the Old Testament.

Even the prophet's name, Hosea, helps highlight the theme of salvation by grace through faith. Indeed, the Hebrew root from which this proper name is built is the primary word group in the Old Testament for "save, savior, salvation." Other names derived from this root, for example, are "Joshua," "Hoshea," and most importantly "Jesus" (cf. Matt 1:21).

The book itself is primarily poetic. Its chapters brim with vivid similes and metaphors. Many of these illustratively depict the LORD in various roles with His covenant people. The book's most pervasive picture is that of God as faithful husband and His people as an unfaithful wife. So the prophecy builds upon the initial imagery of a spiritually "dysfunctional family."

Structurally, the majority of interpreters opt for two major sections, i.e., chapters 1-3 and 4-14. It seems most reasonable to view the book as an intense, real-life drama about unrequited love that unfolds in two episodes:

> (1:2-3:5) Episode one is illustrative, indirectly based upon the unrequited love of the LORD's prophet.

> (4:1-14:9) Episode two is inconceivable, directly based upon the unrequited love of the LORD Himself.

The symbolic action of episode one, in the grand scheme of things, is effectively a warm-up for the tragic reality which is chronicled throughout the second episode. As the book launches, we are prone to think "poor Hosea!" However, we need to focus on the flagrant sins of the theocratic people against their righteous, and yet loving, LORD. Furthermore, it is the better part of biblical wisdom for us to update this scenario implicationally. All too often we are spiritually wayward in the presence of our longsuffering Savior. Therefore, Hosea's calls to repentance should echo down all the corridors of salvation history including ours.

Because of the irregularity of the cycles of predictions of judgment, interspersed calls to repentance, and those mind-blowing reversals which unfold in the sub-structure of each episode, it is difficult to set the whole book into a logically outlined order. However, the following is an attempt to map out the contents of Hosea (using English Bible versifications).

1A. Episode one is illustrative, indirectly based upon the unrequited love of the LORD's prophet (1:2-3:5).

    1B. The LORD's initial commissioning of Hosea to marry Gomer (1:2-2:23)

        1C. The three children born of this marriage prophetically illustrate the coming judgment (1:2-9)

        [A mind-blowing reversal]

        2C. The subsequent hope of a future restoration of a unified nation (1:10-2:1)

        3C. Additional illustrative details of the LORD's coming judgments (2:2-13)

        [A mind-blowing reversal]

        4C. Reassurance of a future restoration (2:14-23)

    2B. The LORD's second commissioning of Hosea, this time to remarry Gomer (3:1-5)

        1C. Its tragic picture (3:1-3)

        2C. Its transitional prophecies (3:4-5)

            1D. Its just judgment (3:4)

            [A mind-blowing reversal]

            2D. Its predicted outcome (3:5)

2A. Episode two is inconceivable, directly based upon the unrequited love of the LORD Himself (4:1-14:9).

    1B. The LORD as Prosecuting Attorney indicts His criminal people (4:1-5:7)

    2B. The LORD as Judge and Jury sentences His criminal people (5:8-14)

3B. The LORD as Parole Board will assess any and all professions of repentance on the part of His criminal people (5:15-7:16)

    1C. His offer of an opportunity for repentance (5:15)

    2C. Their superficial expression of repentance (i.e., their appeal fails) (6:1-3)

    3C. His reasons for rejecting their pseudo-repentance (6:4-7:16)

        1D. Their short-lived loyalty (6:4-11a)

        A mind-blowing reversal: a future restoration (6:11b-7:1a)

        2D. Their apostate hearts (7:1b-16)

4B. The LORD as Executioner orders the punishments of His criminal people to be carried out (8:1-10:15)

Note: The alternations of fitting punishments (e.g., military, political, religious, agricultural, etc.) with the various kinds of crimes committed are exceedingly complex in this section. Nevertheless, even in a synopsis of these righteous judgments (cf. 10:10-15) another mind-blowing reversal pointing to a future restoration associated with repentance slips into the LORD's prophetic pronouncements.

5B. The LORD as Lover restores His criminal people (11:1-14:9)

    1C. A precedent from the past (11:1-4)

    2C. Hope for the future (11:5-14:9)

        1D. This hope is not built upon their initiative (11:5-7)

[A mind-blowing reversal, i.e., the chief mind-blowing reversal of the whole prophecy]

2D. This hope is solely resident in God (11:8-11)

3D. This hope was and is shackled by sin in the past and the present (11:12-13:3)

4D. This hope has been and is kept alive by the LORD's faithfulness (13:4-5)

5D. This hope will be brought to fruition only after the LORD punishes His people (13:6-16)

6D. This hope is offered in connection with genuine repentance (14:1-3)

[A mind-blowing reversal]

7D. This hope ultimately arises from the inexplicable mercy of the LORD (14:4-7)

8D. This hope is attended by an awakening to biblical wisdom (14:8-9)

With these introductory generalities in mind, let's launch into our study of this love beyond degree story. Its theology of sin should humble us, prompting confession. Its theology of salvation should amaze us, prompting gratitude. And its theology of God should overwhelm us, prompting fear and worship.

1 HOSEA 1:1–11

EXPOSITION

(1:1) THE PROPHET AND HIS ERA

Using a typical formula of introduction to one of Yahweh's mouthpieces,[1] we are informed that Hosea was divinely called to his prophetic task. It was previously mentioned that the name Hosea was built from the most conspicuous Hebrew root for *salvation* in the Old Testament.[2] Concerning an immediate genealogical connection, he is said to have been the "son of Beeri." However, this provides us with no help in reference to a more specific identification of our prophet.[3]

The list of kings which helps sketch out a time frame (i.e., "in the days of … ") for Hosea's ministry is not only helpful, but also challenging. These kings were respectively rulers over both the northern and the southern tribes, in which division had arisen with the split that occurred after Solomon.[4] As a matter of fact, there is only one represen-

---

1   Cf. similarly Joel 1:1, Jon 1:1, Mic 1:1, Zeph 1:1, Zech 1:1; etc.

2   For other places where this important root shows up in a proper name, see Num 13:8,16; Deut 32:44; 2 Kgs 15:30; 17:1,3,4,6; 18:1,9,10; 1 Chron 27:20; Neh 10:23.

3   The only other occurrence of this name is for Esau's father-in-law in Gen 26:34.

4   Cf. a similar phenomenon concerning Amos 1:1, remembering that Amos was a slightly older contemporary of Hosea.

tative listed from the north (i.e., "Jeroboam [II], the son of Joash" from Israel), while four are mentioned from the south (i.e., "Uzziah, Jotham, Ahaz, Hezekiah" from Judah). This seems a bit strange since the primary target of Hosea's pronouncements was Israel, sometimes identified as "Ephraim" in the wider application of that designation. Nevertheless Judah is not left off the hook as oracle after oracle goes forth, some of which also include strong invectives against the southern kingdom.

This list of five kings also presents chronological challenges. Just how long was the time frame of Hosea's ministry? If one measured the range of those various reigns from the first years of the earliest of them to the last days of the last of them, we would be looking at a period of time around the century mark. However, if the core of overlap is compressed, yet including the regencies of all five kings, the minimal time for the delivered messages of Hosea would have been around forty-five years.

Most importantly in this era of Hosea's conveyance of God's warnings of coming judgments and of urgings to repent, these two kingdoms continued to be involved in political deal-makings with international powers. Of course, relying on their own plans and efforts at preservation (i.e., *self*-preservation), and not upon Yahweh, would ultimately bring to pass the nearer fulfillments[5] of Hosea's oracles of judgment. God's international instrument of Assyria would secure the downfall of the Northern Kingdom in 722 BC, and His employment of Babylon would do the same concerning Judah (i.e., in three increments: 605 BC, 597 BC, 586 BC).

(1:2–9) A Mandated Marriage and Its Prophetic Progeny

The lead-off word of verse 2 in the Hebrew text is "beginning" or "first," and the subordinate clause that it launches would literally read something like this, "The beginning of the word of the LORD through Hosea." These introductory words probably not only indicate that what immediately follows is an initial revelation of God among *many* subsequent ones, but it especially seems to anticipate the return of a quite similar

---

5   As we will see, several of his prophecies still await final fulfillments in the *eschaton*.

mandate (cf. 3:1ff.). So, verse 2a is rightly regarded as *temporally* setting the context for the command that immediately follows (cf. most modern translations which begin with "When … ").[6]

Just before that command is articulated, its divine origin is reaffirmed in v. 2b: "Now the LORD said to Hosea." The summary statement of divine revelation coming to Hosea in verse 1a is now set into motion with the arrival of the prophet's initial charge. And what a shocking charge it was!

The connotation of the leading words of the LORD's command to Hosea is "get going, marry!" However, rather than receiving an instruction to deliver a *verbal* communication, God calls him to begin his prophetic career with an attention-arresting *prophetic action*[7]: "Go, take for yourself a woman of prostitution, and [have, or, produce] children of prostitution!" This Hebrew root, having to do with prostitution, whoredom, harlotry, will occur twice more in the last line of verse 2, then eighteen more times in the remainder of the book.[8]

Much ink has been spilt concerning the interpretation of this divine command. On the one hand, some have felt compelled 'to protect' God's character, arguing that these words should not be taken literally as divine orders to marry a woman who already had the reputation of and was currently a prostitute. However, if one is committed to the perspicuity of divine revelation, a normal hermeneutic should lead us exactly to that conclusion. Furthermore, if these words are not taken in their straightforward sense, the analogy about to be drawn in the last line of verse 2 and throughout the rest of the book would be at best an anemic parallel.

Indeed, the sublime reason and representational significance of the prophet's initial orders follow with the words "for (or, because, or, since)

---

6   For example, NASB, "When the LORD first spoke through Hosea … ." Loosely analogous would be the two calls and commands given to Jonah (i.e., 1:2 and 3:1), except in that prophet's case it was reissued because of *his* disobedience.

7   For other examples of such symbolic acts see, e.g., 1 Kgs 22:11 (a false prophet); Isa 20; Jer 27-28; Ezek 4:12; etc.

8   See 2:2,4,5; 3:3; 4:10,11,12 (x2),14(x2),15,18 (x2); 5:3; 6:10; 9:1. Note a similar saturation with this repulsive imagery in Ezekiel chapters 16 and 23.

the land (i.e., a metonymy for the inhabitants of the land) practices gross[9] prostitution, (literally) from after the LORD."[10] The brevity of the last phrase crystallizes the meanings of the imagery of this spiritual harlotry. The people of the land had abandoned following after the LORD; they had apostatized. So, fittingly, this graphic picture of prostitution joins ranks with the many other word groups and images that chronicle the treacherous infidelity of God's sinning people.[11]

Hosea does not protest these orders nor is his obedience delayed as indicated by the lead-off narrative of verse 3, i.e., "So he went and he took ... ." These actions conform and thereby confirm that Hosea was following exactly the two commissioning commands of verse 2. The person he "took," i.e., "married," is now identified personally as "Gomer, the daughter of Diblaim." We have no further genealogical information on Gomer beyond her father's name. The only other biblical occurrence of *her* personal name would be that of the grand*son* of Noah (cf. Gen 10:2-3). Obviously there is no connection.

Gomer at this juncture becomes the subject of the final two narrative verbs of verse 3: "And she conceived and bore for him a son." Now the stage is beginning to be set with Hosea's progeny who will dramatically represent the LORD's unfaithful people, whose spiritual adultery is about to be exposed for the purpose of warning and judgment.

Verse 4 launches with a divine directive concerning the naming of the firstborn son of this prostitute. Hosea is commanded by the LORD to name him "Jezreel" (v. 4a).[12] The main verb that comes from the root of this personal name has to do with sowing, scattering, dispersing. It

---

9   I.e., a Hebrew infinitive from the same prostitution word group. It *magnifies* all the more the force of the verb translated here "to practice prostitution."

10 Incidentally, this is the fourth of nearly 50 occurrences of the memorial-name Yahweh in Hosea. In subsequent chapters, although His people are unfaithful, He will remain faithful and merciful as the great "I AM" (cf., e.g., Exod 3:13-15; 34:5-7; etc.). Nevertheless, we're going to observe a most shocking word play on God, the "I AM," in v. 9b.

11 For example, one of these word families will occur in Hos 5:7 and 6:7 and also shows up five times in various forms in the infamous context of Mal 2:10-16.

12 In Hebrew "Jezreel" and "Israel" are close sound-alikes.

most likely depicts a metaphorical scattering (i.e., the dispersion) of God's people among the nations (cf. Zech 10:9). And yet, God's naming of this child in this context is going to set up an astounding antithetical application with Chapter 2, verses 22-23. Therein the LORD reveals that He will ultimately "sow" them back into the Promised Land.[13]

There obviously appears to be more figurative freight regarding this firstborn son's name as indicated by the words that follow the causal "for" (i.e., vv. 4b-5). God's insistence upon this name digs up historical roots involving both prominent persons (e.g. Jehu) and a prominent place of warfare and bloodshed. The rootlets of verse 4 could have tapped into the soils of several different historical situations. However, what is crystal clear is God's imminent coming[14] in judgment: "I will punish" (lit. *visit* [in an adversarial sense]) ... "I will put an end to" (lit. cause to cease) ... "I will break." In a narrower application Yahweh was going to judge the dynasty of Jehu for his carrying out of unrestrained bloodbaths, and in the wider application He was going to terminate the dynasties of Israel (v. 4). That would be accomplished concurrently with the destruction of the nation's military capability (v. 5), i.e., Yahweh was going to "break" their "bow".[15]

Using the same verbs for conception and birth as found in verse 3, but with the addition of the word "again," we next learn about the arrival of a second child in verse 6, this time a daughter. As it was in the case of naming the previous child, "Jezreel," Hosea was commanded by God to name his daughter. Her divinely-appointed name would be even more shocking than her firstborn brother's; she would be called *Lo-ruhamah*,

---

13   So, amazingly, God, by His unfathomable grace, will re-sow them into His Promised Land after His purging judgments are carried out.

14   Cf. the introductory, idiomatic expression (lit.) "yet a little," "soon" in Isa 10:25; Hag 2:6; etc.

15   It is not prophetically insignificant that this last divine judgment is introduced by: "Now it will come to pass on that day that ... ." Most often in the prophets "that day" refers back to or stands for "the Day of Yahweh." "The Day of the LORD" frequently had qualitative applications to various historical times when God dramatically and powerfully broke into human affairs. Also, quite frequently it looks ahead to a final fulfillment in the *eschaton*.

"No Mercy."[16] God's somber explanation of the choice of this particular name is heart stopping: "Since (or because) I will no longer deal mercifully with Israel, for (or indeed) I certainly will not forgive them" (v. 6b,c).

The vocabulary, the grammar, and the theology of verse 6 combine in such a way that the breath of the original hearers must have been sucked out of them. First, the negatives used with the noun "mercy" and with the "no longer" or "not again" are strong and unqualified. Second, the last statement uses the same verbal root for forgiveness, therefore twice emphasizing the futility of hoping for a divine pardon.[17] However, the most astounding feature of Hosea 1:6 is Yahweh's withholding of one of His chief attributes of grace, *rahamim*, His "mercy" or "compassion." It stands preeminently among God's Tender Loving Caring (i.e., TLC) qualities. After all, it was the first of the attributes articulated by the LORD Himself to Moses in Exodus 34:6. The root of this word is related to the word for a mother's womb, yet it conveys a fatherly side to His personal care (cf. Ps 103:8). Furthermore, even in the midst of the rubble of Yahweh's righteous judgment, Jeremiah cries out in Lamentations 3:22b that "His mercies [or compassions] never come to an end" (ESV). But here in Hosea 1:6 they are announced as ceasing; that indeed would be the worst kind of bad news!

Nevertheless, a partial mind-blowing reversal enters the prophetic forecast with the contrastive "But" (or "However," "Yet," etc.) standing at the head of verse 7. This verse might literally be rendered "But unto the house (or, dynasty) of Judah I will extend mercy, and (or, now) I will not save[18] them by means of bow, or sword, or a war (or, a battle) with horses and horsemen." This affirmation is a hands-on application of what God had revealed about Himself to Moses in Exodus 33:19b: "I will be gracious to whom I will be gracious, and I will show compassion

---

16   Taking off on a reversal of this name, cf. Peter's application in 1 Peter 2:10.

17   Cf. NASB's rendering, "that I would *ever* forgive them"; ESV's "to forgive them *at all*"; NIV's, "that I should *at all* forgive them," (italics added to show the sense of how the second verbal from the same root intensifies the leading verb's action).

18   The root of these important deliverance verbs is the same one from which the prophet's name was derived.

on whom I will show compassion[19]" (NASB).[20] His sovereign grace is truly amazing!

One may wonder about the LORD's affirmations and denials of the means found in the last part of verse 7. These words constitute a corrective to what, unfortunately, and all too frequently, characterized His people's response to local and international threats. Instead of fearing and trusting God, they would fear man and trust in the making of covenants with nations that they thought would defend them from an enemy's attack. Isaiah 31:1-3 is one historical case in point about trusting in the wrong object and relying on the wrong things:

> Woe to those who go down to Egypt for help and rely on horses, who trust in chariots because they are many and in horsemen because they are very strong, but do not look to the Holy One of Israel or consult the LORD! And yet he is wise and brings disaster; he does not call back his words, but will arise against the house of the evildoers and against the helpers of those who work iniquity. The Egyptians are men, and not God, and their horses are flesh, and not spirit. When the LORD stretches out his hand, the helper will stumble and he who is helped will fall, and they will all perish together (ESV).[21]

After a notation about the weaning of Hosea's daughter *Lo-ruhamah* (v. 8a), child number three, a second son, is introduced in verses 8b-9.[22] Although the LORD's command to name this boy is not preceded by the addition of the words "to Hosea"[23] it was the father's prerogative to assign

---

19   This is the root from which the prophet's daughter's name was constructed.

20   Remember Paul's application of those words in Romans 9:14-18.

21   Notice especially the parallelisms of v. 3: Egyptians = limited humanity; horses = frail flesh contrasted with God = spirit (i.e., divine power).

22   Once again, the same two verbs chronicle this conception and birth (cf. vv. 3b and 6a).

23   Cf. "to him" in v. 4a and v. 6b.

a child his or her name. And his name would indeed convey a blood-curdling revelation, *Lo-ammi*, "Not My People" (v. 9a).[24]

The divinely revealed rationale for this designation explodes like a nuclear bomb in verse 9b. Its devastating realities are delivered to a seismically rocked audience by several eye-catching phenomena (especially observable in the Hebrew text). First, along with an *objective* negation contained in the name itself, two strong denials follow as an explanation of this appellation. The first of these two affirms the stark reality of that name, i.e., "*You* [a plural pronoun] are *NOT* My People" (v. 9b; italics and caps added). Then comes the corollary negation, "And *I* [a first-person singular pronoun, functioning emphatically] am *NOT* yours" (v. 9b, also italics and caps added). The "yours" translates a typical occurrence of a possessive idiom in Hebrew, i.e., He no longer belongs to them. They have been disowned; they have no claim to Him!

Such drastic pronouncements to many people are theologically unacceptable. Is God reneging on His 'unconditional' promises? Is He defaulting on His 'unconditional' covenants? Does His oath mean nothing?[25] After all, what does Genesis 12:1-3 say? After all, what does 2 Samuel 7:8-17; etc. mean? And what about Yahweh's sovereign election of Israel to be His especially treasured people (e.g., Exod 3:7ff.; 6:2-8; 29:45-46; Deut 7:6-8; etc.)?

Well, God in His inscrutable, sovereign wisdom has often contextually programmed into such promises elements of conditionality. For example, we observe this phenomenon when we compare Genesis 12:1-3 with 17:1ff.; 2 Samuel 7:8-17; then Exodus 3:7ff.; 6:2-8; 29:45-46; Deuteronomy 7:6-8, respectively with Exodus 19:5-6; Deuteronomy 7:9ff. A good passage that helps us return in a more balanced fashion to our text in Hosea 1:9 is Leviticus 26. It contains blessings for covenant obedience and curses for disobedience. Near the end of the section on the blessings of obedience the LORD says this in verse 12 of Leviticus 26: "And I will walk among you and will be your God, and you shall be

---

24   Again, notice 1 Peter 2:10 for an applied reversal of this name's significance.

25   Cf., e.g., Heb 6:13-18.

my people" (ESV). The chapter also goes on to warn: "But if you do not listen to Me and do not do all these commandments … "(Lev 26:14ff.). Other "if" case scenarios of disobedience follow, all of which precipitate severe, divine judgments (cf. vv. 15-39). That's where the astronomical judgment of "Not My People" and "Not your God" comes in as an even more powerful parallel.[26] Yet in Leviticus 26 opportunities are graciously granted for repentance (cf. vv. 40-43), and God reaffirms His promise of restoration (cf. vv. 44-45). So it will be in Hosea with the arrival of another merciful, mind-blowing reversal of the restoration prophesied in 1:10-2:1.

But before we go there, in view of all the prophetic puns, especially relating to the names of these children born to Hosea and Gomer, the prostitute,[27] there seems to be one more nugget of a deeply-embedded wordplay in verse 9. It is found in the last line which is normally trans-lated "and I am not your God." Although the negated state of being verb flows right into its predicate (i.e., "your God"), if we should leave that predicate off for the time being, the first words that those people would have heard after the introductory "and I" would have been the negative "NOT" joined to the following transliteration of the Hebrew verb, i.e., *ehyeh*, i.e., "I AM." Now, indeed, *ehyeh* was the name that God used of Himself in Exodus 3:14, "*I AM* WHO *I AM*" (in Hebrew: *ehyeh asher ehyeh*). This was to be His "memorial NAME to all generations" (Exod 3:15). However, when Moses would relay this personal name of God to His people he would have likely changed its form into a third person construction of the verb *to be*, i.e., *yihyeh* (cf. Yahweh). So ultimately the devastating announcement of Hosea 1:9b amounted to this: "You're not My people and I'm not your Yahweh!"

---

26   However, nowhere in Lev 26 does the language of the pronounced curses go so far as to convey with *seeming* finality the severance of Yahweh's relationship with His apostate people.

27   Just imagine illustratively the summoning of the children of such a dysfunctional family. You would hear again and again, "Come here, 'He sows'!" "Come here, 'No mercy'!" "Come here, 'Not My people'!"

This sounds like a final divorce pronouncement. It seems to be irrevocable. As we have learned from the verses just traversed and will learn from the forthcoming indictments of God's sinful people, Yahweh's grounds were not merely "irreconcilable differences" but exceedingly culpable forms of spiritual adultery. Nevertheless, we will next be hit with a thunderbolt of God's inexplicable mercy with the arrival of the book's first *major* mind-blowing reversal, the bursting forth of Yahweh's unfathomable sovereign grace.

(1:10–11) THE HOPE OF A FUTURE RESTORATION OF A UNIFIED NATION

In an attempt to capture the impact of this prophesied[28] one-hundred eighty degree reversal of fortunes,[29] consider the following rendering:

> Yet (or But) (or Notwithstanding) (or Nevertheless, etc.) the number of the sons of Israel[30] will be like the sand of the sea, which cannot be measured nor counted. Also, it shall come to pass in the place where it was being said to them, "You are not my people," it will be said to them, "(You are) sons of the living God." The sons of Judah and the sons of Israel[31] alike[32] will be gathered together. And

---

28 The leading verbs of these three verses are rightly labeled by older grammarians as "prophetic perfects," i.e., future in fulfillment but as good as done in God's book.

29 The contrasting impact of these words with the dramatic revelations preceding them is also illustrated by the fact of the Hebrew Bible's versification (i.e., they start a new chapter, 2:1-3).

30 Or, more dynamically, "children of Israel" (ESV), "Israelites" (HCSB).

31 Again, more dynamically, "the children of Judah and the children of Israel" (ESV), "the Judeans and the Israelites" (HCSB).

32 I.e., a word in Hebrew that is often left untranslated when combined with a verb and/or its inflected form connoting, among other things, the idea of togetherness. Here it seems best to take the verb as a passive (contextually a divine passive) and the additional term as reinforcing the idea of unitedness.

(or then) they will appoint for themselves one head,[33] and (or then) they will go up from the land because the day of Jezreel will be great. Say to your brothers, "*Ammi*" and to your sisters, "*Ruhamah*"![34]

These words truly reflect the inexplicable yet incontestable compassion of our merciful God.

Going back to Hosea 1:10a, this revelation conveys a staggeringly quantifiable reversal of the preceding judgments that God will bring to pass. For some divine promises of an ultimately incalculable number of chosen people that He would bless, it is incumbent upon us to note the imagery of "sand of the sea" in Genesis 22:17[35] and 32:12.

Moving on to the second part of verse 10, God will also bring about a reversal of reputation. At that very location where in the LORD's judgment it was said of His apostate people that "You're not My people" and that "I'm not your God," they will come to be recognized as being graciously blessed by Yahweh; they will bear the designation "sons of the living God." By His mercy they would again be identified with the omnipotent God who powerfully breaks into time, space, and history (cf., e.g., the corroborations that Joshua mentions in Josh 3:10).

A reunification of north and south is predicted in verse 11a. Historically we need to keep in mind that the monarchy was divided in 931 BC (1 Kgs 12:16) after a previous period of unification under David and Solomon. However, in the future is coming a gathering together[36] of both of these formerly divided nations into the one people of God that He originally brought forth from captivity in Egypt. There

---

33   I.e., "one leader" (NASB), "a single ruler" (HCSB).

34   Respectively, "My people" and "mercy."

35   Notice besides Gen 22:17 "the stars of the heavens" imagery in Gen 15:5; 26:4; 1 Chron 27:23; etc., and also "the dust of the earth" in Gen 28:14.

36   This eschatological gathering of formerly split nations is well captured in the LXX by a future passive verb form which is part of an important word group out of which comes the noun meaning "synagogue." This verb is also intensified by a prepositional idiom in Greek connoting unitedness.

will no longer be dual kingships because they all will submit to "one head," i.e., chief, leader, ruler, and probably herein, king (cf. the parallelism of Job 29:25).[37]

Furthermore, they shall "go up" (or) "ascend from the land" (v. 11c). These words have spawned considerable controversy. Two basic views, among others, have arisen, one emphasizing blessing and productivity *in* the Promised Land,[38] and one arguing for a final, grand "Exodus" *from* the land of captivity to the Promised Land in the last days.[39] The last view seems to have an edge in view of the Bible's many geographical references to "ascending to" the hill country, Jerusalem, etc. It would also conform to a recurrent eschatological pattern, namely the judgment of God's erring people ultimately being followed by a spiritual renewal and physical restoration to the land promised to the patriarchs (cf., e.g., Gen 12:1-3; 15:18; 17:1-8; etc. with, e.g., Exod 32:13). This all being part of "the day of the LORD" is also inferred by the final explanatory clause of v. 11, "for great is the day of Jezreel."

EXHORTATIONS
STARKLY CONTRASTING CHARACTER

In this opening chapter, we are immediately confronted with the starkest imaginable contrasts. The first set of unmistakable opposites is displayed dramatically in Hosea's marriage. As an act of submissive obedience to God's command, Hosea, a holy prophet of God, joined himself in marriage to Gomer, an unholy woman who was apparently already known for her shameless immorality. God chose an unlovely, "used," and possibly even disease-ridden bride for His prophet. She was utterly unworthy of

---

37   Cf. a likely parallel to "David their King" in its eschatological setting of 3:5.

38   Some evidence for this view is mustered in the parallels with our verb "to go up" in Deut 29:23 (therein with a negation).

39   Cf., e.g., conceptual parallels with Exod 3:8 (a causative form of the verb, i.e., "to make to go up"), 17 (an active form as in Hos 1:11) with the subsequent historical reminiscences of Hos 2:15 (an active form) and 12:13 (another causative form).

Hosea's principled compassion and committed love. In contrast, Hosea is depicted as a faithful husband who persistently and compassionately pursues his unchaste wife, who caused him public shame. Hosea and Gomer were the quintessential example of the maxim, "opposites attract." But their polar differences serve to illustrate an even deeper chasm, the vast difference between a holy God and His repulsive people who habitually despise the undeserved grace He continuously offers.

This glaring differential is not limited to the ancient people of God. It is equally true of every sinner born in every age since. The moral gap between a holy God and defiled and corrupt sinners is too vast to be described. Were it not that God Himself took the initiative to send Christ as a perfect sin-bearer and righteous covering, there would be no hope for all the Gomers of the world.

STARKLY CONTRASTING RESPONSES

But the contrasts in chapter 1 do not stop merely at the difference between the *character* of God and the character of His people. We also discover two radically opposite *responses* from God toward the ugliness of His people's chronic sin. First, we read of the promise of severe judgment and rejection by God with words like "I will punish"; "I will put an end to the House of Israel"; "I will no longer have compassion"; "You are not my people and I am not your God" (1:4, 6, 9). This is the natural reaction that we expect from a devoted prophet/husband whose loving overtures have been spurned. And this is the response that we expect as well as from a faithful, compassionate God whose mercy has been so high-handedly rejected by His chosen people. Gloriously, Hosea records a second and completely opposite response that God has toward His people. The predictions of divine doom and utter rejection are followed by equally vivid but unanticipated assurances of God's loyal love and ultimately for the restoration of the nation! Despite His people's constant infidelity and deep rebellion, we hear the Lord's intense assurances of hope with unexpected promises like: "Yet ... where it is said of them, 'You are *not* My people,' it will be said to them 'You *are* the sons of the living God.'" "Say to your brothers, 'Ammi [my people],' and to your sister, 'Ruhamah [mercy]'" (1:10; 2:1, emphasis added).

Knowing what you and I deserve in the light of the severity of our sin, who among us today could object if God were to choose to withhold any additional mercy? No one could legitimately accuse God of injustice if He were to declare that sinners like you and me had been officially disowned. If God were to pronounce that He no longer loved us, who among us would protest that we were somehow just too lovable to ignore? The nature of God's temporary judgment of Israel and Judah's sin as described in this opening chapter touches upon some of our greatest fears and doubts in the Christian life, that we might somehow, one day sin beyond the limits of the grace of God and find ourselves disowned and rejected! The warnings in this chapter send a chill down the spine of any child of God who has an awareness of his own sinfulness and what he justly deserves from God's hand. Where would we be without important Scriptural words like "yet"? Such a small word, yet it is used to introduce an enormous message of hope—the undeserved, unexpected assurance that we will *not* receive what we deserve. This passage is but the first of many such unexpected outbreaks of God's mercy scattered throughout the book that will climax in chapter 14. What wonderful truths we find in Hosea that confront and relieve any fears of rejection by God and induce grateful worship for His unmerited mercy!

Admittedly, these dramatic alternations between sober warnings of disciplinary disaster and profound reminders of unconditional compassion are positively jolting to the reader of Hosea. What are we to make of the stark contrast of divine declaration of coming wrath and judgment coupled with assurances of compassion and healing? God is not fickle or vacillating, is He? Of course not. God's anger toward His people's sin is not a divine temper tantrum from which He must later recover. Rather, God's wrath is a holy, sustained, and principled abhorrence of all that is wicked, defiled, and offensive to His righteous character. Simply put, God, who is sinless and pure, hates sin! The Lord's severe predictions of judgment are not out-of-control declarations which He must later sheepishly retract. Nor are they idle threats by which the Lord attempts to manipulate his people into returning to Him, while never actually intending to bring them about. Rather, all the prophecies of God's plans to chastise His people with captivity and temporary rejection in this book are perfectly measured expressions of His actual intentions. Each of the prophesied, drastic judgments did indeed come to pass. God knows and predicts what is required to cause His people to repent and return to Him, the Lover of their souls.

In your further reading through Hosea you will notice that the warning sections of the book steadily intensify, eventually becoming terrifyingly graphic in their depictions of violent future events. A bit of historical context helps us understand why the warnings come with such ferocious intensity. Hosea was admonishing a generation of Israelites who were enjoying a resurgence of national political power and riding a wave of financial prosperity. In the midst of such political peace and opulence, the doom of the impending judgment of God seemed utterly inconceivable. They had never tasted suffering firsthand; the only spiritual humiliation with which they had any familiarity was that which they had heard through their forefathers' distant stories. Hosea's thunderous forewarnings may have seemed ridiculous to his audience, yet the proximity of that generation to the fulfillment of such dreadful affliction also helps us understand the severity of God's words through Hosea.

But God's judgments on His people are not the end of the story. The LORD will not—could not—utterly annihilate His chosen nation. To do so would be to renege on the promises He made to the patriarchs. However, God loves his people too much to abandon them in their sinful rebellion. His compassion could never indifferently ignore their persistent unfaithfulness. The Lord's affliction of His people is not set in contrast to His love; instead, His chastisement is an expression of His love (Heb 12:6–7). Similarly, God's consoling assurances of ultimate blessing on His children are not a reversal of His intention to bring His people low through suffering. Rather, both the discipline and the restoration are equally reliable, sure words of God; and both are ultimately motivated by incomprehensible compassion described by the hymn writer Isaac Watts as "amazing pity, grace unknown, and love beyond degree."

2 HOSEA 2:1–23

EXPOSITION

(2:1–13) DETAILS OF THE LORD'S COMING JUDGMENTS

Next in 2:1, by a prophetic projection into that blessing stage of the day of the LORD, comes a command of great privilege. The innumerable inhabitants divinely brought back and planted in the holy land will address each other as spiritually and politically unified brothers and sisters calling out to each other "*Ammi*" and "*Ruhamah.*" On that grand day in the future "the living GOD," having finished His purging judgments, will mercifully restore His chosen family.[40]

In 2:2 the compass abruptly turns back 180 degrees to the current situation of gross spiritual defection. Furthermore, it does so with an ironic twist concerning God's confrontation of His idolatrous people.

The oracle begins by calling upon the products of prostitution, the children, to contend or strive with their mother, the adulteress. They function as agents of indictment being employed by their father to confront her. Of course throughout this section (i.e., vv. 2-13) the characters

---

40   It should be noted that, in Paul's emphasizing of God's mercy in its spiritual domain, the apostle extends the application of Hos 1:10 ethnically to the Gentiles in Rom 9:26. Later it will be noted that he employs Hos 2:23 in a similar way in Romans 9:25. This in no way dilutes the spiritual or abrogates the physical blessings promised to the Jews (cf. Rom 9:27-11:29).

on stage are Hosea's children of prostitution, their whoring mother, and
the prophet himself (cf. the "I"'s of vv. 3-13). However, once again,
these historical characters represent the LORD, His part being played by
Hosea and His errant people, their part being played by both Gomer *and*
her apostate children.[41]

Returning to verse 2 the twice repeated command to "contend"
(NASB), or "rebuke" (NIV), or "strive," etc.,[42] is often used in the context of the law court. Gomer's children are being commanded by their
father, Hosea, both to bring an indictment against and to prosecute their
mother. This legal imagery will be picked up later by a noun form, "dispute," or "case," in 4:1 and 12:2.[43] Using the children to prosecute their
mother would seemingly make Hosea's case more compelling.

One should not assume from the causal clause, "because she is not
my wife and I am not her husband," that these words indicate an actual
divorce had taken place. Indeed based upon the attitude and acts of
Gomer (i.e., she representing Yahweh's apostate people) the marriage covenant had truly been violated; however, even though the words of Hosea
(i.e., representing God's words as the nation's Husband) are sharply condemnatory, he/He did not end the relationship as passages like 2:14-23
will document.

In the last two parallel lines of verse 2 the intentionality of the children's suit against their mother is revealed: "that she put away[44] her whoring from her face, and her adultery from between her breasts" (ESV). The
parallelisms between "whoring" (or, "prostitution") and "adultery" and
between "from her face" (or, "presence") and "her breasts" have generated
several different interpretations. These span a continuum from external

---

41   Although the children are used in v. 2 as instruments of confrontation, they also are worthy
      of condemnation (cf. v. 4).

42   The rendering in ESV, "plead," is certainly possible, but it seems somewhat anemic in this
      context.

43   Externally to Hosea, cf., e.g., Exod 23:2-6; Deut 17:8; Isa 3:13; Jer 2:9; Mic 6:1-2.

44   Or, "let her put away" (NASB); or "let her remove" (HCSB).

allurements (cf. 2:13) to her seductive demeanor. Most likely both elements were intended to stand behind this scathing imagery.

Following the laying down of the children's case against their mother, along with its intentionality (i.e., v. 2), an "or else" (i.e., vv. 3ff.) comes into play outlining the consequences should she not repent. And what shocking but appropriate consequences they would be!

Her husband[45] will expose her to great shame: "I will strip her naked and make her as bare as on the day she was born" (NIV).[46] Such humiliation was the ultimate form of punishment in the ancient Near East. The next similes reinforce the seriousness of consequences for refusing to repent. She would be made like the most arid of all deserts, and in that setting would be sentenced to death by thirst. On the applicational level, nationally these words should have brought back to the memory the deprivations of the wilderness wanderings.

Now the instruments of indictment, the children (v. 2), joining their mother, find themselves under the gavel of judgment in verse 4: "Also, I will have no compassion on her children" (NASB). The future promise of 2:1 is still for the future, and the reality of "no mercy" (cf. 1:6) is still applicable, since these children remain "sons of harlotry." They, too, have the heart and habits of their prostituting mother. Indeed a spiritual "like" had produced spiritual "likes."

With the unfolding explanatory clauses of verse 5, more evidence is put forth sealing this woman's indictment. Their mother incontestably was engaging in harlotry; the one who conceived them was acting shamefully.

At this point in verse 5 the internal voicings of her lustful heart are revealed. Literally she muses, "I will walk after my lovers." "To walk" is a common metaphor in the Bible most often speaking of traveling the pathway of one's life. Here "walking" is combined with "after" not

---

45   Remembering here is where the first-person verbs take over (i.e., Hosea, but ultimately representing Yahweh).

46   Cf., e.g., Ezek 16:39; 23:26.

only indicating the direction of her "following *after*,"[47] but also representatively pointing to Israel's spiritual apostasy (cf., e.g., Deut 4:3; 6:14; 8:19; 13:2,6,13; Judg 2:11-12,17; etc.).[48]

Gomer's self-deceptive thinking is noted by the way she perceives her lovers. She looks upon them as supplying all of her basic needs and possibly then some. These things, however, when brought applicationally into their symbolic, nationalistic setting are to be found only in Yahweh God and not in the *Baals* that His apostate people were pursuing. This comes out clearly in verses 6-13.

God's gracious hindrances are affirmed as being brought to bear in verses 6-7a. Because of her perverted thinking and resultant harlotries Yahweh places obstacles in her perverted pathways. Turning to her directly in verse 6a, God literally says, "Therefore (or Consequently), behold,[49] I will hedge your way with thorns" (NASB). Then switching the divine means of hindrance and resuming a third-person designation for the recipient[50] of this pronounced action, the LORD literally says, "and I will wall[51] up her wall,[51] i.e., I will construct a special wall for her for the purpose of impeding her. Indeed this divine intentionality is revealed in the last line of verse 6, "in order that (or so) that she might not find her pathways."

The success of this divine endeavor is prophetically chronicled in the first two lines of verse 7. Although she will be in hot pursuit of her paramours, she will never be able to catch up to them; although she will run after them, she will never be able to find them. Consequently, being frustrated, she has a little talk with herself as she did in verse 5. Here in verse

---

47   Cf. her "pursuing" them in v. 7.

48   The irony of this is likely expressed by a variant reading found in Hos 5:11 wherein Ephraim is shown to be "walking after emptiness" or "following after vanity." This well accords with the OT's many exposures of the culpable stupidity of idolatrous worship.

49   On this attention-grabbing particle in context, compare the interpretively periphrastic rendering of HCSB, "this is what I will do."

50   In Hebrew a second-person singular.

51   The verb and the noun came from the same Hebrew root.

7b her internal deliberations are captured by Yahweh's infallible MRI: "I will go and return to my first husband for it was better for me then than now" (ESV). The Hebrew verb for "return" or "go back" is built upon the primary root for repentance in the Old Testament.[52] Unfortunately this would prove not to be a permanent 180-degree return to God. This sad truth will be borne out by the following context wherein both her faulty knowledge is exposed (i.e., v. 8) and God's subsequent chastisements are revealed (i.e., vv. 9-13).

What she thought about who her providers were (i.e., v. 5) is divinely corrected here in verse 8: "she[53] does not recognize that it was I[53] who gave her the grain, the new wine, and the oil. I lavished silver and gold on her, which they[54] used for Baal" (HCSB). As a consequence, the LORD, the true Provider, says, "Therefore, I will take back[55] (or take) away[55] ... " all those commodities which she had attributed wrongly to her "lovers." Yahweh was going to withhold from her both food and clothing items. Consequently, with the deprival of those materials, she would not be able to cover up her own nakedness.

God's punitive actions become even more tailor made for her adulterous crimes in verses 10ff. Yahweh's first specifically-designed retribution is announced in verse 10: "So now I will uncover (or expose) her immodesty (or lewdness[56]) in the sight (or presence of[57]) her lovers. And no one will deliver (or rescue) her out of (or from) My hand." Once the LORD intervenes by fully exposing her, by unveiling what she is as demonstrated by her polluted pursuits, no man would dare to save her.

---

52   This is the first of 23 occurrences in Hosea.

53   Both pronouns are emphatic in the Hebrew text. The plural form here explicitly documents the ultimate application of this section to God's professing people.

54   The plural form here explicitly documents the ultimate application of this section to God's professing people.

55   I.e., lit., "I will turn (or return) and I will take ... ." The first verb when linked up with a similar form in v. 7 produces a pun. Both occurrences are based on that aforementioned repentance word group.

56   The early Greek translation of the Hebrew text emphasizes *uncleanness*.

57   A common Hebrew idiom; lit., "to (or before) the eyes of."

In verse 11 God plans to stop cold[58] all manifestations of her "exultation."[59] The more specific terms which follow in apposition, "her feasts, her new moons, her Sabbaths, and all her appointed times," represent Israel's whole calendar of religious holidays. For the nation in its sinful estate, to participate in the celebration of the holy days and times would add a most heinous offense to their charges, namely, hypocrisy. Such a divine prohibition of the very practices set up by God Himself, for example, through Mosaic legislations, was not something that was historically unprecedented. The LORD detests disobedience and duplicity; therefore, he refuses all forms of polluted "worship."[60] How dare a nation chasing as a prostitute after "the Baals" (v. 13) come into Yahweh's presence under the pretense of worshipping the only true God!

The judgments of verse 12[61] bring to mind some of the promised curses threatened in Deuteronomy 28:15ff. Apostasy would indeed bring on the severest of divine consequences. And that is what Yahweh is announcing here. To an agrarian society such things as the destruction of the produce from the vine and the fig tree would put the people's very existence into jeopardy. The prophet Habakkuk himself would witness the fulfillment of such a pronouncement against Judah specifically (cf. Hab 1:5; 3:17). Furthermore, the two lines of Hosea 2:12 imply that the land will revert to a wild state (cf. Mic 3:12). The high level of culpability that especially brings on these curses is illustrated right in the middle of verse 12. The prostituting nation's thoughts are once again brought to expression. Speaking not only of the produce of vines and trees but also of her other staples (cf. v. 5), she says, "They are my gift which my

---

58   Lit., "cause to cease" (cf. the same causative form in 1:4c). Also, this same verb and form appears in Ezek 23:27,48 where what God causes to cease is the nation's "lewdness," a synonym of the word encountered in Hos 2:10.

59   Rendered "gaiety" (NASB), "mirth" (ESV), "celebrations" (NIV).

60   Cf., e.g., such cease and desist occasions as the following: 1 Sam 15:22-23; Pss 40:6-8; 51:16-17; Isa 1:10-15; Mic 6:6-8; Mal 1:6-2:3; etc.; even in the NT, cf., e.g., John 2:13-17, *et al.*

61   The spoken oracle delivered by Hosea as contained in verses 11 and 12 (vv. 13 and 14 in the Hebrew text), besides its somber contents, was reinforced by sound-alike verb forms at the head of each respective pronouncement (i.e., verse).

lovers have given to me." The word for "gift" is used most frequently of the "hire" or "wages" of a prostitute (cf., e.g., Deut 23:18; Isa 23:17-18; Ezek 16:34,41[62]; Micah 1:7; and later in Hos 9:1). She still doesn't get it (cf. again v. 5; contra. v. 8)!

Verse 13 of Hosea 2 is definitely climactic. The LORD continues to speak through His prophetic mouthpiece saying, "And (or now) I will visit her concerning (i.e., I will punish her for) the days of Baals to which she was burning incense, and she adorned herself with her nose-ring and her jewelry and went after[63] her lovers, but Me she forgot." This punishment along with a synopsis of the grounds for it is solemnly punctuated by "The Utterance of Yahweh!"

Hosea 2:13 contains the ultimate indictment against the nation: their high-handed worship of false gods. The people had been literally "making sacrifices smoke" to the Baals (cf., e.g., Jer 7:9; 11:12-13,17; 19:4; et al.). These false Canaanite deities were superstitiously looked upon as controlling fertility and productivity. Cultic prostitution was also practiced. This constitutes the cultural framework for Israel's apostate pursuits as conveyed by the Gomer imagery of Hosea 1-3. Israel was so caught up in chasing after these false deities that there could be only one viable conclusion: she had come to the point of deliberately putting Yahweh out of her mind.[64]

(2:14–23) Reassurance of a Future Restoration

It would seem that Hosea 2:2-13 should have been the final nail in the nation's coffin.[65] However, the second mind-blowing reversal in as

---

62   Notice the ironic reversal of who is giving the payment in Ezekiel.

63   Cf. 2:5.

64   Cf. Jer 18:15 in its context. Such forgettings are all the more tragic in view of the fact that Yahweh was to be His Memorial Name, the name by which He was to be remembered perpetually (cf. Exod 3:15).

65   I.e., such would be the logical expectation as built upon the condemning evidences and divine pronouncements of Hos 2:2-13. However, the conjunction "Therefore" (or "That being so") which launches vv. 14-23 shockingly functions in this setting more like a "Nevertheless."

many chapters introduces another breaking in of God's unfathomable mercy.[66] Yahweh, having just leveled against the nation many more evidences of their infidelity, now approaches them in a courting manner.[67] The "behold, I am going to entice her" arrests the reader's attention, although not the nation's back then. This introductory verbal, well translated "allure" (NASB, ESV, NIV, *et al.*), is used in other contexts with meanings ranging from "persuade" to "seduce."[68] Here Yahweh commits Himself to wooing her back to Him as her only truly faithful Husband. Furthermore, He affirms, "I will bring her into the wilderness and will speak (lit.) upon her heart," i.e., talk to her "kindly" (NASB) or "tenderly" (NIV).

Yahweh's inexplicable, unfathomable, loving gestures are backed up by a tangible promise in verse 15a: "There I will give her vineyards back to her and make the Valley of Achor into a gateway of hope" (HCSB). This not only will be a subsequent reversal of God's destruction of "her vines" (v. 12), but also the Valley of Trouble (i.e., Achor) will be transformed into the Door of Hope.[69]

That someday in the future God's love would no longer be unrequited is indicated in verses 15b-16: "And (or then) there (or in that place) she will answer (or respond) (or sing[70]) as in the days of her youth,[71] as in the day when she came up out of the Land of Egypt. Now it will come to

---

66   Cf. Hos 2:2-13 and 2:14-23 with Ezek 16:15-52 and 16:53ff.

67   I.e., actually a *re*-courting mode as indicated by the historical allusions to the Exodus and His wilderness provisions in the following verses.

68   Cf. what Jeremiah boldly accuses God of doing to him in calling him into prophetic ministry (20:7)!

69   It is interesting that fairly often in Scripture the passageway to hope is through trials and troubles (cf., e.g., Rom 5:3-5).

70   This Hebrew root exhibits multiple semantic fields, most of which fit this setting; however, the LXX's rendering of "to be humbled" or "humiliated" does not align with the immediate context.

71   Combining this reference to her "youth," "the wilderness," and other features in the immediate context, obvious parallels with Jer 2:2 come to light.

pass on that day—the utterance of Yahweh—that you will call Me 'my Husband'[72] and will not again call me 'my *Baali*.'"[72]

Although showing signs of compliance, verses 17ff. indicate that it is God who would initiate and enable change. Concerning her switching from "my *Baali*" to "my Husband," Yahweh says in verse 17, "For I will remove the names of the Baals from her mouth, and they shall be remembered by name no more" (ESV). As revealed so clearly to His people, they must not have any other gods besides Him (cf., e.g., Exod 20:2-3). The One and only true God bears the Name to "be remembered," the memorial Name Yahweh (Exod 3:15), and He will step in to do away with any form of polytheistic or syncretistic "worship."

Another eschatological "on that day" stands near the head of verse 18, continuing God's unfathomably gracious commitments to a high-handedly wicked people. In the first part of verse 18 the LORD promises to make a covenant with all the creatures He had originally placed under the vice regency of man (cf. Gen 1:28). Contextually this seemingly would mercifully neutralize the consequences of the judgments previously mentioned in the last part of verse 12.

Furthermore, in the human domain this covenant of Yahweh would establish[73] peace. The language of God's "breaking the bow" used back in Hos 1:5 returns in the second part of 2:18. This time it pertains to the abolishing of all human warfare which will result in a state of true peace.[74]

Once again, shockingly in the larger context of Israel's gross infidelity, God pledges His marital fidelity to them in verses 19-20. Each poetic line[75] in the original text of these two verses begins conspicuously with echoing words of divine commitment: "And (or Now) I will betroth you

---

72   Respectively in Hebrew *Ishi* ("my Husband") … *Baali* ("my Baal," or "master").

73   The last line of v. 18 (v. 20, Hebrew) literally reads: "I will cause them to lie down…."

74   Conceptually, this universal and extended application of safety and peace relates to the individual experience of the psalmist as testified to in Ps 4:8. Furthermore, when these kinds of conditions are set in the context of "on that day," millennial parallels galore arise.

75   There are three of them. Incidentally, the verbs should be construed as prophetic perfects; God's promises are viewed as done deals.

to Myself… . And (or Now) I will betroth you to Myself … . And (or Now) I will betroth you to Myself." In view of the ancient Near Eastern characteristics of betrothal, the LORD is essentially pledging: "I will take you to be My wife" (HCSB).[76]

He qualifies the first voicing of that pledge with "forever." God will not renege on His promise. Then in the second voicing of His commitment He qualifies with some of His precious attributes, i.e., righteousness, justice, loyal love, and a TLC kind of mercy. Finally, He adds to His final "I will" pledge of faithfulness, the antithesis of His people's track record of infidelity. His gracious actions as an initiator will in the future finally have an effect on a previously apostate people: "And (or then) (or so) that you will know [contra. v. 8a] the LORD [i.e., Yahweh]" (v. 20b). They will eventually acknowledge Him as the great "I AM" of Exodus 3. (Cf. Exod 6:7 in its historic context and Jer 31:34 in its New Covenant setting).

God's direct intervention in verse 21 causes the chain reaction which follows in the remainder of verses 21-22.[77] This intervention and its positive consequences are couched historically in the future Day of the LORD, i.e., "on that day." As background, remember that the various ancient Near Eastern agrarian societies sought out fertility gods in hopes of bountiful crops. As pointed out previously this most likely was a significant factor in Israel's apostasy from Yahweh (cf., e.g., 2:5 with the LORD's judgments in vv. 12-13). Here in verse 21 Yahweh now demonstrates that He and He alone controls "nature" so as to bestow the blessing of bountiful crops.[78]

The final link in this chain, "and they[79] will respond to Jezreel," brings back the name of Hosea's and Gomer's first child. Among other features, the Hebrew root of that symbolic name for Israel is "to sow." In judgment God is going to *sow* [in the sense of to scatter, to disperse] His people

---

76   For further justification note the parallelism exhibited in 2 Sam 3:14.

77   This chain reaction is largely maintained by five occurrences of a Hebrew root exhibiting such meanings as "to answer, to respond," etc.

78   Cf., e.g., His providential control in Ps 65:9-13.

79   I.e., the heavens, the earth, and its abundance of produce.

into captivities as He would soon do; however, in mercy, He would in the future *sow* [in the sense of sow as to plant] them back into the Promised Land (cf. v. 23a). And that land will be abundantly productive.

The rest of verse 23 deliberately brings back into the poetic picture the other two children born to Hosea and to Gomer, the prostitute. God promises in verse 23b: "I will have mercy on No Mercy" (ESV). This is a future reversal of His judgment conveyed by the symbolic name of *Lo-ruhamah* for Israel. Finally at the end of verse 23, the third child enters to complete the picture: "And I will say to Not My People, 'You are my people,' and he shall say, 'You are my God'" (ESV). The severance of relationship conveyed by this name, *Lo-ammi*, will also be reversed, and an intimate relationship will be reestablished in the future.[80]

EXHORTATIONS

In this first portion of Hosea, chapter 2 uncovers not only Israel's pursuit of idolatry but also the spiritual and theological assumptions driving their sin. Scripture texts like this one not only expose the false beliefs which were feeding Israel's unfaithfulness, but they help us detect evidences of false worship in our own hearts as well. After exposing the progression of Israel's sin, the passage reveals the Lord's response to the nation's sin and the motivations behind His gracious reactions.

(2:1-13) THE ANATOMY OF ISRAEL'S IDOLATRY

Relational Treachery

Israel's habitual idolatry continues to be pictured in Gomer, the unfaithful wife who runs away from Hosea in breathless pursuit of adulterous relationships. In a sickening display of the hardness of her heart, she betrays her husband and insists, "I will go after my lovers" (v. 5). The LORD contends, "She will pursue her lovers ... she will seek them ....

---

80   Besides the confirmation of this merciful promise found in Hos 2:23, remember a similar assurance of it in 1:10-11.

And follow her lovers" (vv. 7,13). Gomer's act of hunting down other lovers requires her to simultaneously turn her back on Hosea. In like manner, Israel, chasing after other gods, has blatantly rejected her God and betrayed His love, preferring the world's impotent, gilded godlets.

The LORD frequently describes the profoundly grievous nature of Israel's idolatry in terms of deep personal betrayal and appalling relational atrocity. Even in a passage as seemingly unlikely as the giving of the law at Mt. Sinai, the LORD precedes the prohibition of idolatry with a reminder of His relationship to them as a mighty deliverer. God reminds them, "I am the LORD your God, who brought you out of the land of Egypt, out of the house of slavery" (Exod 20:2). The very term "house of slavery" would have recalled bitter memories of the cruel oppression and lengthy misery in Egypt from which God had so dramatically liberated them. Remembering the undeserved favor which the LORD had showered on His people should have also compelled them to obey every word from the mouth of such a mighty Savior. Therefore, disobedience to God's demand for exclusive worship and perpetual spiritual fidelity is not merely viewed by Him as a legal infraction, though it is certainly nothing less than that. Rather, the LORD is appalled that His goodness and love could be met by His redeemed ones with such cold ingratitude and cruel disloyalty. In addition to Hosea, other prophets also castigate Israel for her relational treachery often using the imagery of a rebellious, ungrateful child toward a loving parent (Deut 1:31; Isa 1:2; 30:1,9; Jer 3:14; Mal 1:6).

Misplaced Gratitude

Gomer's decisive rejection of Hosea is driven by the unthinkable assumption that the undeserved blessings, so lavishly bestowed on her by a generous husband, had actually come from adulterous lovers. Gomer arrogantly asserts, "They give me my bread and my water, my wool and my flax, my oil and my drink" (v. 5). The LORD laments that Gomer—and by extension Israel—"does not know that it was I who gave her the grain and the new wine and the oil, and lavished on her silver and gold which they used for Baal" (v. 8). Like Gomer, the people of God actually chose to believe that their prosperity did not come from God Almighty, but from their own hand-gilded idols. Habitually giving credit where credit was *not* due, the nation found themselves caught up in a blindness for which they were directly culpable. They systematically duped themselves into believing that the prosperity they enjoyed was sourced in false gods. Gomer knew better. Israel and Judah knew better. You and I know better as well. Any time that we are tempted to give credit to another for that which only God could accomplish, we are guilty of this same sin.

It should be noted, however, that Israel's practice of such foolish misattribution of God's worth and works to both non-deities and themselves did not signal the complete abandonment of the worship of Yahweh. Rather (and perhaps worse than that), they attempted to blend together the worship of the one true God with the pagan gods of the surrounding nations. While such a mingling of holy and unholy worship may strike us today as unthinkable, it is important to remember that in the world of Hosea's day, worshipping a plethora of gods was not considered exceptionally evil; it was simply customary. Spiritually toxic syncretism, expressly forbidden by God, was imbedded into the fabric of Canaanite culture. Israel's participation in false worship did not seem outrageous; it was a simple matter of accommodating the world around them.

Offering sacrifices to a fertility god when you were desperate to bear children, or to the god of rain when your fields were in danger of drought, displays the crassly, self-serving heart behind all idolatries. In essence, Israel reasoned, "What could it hurt to seek help from Yahweh on the Sabbath and pray to other gods during the week as a safety net just in case God didn't come through?" Such thinking inevitably caused the Lord's people to offer external, perfunctory worship to God, while giving deeper, more loyal, and truer devotion and trust to false gods. Millennia later, the apostles would warn believers of the danger of double-mindedness, being conformed to or loving the world (James 1:8; Rom 12:2; 1 John 2:15). Though devoid of the religious formality of temples and carved idols, the church today often seeks to remain orthodox in its external worship forms while seeking to maintain a comfortable friendship with the world, a friendship that is regarded by the Lord as nothing less than spiritually adulterous enmity with Him (James 4:4).

Such misdirected thanksgiving and amalgamation of true and false worship is proof of the utter corruption of men's hearts and the distilled essence of all idolatry (Rom 1:18ff.). Underneath every gilded statue before which men bow or offer sacrificial gifts is ultimately the worship of oneself. There is little difference between Israel's declaration that idols have given them all their goods and the claim that "my power and the strength of my hand have made me this wealth" (Deut 8:17). Nebuchadnezzar remains the outstanding example of blatant self-worship when he asserts, "Is this not Babylon the great, which I myself have built as a royal residence by the might of my power and for the glory of my majesty?" (Dan 4:30). Often in self-worship we clamor for others to recognize and admire our accomplishments. We insist that people praise us for our pitiful displays of external righteousness and insist that there be grateful applause for anything resembling a sacrifice. Inebriated with a sense of our own supposed greatness, we demand that our craving for praise be satisfied. Our evil hearts covet the glory that belongs exclusively to God. We must repent of such proud, wicked cravings and say with the psalmist, "Not to us, O LORD, not to us, but to Your name give glory because of Your lovingkindness, because of Your truth" (Ps 115:1).

Spiritual Amnesia

Having indicted Israel for both her deep relational betrayal and misplaced thankfulness, finally the LORD diagnoses His people with a severe case of spiritual amnesia. He declares, "[Israel] forgot Me" (v. 13). They forgot God? They forgot the LORD who lavished His love and favor beyond description on them? It would seem impossible to disregard such a gracious God! Yet Hosea's fiery sermons about the dangers of forgetting God were not unique to this prophet. The Old Testament contains many warning flares from the LORD regarding His people's pitiful propensity to forget Him, especially during times of prosperity. It is a particularly prominent theme in Deuteronomy, as the following excerpts demonstrate:

Only give heed to yourself and keep your soul diligently, so that you *do not forget the things which your eyes have seen* and they do not depart from your heart all the days of your life; but make them know to your sons and grandsons. (Deut 4:9, emphasis added)

... watch yourself, that you *do not forget the LORD* who brought you out of the land of Egypt, out of the house of slavery. (Deut 6:12, emphasis added)

When you have eaten and are satisfied, you shall bless the LORD your God for the good land which He has given you. Beware that you *do not forget the LORD* ... (Deut 8:10-11a, emphasis added)

... when ... all that you have multiplies, *then your heart will become proud and you will forget the LORD your God* who brought you out from the land of Egypt, out of the house of slavery. (Deut 8:13-14, emphasis added)

But you shall *remember the* LORD your God, for it is He who is giving you power to make wealth. (Deut 8:18, emphasis added)

See also Judg 3:7; 1 Sam 12:9, Pss 9:17; 50:22; 78:7; Jer 23:27.

These passages reveal an undeniable link between the prosperity of God's people and their willful failure to constantly bring to mind the glorious person and work of God. How sad that still today the Lord's people should be capable of selfishly grasping the physical and spiritual blessings which He so generously bestows, while ignoring the Giver. Rather than responding in grateful worship for the undeserved gifts from God's hand, those same blessings often became the trigger for despising and forgetting God. We cannot afford to remain ignorant of the spiritual danger of prosperity. Riches, and the comfort and ease that frequently accompany them, are often the genesis of a proud despising of God in the heart.

God's Just Response to Idolatry

How does the Lord respond when His people willingly forget Him? First, He declares that He will place massive blockades to hinder Gomer (i.e., Israel) from her breathless pursuit of other lovers (i.e., gods). Two vivid images portray the intentional obstructions the LORD will place between His people and their sinful pursuits: the first, a tall, confining hedge of thorns, and the second, an impenetrable, encircling wall (v. 6). The idea behind both images is that the LORD Himself will create circumstances that will make it impossible to locate, much less travel down, the well-worn paths to idolatry. God will interrupt His people's pathetic quest for sin. He will impede their grievous iniquity. He will make it tough to transgress. Additionally, the LORD declares that He will remove and destroy the very blessings given by His hand that were so erroneously attributed to false gods (vv. 8-10). Further, Israel is warned that the LORD will not only eradicate their false worship, but will also humiliate the nation by exposing their shame before their so-called deities. Finally, the LORD declares that there will be national punishment for the panting pursuits after false gods (vv. 9-13).

The LORD's ultimate purpose in hindering His people's careening path of sin is stated directly when God predicts a day when Gomer " … will say, 'I will go back to my first husband, for it was better for me then than now'" (v. 7). Gomer's words, like a foreshadowing of the thoughts of the prodigal son returning to his father in Luke 15, reveal the redemptive motive of God: to cause His people to repent. God's placement of hedges and walls, His removal of prosperity, and His termination of idolatry in Israel are all designed not merely to express displeasure at their sin, but for the spiritual good of His people, so as to lead them back to Himself.

Despite the nation's disloyalty, God's committed love makes it impossible for Him to react with cold indifference. He cannot respond with disinterest saying, "Go ahead and pursue your lovers unencumbered. Keep bringing your pseudo-sacrifices. Continue the vain attempt to simultaneously worship Me and a multitude of gods." The Lord's perfect lovingkindnesses will never bless and prosper His children in their sin. Instead, He kindly put in place gracious hindrances so that His people would not continue in the hideous delusion that it really does pay to worship Baal. God displays his love for His own by thwarting their clamorous idolatry!

Many years ago I counseled a couple in which the wife admitted to having deep affections in her heart for other men, affections that she was beginning to express with flattering words and thoughtful gifts. The husband responded to her disturbing confession with shocking indifference and without even a hint of jealousy. He informed me that his wife had disclosed such sinful thoughts many times throughout their marriage. Based on his unconcerned response, I could only reach one sad conclusion: he did not deeply love his wife! In contrast to such an unresponsive husband, the sheer intensity of God's love prevents Him from resembling in any way the apathetic husband. When the Lord's people go whoring after other lovers, He does not remain indifferent; instead, He will do whatever is necessary, even if that means afflicting the very people whom He loves, in order to produce a penitent heart that will return to the Lord and lover of their souls.

(2:14–23) GOD'S MERCIFUL RESPONSE TO IDOLATRY

In the previous passage, Hosea prophesied of the severe but ultimately gracious hindrances that God would place between Israel and their chronic idolatry. Further, Hosea announced that the final purpose of the Lord's "sin blockade" was to bring the nation back to Himself. In this passage, the prophet gloriously details the success of that intended reconciliation: God's gracious hindrances led to an even more gracious restoration. The Lord's undiminished desire for a relationship with such disloyal rebels is astounding and reveals much about the nature of His unrelenting love.

God Initiates Reconciliation

Although the stated goal of God's judgment was for Israel to cry out, "I will go back" (2:7), it is God Himself who shockingly and mercifully takes the initiative. Although His love was spurned so grossly, the Lord expresses His desire to pursue a new "courtship" of His people (2:14). God promises to win back the affection of His people through loving deeds of deliverance and tender words spoken directly to the heart of His nation/bride. God does not wait for Israel to call, but rather He takes the lead in bringing about a reunion.

The numerous, rich spiritual blessings with which the Lord woos His people are overwhelming, particularly in contrast to what they actually deserve. God promises the full restoration of prosperity (vv. 15a). He comforts them with the assurance that He will transform the place of calamity, shame, and trouble into a door of deep, spiritual hope (v. 15b). The Lord commits Himself to the removal of every remnant of idolatry (v. 17). He covenants to reestablish temporal security and military peace (v. 18). With unusual intensity, God makes a threefold, absolute, eternal oath of His renewed betrothal to his bride/nation, a vow grounded solely on His righteous character (v. 19-20). He reminds His people that as Creator of the earth, He alone will provide abundant, fruitful harvests (vv. 21-22).

Climactically, the Lord pledges the absolute reversal of the nation's spiritual status reflected in the names of Hosea and Gomer's children. Jezreel, their firstborn, whose name meant "to scatter" or "to sow," indicates that Israel will indeed be "scattered" for a time as an exile, but eventually the Lord Himself will "sow" them back in the Promised Land. The plight of the nation depicted in the daughter named Lo-ruhamah ("not loved") will indeed receive the lavish, compassion she did not expect. Finally, the rejection and temporary abandonment associated with the son Lo-Ammi ("not my people") will be eradicated. What relief for the people of God to learn that they still belong to God, as they rejoiced at the precious words of God, "You are my people." Long before the people of God were anywhere close to repenting, God re-kindles the relationship on His own accord.

These prolific promises of dramatic reversals are not God's embarrassed apology for over-speaking regarding His judgment of Israel. Rather, the LORD's unexpected commitments to bless His rebellious people are an indication of just how unrestrained His love is for His own. God will indeed chastise those He calls His own, but God could not, would not ever renege on the covenant He made with His chosen people centuries beforehand with Abraham (Gen 12:1-3). The future blessings and restoration which were prophesied through Hosea were in some measure bestowed on the nation following their return from exile. However, the use of the unique phrase "in that day," combined with the assurances of complete harmony between men and animals and military peace among nations (Isa 2:1-4; 11:6ff.), clearly indicates that their ultimate, complete fulfillment will not occur until the millennial kingdom.

You and I share with ancient Israelites the humbling knowledge that any reconciliation between themselves and God—any true repentance, or any spiritual progress in holiness—is always the result of Him making the first move. Like the prophet Hosea, the apostle John echoes the theme of God's self-initiating, self-sacrificing love for sinners: "In this is love, not that we loved God, but that He loved us and sent His son to be the propitiation for our sins.... . We love Him because He first loved us" (1 John 4:10, 19). More specifically, verses from Hosea chapter 2 are quoted by both the apostles Paul and Peter in order to demonstrate that followers of Jesus Christ have also been recipients of that same unbelievable, lavish mercy of God. Like Israel, you and I have had our spiritual destinies dramatically reversed by God's powerful and gracious initiative:

> As He also says in Hosea, "I WILL CALL THOSE WHO WERE NOT MY PEOPLE, 'MY PEOPLE,' AND HER WHO WAS NOT BELOVED, 'BELOVED.' AND IT SHALL BE THAT IN THE PLACE WHERE IT WAS SAID TO THEM, 'YOU ARE NOT MY PEOPLE,' THERE THEY SHALL BE CALLED SONS OF THE LIVING GOD." (Rom 9:25-26)

For you once were NOT A PEOPLE, but now you are
THE PEOPLE OF GOD; you had NOT RECEIVED
MERCY, but now you have RECEIVED MERCY. (1
Peter 2:10)

Of course as we read we must keep in mind that the apostles' application
of Old Testament promises to the church does not in any way diminish
the reality of a literal and future fulfillment for the nation of Israel as well.

God Accomplishes Reconciliation

As you read this chapter, you cannot help but be encouraged to see that
the severe chastisement that Israel felt under God's correction will eventually produce an ability and readiness in the fickle hearts of Israel to
perceive, receive, and return to the faithful love of God. In His infinite wisdom, the LORD knew just what would be required to soften
such stubborn sinners and cause real repentance. Hosea 2:15-23 beautifully describes Israel's future reciprocation of God's loving initiative. The
nation will finally respond (possibly "sing") to the LORD with the kind
of heart that characterized them when, as a young nation, they first were
delivered out of Egypt (v. 15b). With undivided loyalty, they will call
the LORD "My Husband" and no longer give even a thought to former
idols (v. 16). In contrast to the earlier indictment of culpable ignorance
(v. 8), finally, they will truly know the LORD (v. 20) and cry out to Him,
"You are my God" (v. 23). Because of God's loving correction and pursuit
of reconciliation, Israel's relationship with God will be restored and her
worship purified. What bounty will follow the abandonment of Baal!
What blessings will follow the ending of blasphemy!

God knows how to select the perfect circumstances to accomplish
His redeeming and sanctifying purposes in our lives as well. The apostle
Paul affirms the spiritual principle that greater spiritual vitality inevitably
follows in the wake of trials, saying, "We also exult in our tribulations,
knowing that tribulation brings about perseverance; and perseverance,
proven character; and proven character, hope; and hope does not disap-
point, because the love of God has been poured out within our hearts

through the Holy Spirit who was given to us" (Rom 5:3-5). Similarly, the Puritan Richard Sibbes encouraged believers to humbly trust that the Lord fully knows just what is needed to help us repent:

> Let us lament our own perversity and say: Lord, what a heart have I that needs all this, that none of this could be spared.... God by his Spirit convinces us deeply, setting our sins before us, and driving us to a standstill. Then we will cry out for mercy. Conviction will breed contrition, and this leads to humiliation. Therefore desire God that he would bring a clear and a strong light into all the corners of our souls, and accompany it with a spirit of power to lay our hearts low. (*The Bruised Reed*, p. 11)

Some two centuries later John Newton wrote this powerful hymn addressing the Lord's sometimes surprising means by which the He leads believers into a deeper love for Himself.

Prayer Answered by Crosses
By John Newton

I asked the Lord that I might grow
In faith and love and every grace,
Might more of his salvation know,
And seek more earnestly his face.
'Twas he who taught me thus to pray;
And he, I trust, has answered prayer;
But it has been in such a way
As almost drove me to despair.
I hoped that, in some favored hour,
At once he'd answer my request,
And by his love's constraining power
Subdue my sins, and give me rest.

Instead of this, he made me feel
The hidden evils of my heart,
And let the angry powers of hell
Assault my soul in every part.
Yea, more, with his own hand he seemed
Intent to aggravate my woe,
Crossed all the fair designs I schemed,
Blasted my gourds*, and laid me low.
Lord, why is this? I trembling cried;
Wilt thou pursue this worm to death?
This is the way, the Lord replied
I answer prayer for grace and faith.
These inward trials I now employ
From self and pride to set thee free,
And break thy schemes of earthly joy,
That thou may'st seek thy all in me.

The undeniable lesson of Hosea chapter 2 is that God, motivated by irrevocable love for His people, will do no more or less than is required in order to draw His wayward people back to Himself. One cannot help but wonder, as Newton said so poignantly above, how many of today's afflictions are sent to us in answer to yesterday's prayer for greater maturity. That is not to say that every affliction a believer experiences is sent by God as a specific correction for sin. But the Scripture does assure us that every trial will refine our faith and draw us to Christ in greater dependence and humility. Trust the Lord robustly, that He may use your present inward trials to wean you from self, pride, and earthly joy.

*A reference to God's destruction of the plant which He had given to the prophet Jonah. The King James translation of Jonah 4:6 reads, "God prepared a gourd." This plant not only provided Jonah with shade, but also inordinate pleasure.

3 HOSEA 3:1–5

EXPOSITION

(3:1–3) A MANDATED REMARRIAGE AND ITS TRAGIC PICTURE

As chapter 3 will symbolically illustrate, the fidelity of the LORD endures until His people finally come home. At the outset of chapter 3 in verse 1 Hosea received new directives from Yahweh God. Hosea's obedience in carrying out those divine orders is personally attested in the next two verses. Finally, in the last two verses of this exceedingly short chapter, prophetic applications are drawn.

Now returning to 3:1, Yahweh spoke personally to His prophet commanding him literally to "again, go; love a woman being loved by a neighbor [i.e., another man] and committing adultery, as Yahweh loves the sons of Israel, while (or, although) they are turning unto other gods, also loving cakes of raisins." This command conceptually parallels the initial command of Hosea 1:2 with the obvious addition of "again." Although the woman is not personally identified by name in 3:1, she should most logically be considered to be Gomer. In this present setting she is described among other things as "committing adultery" (cf. 4:2,13,14; 7:4),[81] a crime punishable by death (e.g., Lev 20:10).

---

81   Cf. the noun form based upon this Hebrew root in 2:2.

This illustrative prophetic action sets up the divine comparison (i.e., the "as … "), which again magnifies the LORD's amazing grace. He ongoingly loves a people bent on "turning to"[82] other deities, a high-handed violation of the first commandment of the Decalogue. The additional mentioning of His people apparently insatiably loving "raisin cakes" is somewhat enigmatic. A variety of cultural and cultic conjectures have been offered; however, because of the low frequency of this combo's occurrences[83] it seems best to restrict conjectures.[84]

As already mentioned, Hosea testified to his own obedience to the LORD in verses 2-3,[85] saying, "So I acquired her for myself for fifteen *shekels* of silver and a *homer*[86]of barley along with a *lethek*[87] of barley. Then I said to her, 'You will remain with me many days. You must not practice prostitution and you will not be with a man, not even I with you.'"

The probable imagery of verse 2 is that of Hosea buying her out of slavery. Although the normal ransom value of a slave would have been 30 pieces of silver,[88] his fifteen *shekels* plus a substantial amount of barley apparently secured the purchase price of this prostitute. Once ownership was transferred to Hosea he laid down the law to her in 3:3. They would cohabit for a long time; she would have to cease from her prostitution; she could not be with any man; and furthermore, during this long period

---

82   The combination of the Hebrew root "to turn" plus the directional preposition "to" or "unto" is often used idiomatically to speak of apostasy (cf., e.g., Lev 20:6; Deut 31:18,20; etc.).

83   Besides here, cf. 1 Chron 16:3; S of Songs 2:5; and Isa 16:7.

84   At the risk of ignoring this seemingly wise advice, it is interesting that two of the four occurrences stand in the historical records about David [as an aside, note the likely prophetic reference to the Greater David in Hos 3:5] distributing what appear to be celebratory gifts to the people upon the return of the ark to Israel. It could be that as Gomer pursued her paramours for her staples (2:5) and any delicacies she might acquire by prostitution, so Israel would try to satisfy her "sweet tooth" in pursuit of idolatrous affairs.

85   Also cf. this prophet's un-Jonah-like *obedience* in 1:3.

86   The volume of a *homer* is 394 liters dry measure.

87   This word occurs only here, and its equivalent volume is not known.

88   Cf. Exod 21:32.

neither would Hosea have intimate relations with her. This protracted period of abstinence begins to make symbolic sense with the arrival of the prophetic applications of verse 4.[89]

(3:4–5) A MANDATED REMARRIAGE AND ITS TRANSITIONAL PROPHECIES

The divinely-engineered deprivations of this verse would severely test the fibers of the nation's wanderlust being. She would surely "live (or dwell) (or remain) without a king and without a prince and without sacrifice and without sacred pillar and without ephod or *teraphim*." The five "and withouts" would have sounded like a dirge to her, like nails in her coffin which would severely restrain her from her idolatrous escapades. For them this would be a time of pain, but in God's plan a time of purging.[90]

These divine deprivations fall into two ancient Near Eastern categories, the political and the cultic. Israel's human government would cease, as would its syncretistic religious activities. There would be no more kings[91] or princes.[92] Both Israel's and Judah's dynasties would end with Yahweh's historical actualizations of these judgments.

Especially abominable to the LORD were the people's pollutions of Yahweh worship with false-god pursuits and practices. Although "sacrifice" and "pillar" and "ephod" could have been used as forms or

---

89   Notice how the "many days" along with the verb "to abide, dwell, remain" explicitly link v. 4 to v. 3.

90   Remember that the "afterward" of v. 5 is coming signaling repentance and restoration.

91   Although Yahweh was the ultimate King of His people (e.g., Isa 43:15; 44:6; *et al.*), early in their national history they demanded "a king like all the nations" (cf., e.g., 1 Sam 8:4-6). This request along with its granting and significance had even been predicted by God (cf., e.g., Deut 17:14; 1 Sam 8:7-9). The lion's share of these rulers were evil and proved to be of no help to the people they governed. God's long, forecasted testing period would eventually prove to be an ironic wake-up-call concerning the futility of a merely human monarchy (cf. Hos 10:3).

92   This word could also be translated more generally as "ruler, chief, captain, official," etc., indicating an across-the-board governmental breakdown. However, the rendering "prince" probably best fits the immediate and larger circle of contexts. The LORD's extended epoch of judgment would allow for no dynastic successor to step in. Note Hosea's other negative linkings of kings and princes in 7:3,5; 8:4; 13:10; etc.

instruments of acceptable worship of the true God,[93] it did not take long until all kinds of religious corruptions crept in. The *teraphim*, variously rendered "household idols" (HCSB), "household gods" (ESV), etc., are always associated with perverted religions. All those things would be cut off for ages until their absence would eventuate in conviction and repentance.

Looking down that long road through God's eschatological telescope, verse 5 reads, "Afterward the sons of Israel will return[94] and seek[95] Yahweh their God and David their king,[96] and they will turn in awe (or dread) to Yahweh and to His goodness[97] in the last days." An earlier prophecy related to this yet future prophecy was issued to the infant nation by Moses all the way back in Deuteronomy 4:29-30: "But from there[98] you will seek the LORD your God, and you will find Him if you search for Him with all your heart and all your soul. When you are in distress and all these things have come upon you,[99] in the latter days you will return to the LORD your God and listen to His voice" (NASB).

The reference to "David their king" is obviously messianic. The cutting off of "king" and "prince" would be for "many days" (3:4), but not forever. In the "later days" of verse 5, after their purging, the people of God would turn to the King of kings and the Prince of princes, i.e., the "Prince of peace" of Isaiah 9:6. The intricacies of salvation history

---

93   Cf. respectively, e.g., "sacrifice" in Lev 7:11; "pillar" in Gen 28:18-22; 31:13; "ephod" in Exod 28:4.

94   This is the primary Hebrew root for repentance in the OT. One day those chosen people *will* respond to this book's closing urgings to "return" (cf. Hos 14:1,2).

95   They would finally respond to commands to "seek" the LORD (cf., e.g., Zeph 2:3).

96   Cf. Yahweh and "David their king" in Jer 30:9.

97   The "good" or "goodness" of Yahweh is one of His most circumscribing attributes (cf., e.g., Exod 33:19; Ps 119:68; also cf. a connection with fear and dread in Jer 33:9).

98   Cf. Deut 4:27-28 as the nation where the divine judgments of Hos 3:4 would take place.

99   Cf. again Hos 3:4.

are all eventually messianically oriented (e.g., Seed/seed theology,[100] the biblical covenants, etc.). The linking together of the promissory covenants and descendants (i.e., seed[101]) which would ultimately issue in the Descendant is crucial if one is to understand a fulfillment in the first coming of Christ. Carefully consider the following *selected* links in this messianic chain: Genesis 3:15; 12:1-3; 17:1-5,21; 17:21; 21:12; 35:10-12; 49:10; Exodus 2:24-25; 2 Samuel 7:8-16; Matthew 1:1-16; Luke 3:23-38; *et al.* Yet, as the New Testament makes abundantly clear, King Jesus was rejected by the masses of Israel (cf., e.g., Matt 27:11,29,37,42; John 19:15; Acts 2:22-23; 3:11-15).

Virtually unforeseen in the Old Testament and throughout most of Christ's earlier earthly ministry was the fact that there was to be a second coming[102] (cf., e.g., Luke 24:25-26; John 14:3; Heb 9:28; 1 Peter 1:11). It will be at a stage of this yet future coming that the remainder of the covenant promises will be fulfilled, including the restoration of the Davidic dynasty with the Greater David Himself ascending to the throne and ruling upon the earth. Indeed, it is this future era that Hosea envisions in 3:5. A selected sampling of similar prophetic anticipations includes Isaiah 11; Jeremiah 23:5-6; 30:8-11; 33:23-26; Ezekiel 34:20-24; 37:24-28; Amos 9:11-15; *et al.*

EXHORTATIONS

Chapter 3 is the final portion of Hosea to use the three-dimensional pageantry of the prophet's marriage and family life as a vivid metaphor to portray the spiritual unfaithfulness of Israel and Judah. In the next eleven chapters of the book, God will address His people's sin even more directly without the living metaphor of wayward Gomer and her children with

---

100   The Seed refers to the *One, The* Messiah, and "seed" refers to the *many* (cf. e.g., Gen 3:15 and Gal 3:16 with v. 29).

101   Later in the covenants that were to be the "GPS" of salvation history the terminology is picked up in the context of a special dynasty (cf. esp. 2 Sam 7).

102   Remember that one of the messianic designations in the Bible is "the Coming One." He will also come again!

such meaning-laden names. In this short chapter the reader is thrust from the beauty of God's promises of a future re-restoration between Himself and Israel back into the present, ugly reality of the nation's infidelity. In this last marital scene, Hosea once again displays an incredible, devoted love to an unthinkably cruel adulteress. In so doing, he magnifies four characteristics of the boundless love of God for His people.

(3:1) RELENTLESS LOVE

As this chapter opens, the habitual pattern of Gomer's marital unfaithfulness remains unchanged. In verse 1 the LORD commands Hosea, in the face of Gomer's repetitive sin, to be perpetually tenacious in his loving pursuit of his wife: "Go again, love a woman who is loved by her husband, yet an adulteress." The reason it is imperative that Hosea "go again" and seek his straying wife is stated explicitly by the LORD in the second half of verse 1, " ... even as the LORD loves the sons of Israel, though they turn to other gods ... ." Hosea must repeatedly pursue Gomer in order to paint a true portrait of the relentless love of God. Hearing this command to love an undeserving wife and the important rationale behind it, you cannot help but hear what the apostle Paul would later write on marriage: "Husbands, love your wives, just as Christ also loved the church" (Eph 5:25). But it is even more meaningful for you and me to be humbled by the truth that God's relentless love sought us out while we were lost:

> For while we were still helpless, at the right time Christ died for the ungodly. For one will hardly die for a righteous man; though perhaps for the good man someone would dare to die. But God demonstrates His own love toward us, in that while we were yet sinners, Christ died for us. Much more then, having been now justified by his blood, we shall be saved from the wrath of God through Him. For if while we were enemies we were reconciled to God through the death of His son, much more, having

been reconciled, we shall be saved by His life. (Rom 5:6-10)

It is the joyful testimony of every true believer that the Lord sought them and lovingly rescued them while they were more like Gomer than they would care to remember or admit!

(3:2) REDEEMING LOVE

Hosea records his response to God's command to love his adulterous wife yet again. You would expect the text to read, "So I, Hosea, obeyed God and went and loved just such a woman." But instead it reads, "So I went and bought her for myself" (v. 2). The act of acquiring Gomer, presumably from the slave market, is synonymous with love in the mind of the prophet. Hosea demonstrated his obedience to God's command to love his wife in a sacrificial, merciful act of generosity; he purchased her for himself. Redeeming Gomer was love in action. Of course, Hosea's actions were a portrait of God's mighty redemption, His ransom if you will, of His own people.

The precious doctrine of redemption is a major theme that runs through both the Old and New Testaments. The Mosaic law commanded that in the tragic event that someone lost their home and property due to poverty, a member of the family was obligated to mercifully repurchase or "redeem" that land for the relative who had experienced the loss (Lev 25:25). When family members became aware of the needs of their relatives, they were expected to involve themselves in relieving the suffering. They were to say, in essence, "Because we are family, your plight is my plight, I cannot just stand by and let this happen. I will, from my own resources, acquire your land for you and give it to you as a gift." Boaz is the preeminent example of a loyal and merciful kinsman redeemer in the Scriptures (Ruth 2:20; 4:4,6). As a member of Ruth's extended family, when Boaz became aware of her distress, he kindly chose to make Ruth's burdens his own. He freely assumed her indebtedness and financial needs and in loving generosity paid whatever was required to remove her vulnerability.

In the New Testament, Jesus referred to Himself as the ultimate Redeemer of sinners, claiming "The Son of Man did not come to be served, but to serve and to give His life a ransom for many" (Matt 20:28). Just as Hosea had to pay a price to purchase Gomer, even so the Lord Jesus would make His own life the payment price to buy back His spiritually enslaved people. The apostle Paul frequently affirmed that Christ Jesus "gave Himself for us to redeem us from every lawless deed" (Titus 2:14) and came to earth to "redeem those who were under the law" (Gal 4:5). Paul gloried in the thought that all believers "have redemption through His blood, the forgiveness of our trespasses" (Eph 1:7). He clearly taught the link between redemption and holy living, reminding believers that they had "been bought with a price: therefore glorify God in your body" (1 Cor 6:20). Peter reminds persecuted believers that "you were not redeemed with perishable things like silver or gold ... but with precious blood, as of a lamb unblemished and spotless, the blood of Christ" (1 Peter 1:18-19).

What went through Gomer's mind as she watched her husband exchange silver and barley for her freedom? Hosea, the man to whom she had given herself freely in marriage, now has to pay for the "honor" of marriage to a woman like herself! Was she grateful? Humiliated? Repentant? The text does not say. But regardless of how Gomer did or did not react, you and I, seeing ourselves in Gomer's unfaithfulness, have the opportunity to respond appropriately to God's extravagant, redeeming love. The only appropriate reaction to the exorbitant price paid for rebellious sinners like you and me is a life filled with praise, worship, faith, submission, and obedience!

(3:3) RESTRICTING LOVE

Having paid the redemption price for Gomer's freedom, Hosea now demands change. With intensity of words more resembling a judicial sentence than a marital conversation, Hosea declares that Gomer will be deprived, for an extended period of time, from intimacy with any man, including Hosea himself. There would be no more prostitution, adultery, or illicit relationships. Even legitimate marital relations would be withheld from Gomer. This long-term deprivation was yet another 3D prophecy being lived out in Hosea's pathetic marriage before the watching eyes of the nation. Because of their sin, Israel too would suffer as God withheld His blessing on them for a protracted period of time. God would remove Israel's earthly kings and princes which the people had sinfully preferred over His perfect, unmediated kingship (1 Sam 8:7). As Gomer would not have access to her rightful husband, God would also eliminate the legitimate priestly leadership whom He had appointed, leaving the nation without spiritual direction and devoid of revelation. Similar to the way Gomer would be prevented from her habitual pursuit of prostitution, Israel's adulterous pursuit of idols would also be eradicated, leaving the people without access to her spiritually adulterous partners. No more "toxic cocktails" blending the worship of Yahweh, Baal, and a plethora of other idols!

How humbling for you and me to realize that God's restricting love that withheld blessings from Israel ushered in a unique period of Gentile evangelism through which most of those who will read this book came to saving faith in Jesus Christ! In Romans chapter 11 Paul notes how Israel's affliction became the occasion for Gentile blessings:

> By [Israel's] transgression salvation has to come to the Gentiles (v. 11)

> Now if [Israel's] transgression is riches for the world and their failure is riches for the Gentiles, how much more will their fulfillment be! (v. 12)

> [Israel's] rejection is the reconciliation of the world (v. 15)

> [Gentiles] have been shown mercy because of [Israel's] disobedience (v. 30)

The apostle goes on to warn the Gentile church at Rome, and by extension, you and me, of the human heart's tendency to be spiritually presumptuous by wrongly assuming that we are somehow superior to disobedient Israel:

Do not be arrogant toward the branches [Israel] (v. 18)

Do not be conceited, but fear (v. 20)

Behold then the kindness and severity of God … continue in His kindness; otherwise you will be cut off (v. 22)

Do not be wise in your own estimation (v. 25)

These verses call you and me to humbly avoid the sin of spiritual presumption, knowing that we today are capable the same hard-hearted unbelief that led to God's discipline of Israel. How grateful we should be that God has not treated us with equal severity for our unbelief!

(3:4–5) RESTORING LOVE

Finally, we see that God's love is marked by restoring power. Once again, there is another unforeseen outbreak of good news! God declares that following His appointed and perfectly measured withdrawal of His blessings, Israel would indeed repent of their sin and seek Him with trembling. Israel would also turn to their Messiah, the ultimate King David. The use of terms like "afterward" and "the last days" (v. 5) indicate that Hosea was referring to Israel's future reception of Christ at His second coming and reign over the earth from David's throne. As we saw in chapter 2, God, in His wisdom, knows exactly what is needed to soften the hearts of His people.

One final observation about this short chapter: note that the text says that in the last days Israel will "come trembling to the LORD and to His goodness" (v. 5). The thought of coming into the awesome presence of the LORD with trembling seems to make sense, but what are we to make of God's people trembling before the *goodness* of God? Perhaps we would naturally assume that we should celebrate God's goodness with rejoicing or singing, but not with trembling. In a similar way, the apostle Paul spoke of a sober response to God's kindness. In Romans 2:4, he warns, "Or do you think lightly of the riches of His kindness and tolerance and patience, not knowing that the kindness of God leads you to repentance?" This passage requires each of us to ask truly heart-searching questions: "Is it a small thing to you that God has shown you undeserved kindness though you have been like spiritually unfaithful Gomer? Has God's patience with your disobedience and rebellion somehow gotten pushed to the periphery of your spiritual vision? Has the high price paid to redeem you somehow slipped off your radar? Before goodness of such magnitude, how could we do any less than tremble!

4 HOSEA 4:1–19

EXPOSITION

(4:1–19) THE LORD AS PROSECUTING ATTORNEY INDICTS HIS CRIMINAL PEOPLE

Chapter 4, however, returns to Hosea's time and the old story of an impenitent people. Both chapter 4 and chapter 5 of Hosea launch with the same command, "Hear!" The immediate application based upon the employment of the noun of direct address in 4:1 is to the people in general. In 5:1a the target group of this warning to pay close attention is initially "O priests"; however, in the next two lines, which use essentially synonymous commands of paying careful attention to, the target audience is first expanded once again to the nation (i.e., 5:1b) then restricted politically to the king and his dynasty (i.e., 5:1c). So swirling around throughout chapters 4 and 5 are Yahweh's divine indictments of both the people and their supposedly spiritual and political leaders. All of them will be shown to be theocratically guilty of high treason.

Hosea 4:1b establishes the main imagery that governs the prophet's oracles in 4:1–5:7, namely, Yahweh was the Prosecuting Attorney who was against them.[103] Furthermore, the evidences backing up His indict-

---

103 This law-court imagery utilizing the Hebrew root *ryb* was introduced in 2:2 wherein the children were to contend with their mother. Herein the LORD Himself assumes the role of Prosecutor, personally bringing His case against the people.

ments are incontestable. So all the people of the nation were to pay their undivided attention to what follows "*because* Yahweh has a *case* (or *charge*) (or *law-suit*) with[104] the ones who dwell in the land"(emphasis added).

Next in the remainder of verse 1 and in verse 2 some sample evidences are leveled against these people to support the LORD's case. The last two lines of the first verse bring up condemning omissions.[105] There nowhere existed among the people throughout the land any "truth" (or "faithfulness"[106]); any "loyalty" or "loyal love" (or "steadfast love" [ESV]) (or "faithful love" [HCSB]) (or "loving-kindness"[107]); nor any experiential "knowledge" as evidenced by a due *recognition* of God.[108]

The abominable evidences of pandemic wickedness mentioned in verse 2 were all prohibited by antecedent divine revelations.[109] It seems best to construe these five foul descriptives of the people with the verb that follows: "Cursing, lying, murder, stealing, and adultery are rampant" (HCBS). [110] That this constituted a panoramic state of affairs is confirmed all the more by the last divine assessment which reads literally, "and bloodshed touches bloodshed," i.e., "so that bloodshed follows bloodshed" (NASB). An unbroken chain of murderous bloodshed is documented.

The "Therefore" or "Consequently" at the outset of verse 3 shows what such anarchy produces. This verse begins and ends with attention-arresting personifications: "Therefore the land mourns, and all who dwell

---

104   This preposition may be contextually glossed as "against" (cf. NASB, NIV, HCSB, *et al.*).

105   Three times a Hebrew particle of *non-existence* is joined to crucial characteristics of spiritual integrity, thereby negating them.

106   The so-called *amen* word group in Hebrew, conveying the concepts of faithfulness, steadfastness, reliability, trustworthiness, truth, truthfulness, etc.

107   The exceedingly rich root *hsd*, which embodies elements of grace, love, kindness, mercy, etc.

108   Cf. the near context, i.e., v. 6. Sadly the people did not exhibit what God desired. However, remember that one day in the future the LORD Himself would bring about such a knowledge (cf. 2:20). Cf., e.g., Isa 11:9 in context.

109   Either explicitly in the Decalogue or implicitly in other contexts of divine displeasure.

110   The word literally conveys "to break through," i.e., so as to spread out, increase, etc.

in it languish,[111] and also the beasts of the field and the birds of the heavens, and even the fish of the sea are taken away" (ESV).[112] The sin of those dwelling in the land caused misery not only for themselves but also for the rest of creation. Conceptually, this brings to mind the "groanings" of redeemed, but not yet glorified, humanity and also the rest of non-human creation in Romans 8:19ff.

The law-court language returns in verse 4 (cf. v. 1). However, the Hebrew text of the last line of this verse has been disputed and therefore variously translated as indicated by a comparison and contrast of two modern versions:

> But let no man bring a charge, let no man accuse another, for your people are like those who bring charges against a priest. (NIV)

> Yet let no one contend and let none accuse, for with you is my contention, O priest (ESV).

The NIV (and the NASB) more closely follows the difficult line of the Hebrew text as it stands without resorting to some of the suggested emendations. Although the singular "you" of the lead-off verb of verse 5 could refer to the "no man" or "no one" as representative of all the people (i.e., v. 4a), the ESV apparently thought it was better to take it as pointing to the priest, especially when verse 5 goes on with the words "and *also* the prophet" (emphasis added).

What do we make of all this? Undoubtedly the LORD is putting a special focus on the responsibilities, failures, and culpabilities of the priesthood in 4:4-6 (cf. also His first direct address in 5:1a). Spiritual leaders are held to the highest level of accountability because, in God's words through Malachi, "the lips of a priest should preserve knowledge, and men should seek instruction from his mouth; for he is the messenger

---

111 Or, "waste away."

112 A biblical expansion of the effects of a sinning people may be noted in Isa 24:4ff.

of the LORD of hosts" (Mal 2:7). However, as in Hosea's day so also in Malachi's, "'But as for you [i.e., the priests of Mal 2:7], you have turned aside from the way; you have caused many to stumble by the instruction; you have corrupted the covenant of Levi,' says the LORD of hosts" (Mal 2:8). So, although the priests had such a negative impact on the nation in general during the time of Hosea's ministry (cf., e.g., 4:6), the people could not merely have passed the buck, thinking that they, as victims, were off the hook. There was more than enough culpability to go around to every individual of the nation. Therefore, it is best to take verse 4 as a prohibition of any and every person in the nation who might desire to bring an accusation against the priests. The LORD God will personally take care of that through Hosea, His prophet.[113] And so He does in verses 5-6:

> So you[114] will stumble by day, and the prophet[115] also will stumble with you[116] by night; And I will destroy your mother.[116] My people are destroyed for lack of knowledge. Because you[117] have rejected knowledge, I also will reject you from being My priest. Since you have forgotten[118] the law of your God, I also will forget your children. (NASB)

---

113 Cf. also the overall context of Malachi.

114 Once again, this "you" refers to the priest (i.e., all the priests of Hosea's day).

115 In reference to the false prophets who often were stationed as court prophets (cf., e.g., the situation under Ahab in 1 Kgs 22).

116 In Hebrew the "with you" in the first line of v. 5 and the "your mother" in the second line are pronounced the same, heightening the gravity of this oracle of judgment by these sounds in their ears!

117 An emphatic "you" in the Hebrew text.

118 I.e., not amnesia, but a deliberate disregard of God's instruction. Notice that this act of priestly mutiny sets up a *lex talionis* execution of divine justice.

Both "your mother" in verse 5 and literally "your sons"[119] in verse 6, whether these designations be taken literally or figuratively or a combination thereof, announce a cutting off at both ends of any priestly heritage.

In verses 7-10 of chapter 4 more high-handed evidences of priestly apostasy are brought forth by the Prosecuting Attorney. Verse 7 presents a bit of a textual challenge as can be seen from the following two renderings:

> The more the priests increased, the more they sinned against me;[120] they exchanged their Glory for something disgraceful. (NIV)

> The more they increased, the more they sinned against me;[120] I will change their glory into shame. (ESV)

There are obviously no insurmountable problems in translating and understanding verse 7a. However, concerning verse 7b the NIV's rendering does not follow the Hebrew text as written but goes by a scribal suggestion[121] along with a couple of early translations. However, the text just as it stands (cf. the rendering of ESV) makes perfectly good sense, and it sets up a normal pattern of the exposure of a sin followed by its just judgment. In the context of the ancient Near East, it was a most dreaded judgment. Yahweh was going to change their religious position of prominence and prestige into one of disgrace. He often levels the same kind of judgment on offending individuals, groups, or nations (cf., e.g., Hab 2:16).

Verse 8 picks up the most common Hebrew root for sin (cf. v. 7a); however, here it appears as a noun form. Even more noteworthy, it introduces one of Hosea's famous puns. Paradoxically, this noun may refer to either a sin committed or to the prescribed *offering* necessary to atone for that sin, namely, "the sin-offering." But herein God through Hosea confronts the priests with a scathing double entendre. In contributing to the

---

119 Most often rendered "children" in modern versions.

120 The "against Me" represents an exposure of high-handed sin, which also appears in such passages as 1 Sam 2:25; 1 Kgs 8:46; Ps 51:4 [v. 6, Hebrew.]; etc.

121 One of 18 throughout the whole of the OT suggested by them.

covenantal infractions of the people, these priests were insuring a plentiful diet for themselves. Indeed God had set up many of the ordained sacrifices secondarily in order that they and their families would live by designated portions of them. The priests of Hosea's day were wickedly behaving like the sons of Eli in a former era (cf. 1 Sam 2:12ff.). They were abusing 'the system'!

Verse 8b simply reinforces the fact that they were acting, in some way, as catalysts for the people's sin. Here the term for sin is heightened, conveying the ideas of perversity, iniquity, or moral crookedness.[122] The priests' twisted example, as the proverb of verse 9a indicates, was replicated in the people: "And it will be, like people, like priest" (NASB). This brings divine judgment upon all parties; literally, "therefore (or consequently), I will visit[123] upon them[124] their ways and return to them their deeds." This is the language of payback.[125]

Some resultant conditions of this divine judgment are listed in the first two lines of verse 10. Ironically, "they will eat [cf. v. 8] but never be satisfied; they will practice prostitution[126] but never increase."[127] All their efforts at self-satisfaction would be frustrated by Yahweh's interventions of judgment. Furthermore, in this context (cf. v. 14), the reference to playing the prostitute would have likely involved the common pagan practices of cultic prostitution. Such practices, associated with the so-called gods and goddesses of fertility, were looked upon as a means

---

122 The Hebrew root in its verbal manifestations often conveys a bending or a twisting.

123 Continuing the pattern of prophetic perfects (i.e., although actualization was reserved for the future, in God's book it was as good as done).

124 Continuing a pattern of collective singular suffixes (i.e., "them" for "him").

125 Cf. the verb to visit as *punish* in v. 9b with occurrences in 1:4; 2:13 [v. 15, Hebrew]; 8:13; 9:9; 12:2 [v. 3, Hebrew]. Also cf. the concept of payback in Deut 7:10.

126 This root, vital to the understanding of the whole prophecy, occurs in high concentrations in 4:10ff. (e.g., 4:10,11,12,14,15,18; 5:3,4). Another essentially synonymous term will join it in 4:14.

127 This last verb more literally means to break forth (cf. its occurrence in 4:2), and in certain contexts would convey a breaking forth out of the womb, i.e., here with the negative, there will be no births.

to higher productivity. No wonder the only true and living God would render futile such abominable efforts. Indeed all their perversions were the result of an abandonment of obedience to Yahweh (v. 10c). Verse 11 mentions a few of the things that had dulled their senses, resulting in such gross disloyalty: "Prostitution and wine and new wine take away[128] sense (or understanding)."[129]

As already intimated, verses 12-14 identify the professing people of Yahweh as idolaters. The first two lines of verse 12 take up a common prophetic polemic, the stupidity of idolatry: "My people inquire of their wood,[130] and their stick (or staff) (or rod[131]) informs them." On how nonsensical this truly is, compare the excoriations coming from some of Yahweh's other prophets, for example, Isaiah 44:9-17; Jeremiah 10:1-14; Habakkuk 2:18-19; et al. The last part of Hosea 4:12 attaches rationale, or should we say, ir-rationale to this culpably pitiful situation: "For a spirit of whoredom has led them astray, and they have left their God to play the whore" (ESV).

Verse 13 puts a special focus on places of worship. Although the two terms for sacrificing in verse 13a were used for stipulated practices in Yahweh worship and although many of the patriarchs sacrificed on high places, prior to the Tabernacle and Temple becoming centers for prescribed worship, the vast majority of such references as these were to false worship practices in unauthorized places. Jeremiah 3:6 succinctly summarizes all similar lapses into false worship: "Have you seen what faithless Israel did? She went up on every high hill and under every green tree and she was a harlot there" (NASB).

The mentioning of prostituting "daughters" and adulterous "daughters-in-law" at the end of verse 13 introduces an interpretive problem with the arrival of verse 14. The text of verse 14a reads "I will not bring punishment upon your daughters when they commit prostitution nor upon

---

128   The verb indicates characteristic action.

129   Lit. "heart."

130   I.e., a carved piece of wood, a wooden idol.

131   Many suggest a "divining rod."

your daughters-in-law when they commit adultery." What?! Is the God of perfect justice here failing to carry it out? Although it may not be logically possible to vindicate Yahweh with dogmatic defenses, several considerations may be brought to bear. First and foremost is the fact that God does not have a need for any puny creature to defend Him in view of such a pronouncement. Also, it must be noted that the suffixes which are translated as "your" on both "daughters" and "daughters-in-law" along with the pronoun and verbs of the next line are all masculine plurals.[132] Therefore, it was the males of this sinful society who were going apart with[133] prostitutes and who were sacrificing with temple prostitutes. However, the last line of the verse[134] along with all the rest of the book's pronouncements of judgment seem to be all-inclusive. Consequently, verse 14 could be pointing, by an inferred comparison, to the higher level of accountability and culpability of those men. Or, it might be that God was going to punish them by not stopping, at least not immediately, the gross practices of their own family members. After all, the male family "models" were occupying themselves with cultic prostitutes of false religions.

A temporary differentiation[135] between the Northern Kingdom's and the Southern Kingdom's degree of culpability occurs with the arrival of verse 15. The verse begins with the unequivocal exposure of idolatrous sin in the North: "Although you, Israel, are characterized by playing the prostitute ... ." Continuing with a focus on the Southern Kingdom, verse 15b says, "Don't let Judah become guilty!" (HCSB). The implication is that the inhabitants of the South had not yet come to the point of incorrigibility.

The second half of verse 15 singles out two worship locations which historically had shifted from places where legitimate worship had

---

132 In order to avoid confusion, most English translations instead of translating these words literally, which would lead to ambivalence (i.e., "and they themselves ... "), appropriately render with the gloss "and the men themselves ... ".

133 I.e., separating themselves to be intimate with.

134 I.e., "People without discernment are doomed" (HCSB).

135 It is temporary because by the time Hos 5:5 arrives, any potential defense of Judah falls by the wayside.

occurred in earlier days to abominable syncretistic centers. Gilgal (most likely) and Bethel were located in the southern part of the Northern Kingdom. Gilgal was originally established as a memorial location after Joshua had led the people into the Promised Land. A member from each tribe had been ordered to take a stone from the middle of the Jordan through which they had crossed over on dry land. Then Joshua "set up" those twelve stones at Gilgal, the nation's first place of bivouac west of the Jordan. However, there is also a historically significant feature pertaining to the name Gilgal in Joshua 5. This chapter records Joshua's circumcision of all the males after which we learn that the name "Gilgal" was a divinely-crafted pun based upon the Hebrew verb from which the place name was derived (i.e., Josh 5:9).

Now Bethel is a different story. Someone will likely say, "Bethel; where's that found in Hosea 4:15? The other place name mentioned is Beth-aven! And I looked it up in several Bible atlases and found no such place!" Well, Yahweh is at work again in His crafting of another intensely scathing pun. A town originally named Luz was renamed Bethel, "house of God," by Jacob[136] to whom the LORD had revealed Himself in a dream (Gen 28:10-22). After that dream, which reiterated the Abrahamic promises being passed on to Jacob, this patriarch recognized the place as being holy, so he set up a pillar-stone designating it "God's house."

So what had started out as a sacred place where acceptable worship was offered to Yahweh had turned into a "House of Iniquity" (or Wickedness) (or Deception)." This shift had taken place right after the kingdom split. Jeroboam I was quick to set up centers featuring the worship of golden calves, one in Bethel and one in Dan (cf. 1 Kgs 12:25-33). This established the false, idolatrous cult that persisted in the Northern Kingdom. Consequently, the designation "Beth-aven" (cf. also Hos 5:8; 10:5) is one of the most damning indictments issued by Yahweh through His prophet to His radically apostate people. The depth of this depravity is revealed at the very end of verse 15 as they, while worshipping calves, were ratifying oaths in the Name of Yahweh.

---

136 The "Jacob" later renamed by God "Israel" (Gen 32:27-28).

Verse 16 begins and ends with linked similes, the second of which is embedded in a rhetorical question: "For Israel is as obstinate as a stubborn[137] cow. Can the LORD now shepherd them like a lamb in an open meadow?" (HCSB). A nation with a reputation of stubbornness (cf. Ps 78:8; Isa 65:2; Jer 5:23; 6:28; etc.) is here poetically depicted as ever resisting divine shepherding. According to Paul such stubborn hearts are ultimately "storing up wrath ... in the day of wrath" (Rom 2:5)!

Ephraim (v. 17), occurring 36 times in Hosea, is not merely a tribal designation, but most often represents the whole Northern Kingdom. Here that nation is denounced as being "united with" or "joined to" idols. This mutinous condition is met with a divine pronouncement of judgment: "Leave him alone!" In essence Yahweh is saying, "You want it; you got it!" A theologically analogous pronouncement may be observed in the "God gave (or delivered) them over" chorus near the end of Romans 1 (cf. vv. 24,26,28).

Although the Hebrew text of verses 18-19 presents several interpretive challenges, the gist of these last two verses of chapter 4 focuses on the results of the nation being left alone to their unbridled lusts. In verse 18 that focus is upon their ever-deepening plunge into depravity, while in verse 19 it is upon the consequent judgment that will come to pass because of such heinous declensions:

> Even when their drinks are gone, they continue their prostitution; their rulers clearly love shameful ways. A whirlwind will sweep them away, and their sacrifices will bring them shame[138] (Hos 4:18-19, NIV).

---

137 Cf., e.g., ESV "stubborn ... stubborn," a translation indicating the descriptive participle and the verb as deriving from the same Hebrew root. It should also be noted that v. 16a contains several (not just two) sound-alikes in the original Hebrew text, which would have intensified the oracle's impact.

138 Although Yahweh would employ instruments of judgment (cf. Assyria in Isa 10), He would be the ultimate Agent behind them all (cf., e.g., "the wind of the LORD" in Hos 13:15 and His changing of their glory into shame in 4:7).

EXHORTATIONS

As we move into chapter 4 of Hosea, we enter a new section of the book marked by several changes. First, while you will notice the absence of any further mention of the marriage and family of Hosea and Gomer, you will note that the theme of the nation's idolatry, couched in the metaphor of marital infidelity or prostitution, remains prominent. Adultery and harlotry are mentioned a dozen times in chapter 4 alone. These references to immorality describe Israel's physical and spiritual unfaithfulness. You will also note in this portion of the book that the descriptions of Israel's grotesque iniquity and God's severe judgments become increasingly graphic. Alongside such sobering intensifications, there is a noticeable decrease in the frequency of the assurances that God will ultimately show mercy and bring about Israel's repentance. Chapters 4 through 14 are by no means devoid of the comforting promises of God's future kindness to Israel; however, the cross-fade of increased indictments of sin and fewer words of comfort make the next several chapters very dark reading. May the Lord use these passages to cause us to truly hate sin and perceive the horrible offense that all transgressions are to our holy God.

As chapter 4 opens, Hosea commands that Israel listen as he announces that the LORD, like a prosecuting attorney, judge, and jury all rolled into one, has a case against His people. Through Hosea, the LORD begins with general indictments and, as the chapter unfolds, specific charges are laid at the feet of Israel's spiritual leaders and, in turn, the nation who followed them. Central to each of the accusations is the nation's willful rejection of the knowledge of the LORD, demonstrating the inseparable link between Israel's compromised theology and their sinful lifestyle and conduct. Each set of censures also warns of horrible results of such culpable ignorance. At times the consequences depicted are simply the inevitable after-effect of certain sins, yet at other times they are the active judgments of the LORD Himself. Let's take a sober look at the danger of hardening our own hearts against truth and the inescapable moral decay that follows in its wake.

LACK OF KNOWLEDGE OF GOD

Though the LORD has declared that there would be a time in the future when Israel would truly know her God (2:20), the dominant theme of the entire chapter is that at present "there is no ... knowledge of God in the land" (v. 1). Even the priests and prophets are rebuked for their rejection of spiritual truth. The LORD describes them as having forgotten His law, no longer giving heed to Him (v. 6). The result was that those under such derelict spiritual leaders were "destroyed for lack of knowledge" (v. 6), and bereft of spiritual understanding, the people of God were utterly ruined (v. 14). God brings a similar accusation against spiritual leaders in Psalm 50 when He asks "What right have you to tell of My statutes, and to take My covenant in your mouth? For you hate discipline, and you cast My words behind you" (vv. 16-17). Israel "knew" God and His word well enough to quote it and teach it, but in their lives they despised it and turned their backs on those very words.

This accusation is somewhat problematic because, in one sense, Israel could not really be accused of actual ignorance of God since He had revealed Himself to Israel for centuries through His mighty deeds and amazing promises going back as far as Abraham. Indeed, "they were entrusted with the oracles of God" (Rom 3:2). Keep in mind that the Lord does not accuse His people of a lack of religious zeal or spiritual activity. Rather, He condemns them for their lack of true knowledge of Himself. As already noted, Israel had not abandoned their outward worship of the LORD, but inwardly their lack of devotion proved they lacked any genuine faith in God, though they busied themselves with their quasi-obedient offerings.

So in what sense were they guilty of a lack of knowledge? Israel's "ignorance" was actually a failure to believe and obey the knowledge of God which they so richly possessed. Commenting on Israel's response to the knowledge of God that Israel received so dramatically at Mt. Sinai, the author of Hebrews warns, "the word they heard did not profit them, because it was not united by faith in those who heard" (Heb 4:2). At the end of the Sermon on the Mount, Jesus says with piercing clarity that those who claim to know God intimately, referring to Him as "Lord,

Lord," and yet live in habitual disobedience will be cast away from the presence of the Lord forever, because He did not know them (Matt 7:21-23)! The prophet Jeremiah also proclaimed the high value God places on true knowledge of Himself:

> Let not a wise man boast of his wisdom, let not the mighty man boast of his might, and let not a rich man boast of his riches; but let him who boasts boast of this, that he knows and understands Me, that I am the LORD who exercises lovingkindness, justice, and righteousness on earth; for I delight in these things, declares the LORD. (Jer 9:23-24)

Having turned their backs on the riches of spiritual truth entrusted to them, Israel certainly could not boast that they had any knowledge of their LORD.

Can you boast that you possess an intimate knowledge of God? Are you careful to activate your "faith muscles" in response to every word of God? Do you take advantage of opportunities to "grow in the grace and knowledge of our Lord Jesus Christ" (2 Peter 3:18)? Does active, submissive obedience to divine revelation characterize your life? If not, beware, for where neglect of spiritual knowledge and privileges exists, a dreadful list of attendant sins inevitably follow.

THE INEVITABLE MORAL DECAY

A survey of chapter 4 quickly reveals that Israel's unseen rejection of the knowledge of God in their hearts led to a plethora of other sins in their visible lives. Among those multiplied sins were profane speech, deceptive words, physical violence, perpetual bloodshed, drunkenness, prostitution, and adultery (vv. 2,11,13). Having departed from their God, the nation flagrantly joined herself to false gods because "a spirit of idolatry has led them astray" (v. 12). Amid multiplied sacrifices, burning incense, and the religious immorality of temple prostitution, Israel sought their spiritual guidance from man-carved statues and sacred sticks. In a disastrous violation of their covenant with the LORD, Israel was indeed "joined to idols" (v. 17). The priests did nothing to stem the tide of the nation's descent into wickedness. Rather, they gorged themselves upon the people's sin with greedy cravings (v. 8). The hideous corruption showed itself in Israel's civil leaders as well, who dearly loved the very sin that should have brought them shame (v. 18).

The New Testament also reveals the strong connection between what we know and believe and how we live. The apostle Paul frequently describes sound doctrine as healthy, clean, disease-free teaching that leads to healthy, clean, holy living. Minds that feed upon true doctrine give rise to "love from a pure heart and a good conscience and a sincere faith" (1 Tim 1:5). Knowledge of truth produces temperate, dignified, sensible, reverent, pure, and kind God-honoring lives that are robust in faith, love, and perseverance (Titus 2:1-5). The opposite is also true. Unsound doctrine—teaching that is diseased, or corrupt—leads to contaminated, unholy living. Lawlessness, rebellion, patricide and other forms of murder, homosexuality, kidnapping, lying, and perjury are listed as sins that are "contrary to sound doctrine" (1 Tim 1:8-10).

We live in an age in which doctrinal preaching and teaching have fallen on hard times. Intolerant of biblical preaching and wishing to have their ears tickled, many so-called Christians have collected for themselves preachers whose messages do not require their listeners to part with their cherished sinful desires in order to follow Christ. Adding to that, many professing believers today have a penchant for following celebrity pastors with whom they have no real relationship, shepherding or accountability, and the results have been disastrous. Starved of clear and compelling biblical instruction in the name of "reaching the lost" on Sundays, the church has become anemic and stunted in her growth. Failing to mortify her love of the praise of men, a worldly church is unwilling to bear any reproach for Christ (Heb 13:13) and is crippled in her gospel witness. Having domesticated doctrine of any possible offense to the culture, churches find themselves incapable of obeying Jesus' command to teach men "to observe [obey] all that I commanded you" (Matt 28:20). Unsound doctrine has indeed produced an unsound church.

If you are a part of a church that prioritizes the preaching and teaching of sound doctrine from the Scriptures, you should thank the Lord and pray for the protection of your leaders. If you have had a tendency to downplay the critical nature of learning biblical truth, then repent, and with greater intentionality pursue opportunities to learn true doctrine. Are there activities in your life that might need to be diminished or eliminated in order to have the time you need to grow in a true knowledge of God? Can you cry out like Paul, "I count all things to be loss in view of the surpassing value of knowing Christ Jesus, my Lord" (Phil 3:8)? No sacrifice could be too great to gain the knowledge of Christ. The godly life that will be the result of knowing Him better will bring Him much glory!

THE SEVERE PRICE FOR SUCH IGNORANCE

Woven throughout this passage are the warnings about what Israel will suffer for their culpable ignorance of their God. Some of that misery will come as the natural outcome of sin. In a cause and effect relationship, the people who turn from God's truth will stumble without spiritual guidance and direction and eventually will become like a stubborn animal which refuses to be shepherded (vv. 5,16). Grievously, others who observe such sin will be tempted to follow (v. 15; see also Ps 73:15). Further, because of Israel's vain attempt to be led by lifeless idols, they lost all spiritual understanding (v. 14) and were left with a futile life, devoid of satisfaction (v. 10; see also Isa 55:1-2). Despite the rich variety of divine revelation that had been entrusted to Israel, their spiritual blindness is a sobering reminder that you may have a dozen Bibles on your shelf and even have one open on your lap, but due to unbelief, still be doomed to be undiscerning!

In addition to Israel experiencing the predictable consequences of their sin, Hosea also warns that they will suffer the active judgments of God as well. The LORD prophesies drought that will threaten the life of man and beast alike; the land without knowledge of God would become a land without water. With biting irony the LORD promises punishment in like kind for Israel's waywardness. As the priests destroyed God's people by depriving them of knowledge, so He will destroy their mothers (v. 5). As Israel's priests rejected knowledge, so the LORD will reject them as His priests and forget their children, just as they had forgotten His law (v. 6). Because of their corruption, the Lord promises to turn the glory of the ministry of both priests and prophets alike into shame (v. 7). However, the most disheartening prediction of the chapter comes in verse 17 when the Lord states that because His people have formed a treacherous union between themselves and idols, He will simply leave them alone, alone with the god of their choosing. Alone, without any hope of God's leadership, provision, or protection. Can there be any more terrifying thought than being abandoned by God to one's sin?! This solemn chapter closes by likening those under the weighty judgment of God to the victims of a tornado or hurricane. Israel's pangs of shame over sacrifices she offered on pagan altars would overwhelm her as she is carried away to death in the tempest of God's wrath.

The equally sobering opening chapter of Romans is in many ways the New Testament counterpart to Hosea, chapter 4. Like the prophet of Israel, the apostle Paul condemns all men as guilty of rejecting the knowledge of God. He declares that all sinners "suppress the truth in unrighteousness, because that which is known about God is evident within them; for God made it evident to them. For since the creation of the world His invisible attributes, His eternal power and divine nature, have been clearly seen, being understood through what has been made, so that they are without excuse" (vv. 18-20). Paul's teaching also follows that of Hosea in presenting the descent into deeper sin and moral perversion that follows the rejection of the truth of God in exchange for a lie. Finally, Paul's warning of the judgment of being given over to gross sins by God also reflects Hosea's message that God will abandon Israel to her chosen sinful life for a time (vv. 21-32).

It is good for us to be sobered by portions of Scripture like these. The chapter began with the LORD's command to "listen to the words of the LORD" (v. 1). Are you willing to listen to words like these and learn from them? Admittedly, most of us would prefer to read and meditate on more positive passages of Scripture. You may be tempted to wonder why

God's Word would have to contain so many negative verses. To be honest, the Bible can be very negative because it addresses the most negative subject in the universe, sin! And it does so on practically every page. But the Scriptures are not negative in the ultimate sense, because they also detail what God has done in Christ to save us from our enslavement to sin and its grim, eternal consequences. Portions of Scripture like Hosea 4 will seem unnecessarily negative only when we, in our pride, want to believe that we are not as bad as those Israelites! But a humble heart sees itself on every page of Hosea! If you are trusting in Christ's payment on Calvary for your sin today, you do not have to fear eternal judgment for your sins. However, if you are not responding to the revelation that He has given you, then theses verses are a plea for you to avoid the chastisement of God as a believer. Take care that you do not make yourself like a stubborn animal that refuses God's leadership and protection by ignoring the truth He richly pours into your life day by day.

5 HOSEA 5:1–15

EXPOSITION

(5:1–15) THE LORD AS JUDGE AND JURY SENTENCES HIS CRIMINAL PEOPLE

As previously noted, the priests are singled out in the first line of 5:1. They are quickly joined by the whole nation in line two, followed immediately by the political leadership. Each of these addressees is commanded to pay strict attention[139] to the indictments which follow. Indeed "the judgment" would be aimed at every level of the sinful society (cf. vv. 1a, 2b).[140]

Verse 1 climaxes with two occurrences of a prevalent biblical image, that of a hunter or trapper.[141] Although the geography and specific incidents mentioned in these last two lines of verse 1 are open to several interpretations, what God is exposing is the people's and especially their leaders' wicked craftiness.

---

139   Respectively, "Hear!," "Pay attention!," "Give ear to!"

140   It is possible that Hosea may have been employing another double entendre when he brings in the Hebrew noun for "justice" or "judgment." The nation's leaders would have been responsible for exercising justice (i.e., justice "belonged to" them; cf. Mic 3:1), but in the absence of such governance which had led to the degradations of the whole of society, the LORD God was preparing "judgment" for them.

141   Cf., e.g., Pss 9:15; 35:7; 57:6; 119:110; 124:7; 140:5; etc.

The Hebrew text of 5:2a is very challenging; however, it seems to be a moral summary of all previous indictments: "And the revolters have gone deep into slaughter" (ESV).[142] This all-encompassing indictment brings on the promise of a personal, divine retribution; literally, "I will be a chastisement for all of them."

This solemn declaration is once again undergirded by more of Yahweh's omniscient insights into the character of the nation in verse 3. There is no way of escaping notice under God's infallible MRI: "I know Ephraim, and Israel is not hidden from Me" (v. 3a, NASB).[143] What the Lord sees with perfect resolution is their track record of spiritual prostitution, which has led to a condition of spiritual defilement (v. 3b,c). They had become unclean, impure. A passage quite similar to Hosea 5:3 is Psalm 106:39; however, it reads in reverse order: "They defiled themselves by their actions and prostituted themselves by their deeds" (HCSB).

Further commentary on this tragic situation is added in Hosea 5:4. It begins, "Their deeds do not[144] permit (or allow) them to turn (or return) to their God." Then verse 4b supplies the reason for this settled condition of apostasy: "Since a spirit of prostitution[145] is in their mindset, consequently they do not acknowledge Yahweh." This not acknowledging the LORD has already been noted as one of the prophecy's major indictments (cf. 4:1,6). So the impact of Hosea 5:4 could be summed up with our contemporary proverb that their actual deeds were speaking louder than their words,[146] and, we might add, along with their hypocritical motions in the context of supposed Yahweh worship.

---

142 Or, by changing in Hebrew the final t-sound in the word for "slaughter" to another t-sound, "The revolters have gone deep into *corruption*," or "depravity" (NASB). This rendering would align quite well with Hos 9:9a: "They have sunk deep into corruption" (NIV).

143 The synonymous parallelism is enhanced all the more by the chiastic ordering.

144 Another objective negation.

145 Cf. 4:12.

146 Esp., cf. 6:1ff.

Further incriminations are brought to light in verse 5: "And the arrogance (or pride[147]) of Israel testifies against it;[148] both Israel and Ephraim[149] will stumble because of their iniquity; Judah will also stumble[150] with them."[151] These stumblings would lead to the respective falls, first of the Northern Kingdom, then of the Southern Kingdom. In verse 6 it becomes obvious that the LORD will judge them for pseudo-worship. Indeed, "With their flock and their herd (of cattle) they will go to seek Yahweh, but they will not[152] find (Him); He has withdrawn (Himself) from them." They set out on an utterly futile seek-and-find mission of "worship." God was in hide-and-seek mode because of their spiritual adultery. Often the Bible urged people to seek God in order that they might find Him. For example, compare the first part of the "if" scenario of 1 Chronicles 28:9 and 2 Chronicles 15:2: "If you seek Him He will let you find Him … " (1 Chron 28:9; 2 Chron 15:2, NASB). However, a "but if" immediately follows: "But if you forsake Him, He will forsake you" (2 Chron 15:2, NASB). From the leadership level downward the prostituting people of Hosea's day had indeed forsaken the LORD. How presumptuous of them to imagine that going through the motions of sacrificing would have been acceptable worship to the only true God! They had totally disregarded the timeless application of the reprimand[153] that had been given to Saul through God's mouthpiece, Samuel:

---

147 See sample negative settings of this word also in Ps 59:12; Prov 8:13; 16:18; *et al.*

148 Very lit., it's "in (the nation's) face"!

149 In this immediate setting Ephraim seems to designate the tribe as a *part* of the Northern Kingdom.

150 This "prophetic perfect" tense is another one of those it's-good-as-done affirmations. The verb is quite obviously built upon the same Hebrew root as the preceding imperfect tense verbal form.

151 Remember that this promise of divine judgment shows that eventually Judah would not heed the warning posted for them in 4:15.

152 Another occurrence of the strong negative.

153 Besides 1 Sam 15:22-23, once again call to mind Pss 40:6-8 [cf. a Messianic application, Heb 10:5-7]; 51:16-17; Isa 1:10-15; Mic 6:6-8; *et al.*

> Does the LORD take pleasure in burnt offerings and sac-
> rifices as much as in obeying the LORD? Look: to obey is
> better than sacrifice, to pay attention [is better] than the
> fat of rams. For rebellion is like the sin of divination, and
> defiance is like wickedness and idolatry. Because you have
> rejected the word of the LORD, He has rejected you as
> king. (1 Sam 15:22-23, HCSB)

Another summation of their multiple transgressions is found at the
outset of verse 7: "They have dealt treacherously with[154] Yahweh" (cf. also
6:7). The emphasis is clearly upon their spiritual infidelities. Married to
Yahweh God, bound to Him by covenantal relationship, they were prostituting themselves to false gods. A tangible evidence of their faithlessness
immediately follows in verse 7b; "Indeed they have given birth to alien
sons." This affirmation of a reality ties back into the symbolic progeny
born to Hosea by Gomer the prostitute.[155] Quite often God's people
were warned about foreign or strange or alien marriages in that they
would lead to apostasy (cf., e.g., Exod 34:11-17; Deut 7:3-5). Solomon
himself had fallen into this disastrous snare (i.e., 1 Kgs 11:1-10). There
were also clear warnings about relationships with *strange* women, i.e.,
prostitutes (cf. Prov 2:16; 5:3; 7:5; *et al.*). Furthermore, engaging in relations with cultic prostitutes would result in a syncretistic abomination.
So God, through Hosea, in verse 7b shows that these resultant progeny
were the products of perverse parents.

The last line of verse 7 brings to bear God's tailor-made judgment
that He will actuate in view of their thoroughly warped worship, *supposedly* of Him. Fittingly, it is quite ironic: "Now a new moon (i.e., celebration or feast)[156] will devour them with their portions." They will be

---

154 This preposition coupled with this particular verb approaches an abusive connotation (cf.,
     e.g., Judg 9:23; Jer 3:20; 5:11; 12:6; Lam 1:2; Mal 2:10,14,15,16; *et al.*). It also carries with
     it overtones of betrayal (cf. the rendering in HCSB).

155 Cf. esp. Hos 1:2, "children of prostitution."

156 Cf. 2:11.

feasted upon by Yahweh's marauding instruments of judgment to the point of their tribal "allotments," or "portions"[157] being gobbled up.[158] It is possible that there might even be, in the light of a narrower focus on the priests in chapters four and five, a corollary judgment on them. Their "share" or "portion" as had been provided by divine legislation (cf., e.g., Lev 6:16-18) would also be brought to an end by Yahweh's appointed "devourers."

With the arrival of Hosea 5:8 the LORD through His prophet goes into taunt mode. These commands, like the ones found, for example, in Nahum 3:14, brim with divine sarcasm. Later a similar sarcastic taunt will show up in Hosea 8:1a. In the context before us Hosea 5:8 reads: "Blow the horn in Gibeah, the trumpet in Ramah. Sound an alarm at Beth-aven: Behind you, Benjamin!" (NASB). The sounding of the *shofar* and/or trumpet served primarily two basic functions, to muster the people for battle or to assemble them for non-hostile purposes such as communications, movement, worship, or the like.[159] Here the former case scenario is indicated by its setting.

The towns that are mentioned represent a circuit of close geographical proximity lying near the border of the Northern and Southern Kingdoms. Although we can't be absolutely sure about their connection to a historic battle, the people of Hosea's day would have been able to bring to mind such an indelible past crisis.[160] However, although a specific historic episode would have likely registered in the people's mind, it would quickly vanish in view of the pronounced judgment of Yahweh which is to come upon them in the future. And it is precisely this reality that is taken up in Hosea 5:9ff.

---

157 Note the original territorial assignments to the tribes under Joshua (chs. 13-19).

158 It is interesting to note what Habakkuk says about the Babylonians whom God would use to carry Judah away into captivity: "Their share (or portion) is fat and his food is abundant" (Hab 1:16).

159 Cf., e.g., the legislation for blowing the trumpets in Num 10:1-10.

160 Cf., e.g., the phrase "the days of Gibeon" in Hos 10:9, which has led some to posit the occasion recorded in Judg 19-21.

According to prophetic precedent, divine pronouncements of severe judgment are documented as perfectly just in view of the high-handed crimes committed. Hosea 5:9a launches with these chilling words: "Ephraim will become a horror (or an astonishment) (or a waste) (or wasteland)[161] on a day of reproach (or reprimand) (or rebuke) (or correction)."[162] This last phrase mercifully intimates that the day of the LORD in this context will not be a day of total destruction but a day of severe discipline.

In verses 9b-10a the scope of the application of Yahweh's judgments is broadened along with a specific clarification that the Southern Kingdom would not be exempted: "Among the tribes of Israel I proclaim what is certain.[163] Judah's leaders are like those who move boundary stones" (NIV). This last criminal indictment was particularly heinous in God's eyes (cf. two of His several warnings against moving boundary markers in the curse context of Deut 27:17 and the wisdom context of Prov 22:28).

This indictment precipitates (pun intended) the divine response of verse 10b, "Upon them[164] I will pour out My overflowing rage (or fury) like water." This term for God's intense wrath is used as a synonym for the Day of the LORD (cf. the day of Yahweh's fury in Job 21:30; Prov 11:4; Ezek 7:19; Zeph 1:15,18).

The exposing spotlight of God's sure judgment is refocused on Ephraim in verse 11a: "Ephraim is oppressed, crushed in judgment" (HCSB). These words likely represent divine judgment as based upon the curse of Deuteronomy 28:33: "A people whom you do not know shall eat up the produce of your ground and all your labors, and you will never be anything but oppressed and crushed continually" (NASB). The reason for this particular curse upon the Northern Kingdom follows in

---

161 On this very string of words from the Hebrew text, see Deut 28:37; 2 Kgs 22:19; Isa 5:9; Jer 25:11; Zeph 2:15; etc.

162 Cf. a twin sister noun as one of the primary discipline terms in Prov 3:11; 5:12; 10:17; 12:1; 13:18; 15:5,10,32.

163 Cf. this descriptive participle used both of God Himself (e.g., Deut 7:9) and words from His Word (e.g., Ps 19:7 [Hebrew, v. 8]).

164 Emphatically placed first in the Hebrew text.

verse 11b; however, the last word of the Hebrew text is quite challenging, leading to the following attempts to translate it:

> Because he was determined to follow *man's* command (NASB).

> because he was determined to go after filth (ESV).

> for he determined to follow what is worthless (HCSB).

A few versions including the early Greek translation rendered the problem word in Hebrew with a term that was often used to refer to idols. If that be the case, this particular indictment would highlight the nation's violation of the first and second commandments. Documentations of the nation's idolatry indeed pepper the whole prophesy of Hosea.

Fitting consequences, borne along by two graphic similes, follow: "Therefore, I am like a moth to Ephraim, and like rottenness to the house of Judah" (NASB). On these two descriptives being experienced by an individual, remember Job's painful testimony in 13:28: "Man wears out like something rotten, like a moth-eaten garment" (HCSB). The common denominator of these two similes in Hosea 5:12 is one of irreversible consumption.

All human remedies, no matter how powerful they might appear, would prove to be futile for both degenerating kingdoms.[165] That indeed is the frustrating reality of verse 13, which reads: "When Ephraim saw his sickness, and Judah his wound, then Ephraim went to Assyria, and sent to the great king. But he is not able to cure you or heal your wound" (ESV). Historically, both kingdoms tried to cut deals with Assyria but they needed to learn the ultimate lesson that they must flee to Yahweh alone, who is both Helper and Healer.

Since they had not yet learned that lesson, Yahweh would assume another *ultimately* merciful role of a rapacious beast who would tear them to pieces. This is where the imagery of the lion, the king of beasts,

---

165 Cf. the condition of God's people in Jer 30:12-15 plus His ultimate healing in 30:16ff.

enters via another simile: "For I will be like a lion to Ephraim and like a young lion to the house of Judah. I, even I, will tear and go away; I will carry off, and no one shall rescue" (Hos 5:14, ESV). The first two synonymous lines indicate that both the north and the south shall succumb to the same Predator. He and He alone as "lion" and "young lion" will successfully kill and drag away the carcasses, and there will not be any deliverer.[166]

Then God, depicted as King of predators, will return to His place (i.e., the lair imagery of v. 15a). However, He has not fully and finally separated Himself from His sinful people as indicated by the "until," which governs the last part of verse 15: "until which (time) they will acknowledge their guilt (or confess their culpability) and seek My face; (and) in their straits (or distress) diligently seek Me." A time of acknowledgement and repentance is still available. The first three verses of chapter 6 show what this kind of repentance should sound and look like.

EXHORTATIONS

As in the previous chapter, this passage begins with a command for Israel's priests, people, and kings alike to listen attentively to the LORD's pronouncement of His summary judgment against them. All three groups are condemned for the covert nature of the sin into which they have sunk deeply (vv. 1-2). Following this summary statement, the chapter emphasizes two threatening certainties: God's absolute knowledge of every aspect of Israel's sin (vv. 3-8) and the absolute certainty of the coming judgment from LORD's hand (vv. 9-15).

(5:3–8) GOD'S ABSOLUTE KNOWLEDGE OF SIN

The emphatic "I know" of verse 3 places God's full knowledge of His people's sin in ironic contrast to Israel's lack of knowledge of God so frequently mentioned in the opening chapters of this book. Though Israel may not know God, He reminds them that He certainly knows them!

---

166 On similar pronouncements cf. Deut 32:39 and Mic 5:8 (v. 7, Heb).

Though their sin may have been committed with stealth and craftiness, they cannot hide from an omniscient God. There is no pulling the wool over His eyes. He is not blind to how they had defiled themselves while playing the harlot with the false gods of the surrounding nations (v. 3; cf. Ps 106:34-39). He knows that "the pride of Israel testifies against him" (v. 5) and that their hearts determined to follow after anything or anyone other than the LORD (v. 11). Yet, despite the profound level of corruption to which Israel has descended, they continue to go through the motions of seeking God in public worship during the appointed festivals, only to find that He has withdrawn Himself from them (v. 6). In yet another alarming irony, the people of God will find that in the midst of their disingenuous, joyful feasting, they themselves will be consumed by the LORD's devastating judgment (v. 7).

Ultimately, the LORD offers the terrifying assessment "their deeds will not allow them to return to their God" (v. 4). Possessed by a "spirit of harlotry," their hearts have been rendered incapable of repenting. Of their own volition, Israel is not only unwilling, they are unable to repent (cf. 1 Cor 2:14). Without the intervention of God, Israel's state is indeed hopeless! The Scriptures teach that this double jeopardy is true of all men. Jesus warned that "everyone who commits sin is the slave to sin" (John 8:34). The apostle Peter wrote, "by what a man is overcome, by this he is enslaved" (2 Peter 2:19). Similarly, Paul reminded the believers in Rome:

> Do you not know that when you present yourself to someone as slaves for obedience, you are slaves of the one whom you obey, either of sin resulting in death, or of obedience resulting in righteousness? But thanks be to God that though you were slaves in sin, you became obedient from the heart to that form of teaching to which you were committed... .(Rom 6:16-17)

While all sinners are commanded to repent of their sin, redeemed sinners cannot take personal credit for their emancipation from sin's mastery.

Left to ourselves, each of us would gladly have remained a slave to sin. The glory for our redemption belongs to God alone!

(5:9–15) GOD'S ABSOLUTELY CERTAIN JUDGMENT

In response to Israel's great moral evil wrapped in the veneer of religious duplicity, God offers the following unqualified certainty of the judgment: "Ephraim will become a desolation in the day of rebuke; Among the tribes of Israel I declare what is true" (v. 9). The LORD uses three haunting images to portray such certain, future desolation. All three diverse images share the common idea of overwhelming power that brings about irreversible devastation. The first is that of an overwhelming flood: "On them I will pour out My wrath like water." God's people will be oppressed and crushed under the tsunami of God's anger (vv. 10-11).

The second picture of coming judgment is that of an insipid moth, that silently, slowly brings about rottenness and ruin (vv. 12-13). One possible alternative translation for the word "moth" would be "maggot," which brings to mind repulsive images of rotting refuse or putrid flesh. Eventually, the hidden devastation wrought by God from the inside out comes undeniably to the surface, and still Israel does not turn back to God in humble contrition. Instead, hoping for relief and healing, they turn to Assyria, a powerful, pagan nation, which is unable to reverse the rottenness brought about by God's mighty hand.

Finally, God's fearful judgment is wrapped in the image of a ravenous lion. "For I will be like a lion to Ephraim and like a young lion to the house of Judah. I, even I, will tear to pieces and go away, I will carry away, and there will be none to deliver" (vv. 13-14). The LORD's devastation will be swift and unsparing. It would be safer to be trapped in the merciless jaws of the king of beasts, than to be locked in the deadly grip of God's intense judgment! As a lion returns to its lair after the kill, the LORD warns, "I will go away and return to My place" (v. 15; cf. v. 6; 4:17).

Gloriously, the chapter ends with a glimmer of hope! Though not as lengthy or developed as some of the other divine consolations of chapters 1-3, the wonderful word "until" in verse 15 signals that all is not lost for this habitually unfaithful nation. The LORD declares, "I will go away and return to My place *until* they acknowledge their guilt and seek My face; in their affliction they will earnestly seek Me" (v. 15, emphasis added). With these words, the LORD states that the purpose of His chastisement (v. 2), withdrawal (v. 6), rebuke (v. 9), and judgment (v. 11) is to bring them to repentance. Why does God have to come like an overwhelming flood, a ruinous moth and predatory lion? Because He knows exactly what it will take to bring wayward, unloving hearts to see their sin and seek the Savior.

Through their rebellious choices, Israel brought on themselves increasingly intense forms of judgment. How much better it would have been for them to repent at the first pang of conviction of sin or with the first prophetic voicing of God's disapproval. Speaking through David, generations before the ministry of Hosea, the LORD reminds all of us that our choices affect the nature of His leadership in our lives.

> I will instruct you and teach you in the way you should go; I will counsel you with my eye upon you. Do not be as the horse or the mule which have no understanding, whose trappings include bit and bridle to hold them in check, otherwise they will not come near you. Many are the sorrows of the wicked, but he who trusts in the LORD, lovingkindness shall surround him. (Ps 32:8-10)

This psalm teaches us that our rebellion and disobedient choices often require God to lead us through painful bit and harsh bridle in order to bring us near to Himself. Israel chose the bit and bridle. They chose the overwhelming flood, the rot-inducing moth, and the predatory lion. Given the current state of your heart, what method will God have to use to keep you close to Himself? Which tools will your loving Father have to use until you confess your guilt and earnestly seek His face? Learn from Israel's and Judah's destructive choices and the resulting, unnecessarily harsh chastisements, and keep your heart humble and easily led!

6 HOSEA 6:1–11

EXPOSITION

(6:1–11) THE LORD AS PAROLE BOARD WILL ASSESS ALL PROFESSIONS OF REPENTANCE ON THE PART OF HIS CRIMINAL PEOPLE

Hosea 6:1-3 contextually could be taken in one of two basic ways. Either as an actual response on the part of the people who were just shaken up by the pronouncement of these impending judgments or by God through the prophet sketching out some indications of what genuine repentance would look like. In view of the historical track record of both Judah and Israel, these options seemed to be a moot point as indicated by the continuing exposures of their sin and resistance in verses 4ff. Nonetheless, implicationally it is to our profit to pay attention to these first three verses of chapter 6:

> Come, let us return[167] to the LORD. He has torn us to
> pieces but he will heal us; he has injured us but he will

---

167 Once again the work-horse term for repentance in the OT, occurring as a verb or verbal 23 times in Hosea, beginning in 2:7 and ending in 14:7 (v. 8, Hebrew).

bind up our wounds.[168] After two days[169] he will revive; on the third day[169] he will restore us, that we may live in his presence. Let us acknowledge[170] the LORD; let us press on to acknowledge[170] him. As surely as the sun[171] rises, he will appear; he will come to us like the winter rains, like the spring rains that water the earth[172] (NIV).

Only by a hot pursuit to know the LORD experientially (v. 3a) will we ever receive His blessings.

The Siamese twin interrogatives addressed respectively to Ephraim and Judah in verses 4a,b do indeed shatter any potential optimism introduced by the "until" turn-around scenario of 5:15ff. Anthropopathically conceived, we might take them as expressing exasperation and frustration on the part of God. However, God is not caught by surprise concerning feigned repentance. Consequently, these questions are divinely-crafted rhetorical probes which launch yet another series of evidences, indictments, and judgments.

Yahweh's first piece of evidence with an indictment is summarized in verse 4 c,d. It chronicles the nation's convicting pattern of disloyalty. Their love for God, their loving-kindness, their faithful commitment, etc.,[173] is likened to two common scenarios about quickly dissipating sources of moisture. It seems to be abundantly present, but before you know it, it vanishes. As a consequence of their historic apostasies, God sent His prophets whose words were intended to hack into sinfully resistant people (v. 5a,b).

---

168 V. 1 obviously picks up the terminology of the preceding context (cf. esp. 5:14).

169 On these kinds of enumeration patterns indicating some sort of an eventual arrival at a *terminus*, cf., e.g., Prov 6:16; 30:15-21; etc.

170 Lit., know.

171 Technically the Hebrew text reads "dawn."

172 These agrarian similes represent absolutely vital benefits that Yahweh will pour out on a reconciled people.

173 Once again, showing up is the lofty term *hesed*, which often relates to covenant commitment.

That this prophetic ministry was being carried on through Hosea in reference to his current audience is indicated by a genuine summary of such confrontational encounters as indicated in verse 5c. The Hebrew text as it stands reads literally: "And Your/your[174] judgments (are) light (that) go forth." However, the early Greek translation, based probably on a simple redivision of the Hebrew consonants, renders this line, "And My judgment goes forth as light."[175] Being next in line, that judgment is what also awaits the recalcitrant nations of Hosea's day.

Verse 6 contrastingly picks up on the lack of loyal-love[176] exposed in verse 4 with this frequently revealed corrective: "For I desire (or take pleasure in) (or delight in) loyal-love and not sacrifice, and (in the) knowledge of God more than (or rather than) whole burnt offerings." As already observed, this statement and similar phrasings of it are designed to shockingly expose hypocritical worship and feigned obedience (cf., e.g., 1 Sam 15:22-23 in its clear context; Pss 40:6-8; 51:16-17 [vv. 18-19, Hebrew]; Isa 1:11 in its exposing setting; Amos 5:21-24; Mic 6:6-8; etc.). Merely going through liturgical motions is an abomination in the eyes of God. Like true discipleship in the New Testament (cf., e.g., Matt 10:37-39 and Luke 14:25ff.), God's scriptural revelation of priorities must reign and rule in the heart. Here they obviously did not, as indicated by the following indictment.

Verse 7, employing high-handed terms for sin, exposes their rebellion; the indictment reads: "But they, like Adam, have violated the covenant; there they have betrayed Me" (HCSB). The analogy is graphic. Just as Adam violated the explicit commandment of God given to him in Genesis 2:17, so had these people violated God's specific laws through Moses. Because of those published stipulations, such infractions were not merely general failures,[177] but explicit infractions of divine man-

---

174 The suffixed pronoun could be construed as either God's judgments or simply the judgments upon Israel (cf., e.g, NASB).

175 Cf. most modern versions (e.g., ESV, NIV, HCSB).

176 I.e., *hesed*.

177 Cf. the *hata* word group in the OT and the *hamartia* word group in the NT.

dates.[178] Here Hosea throws God's floodlight on the people's gross sins appropriately identified respectively as deliberate transgressions [crossings over] of Yahweh's revealed laws and as acts of treachery. Incidentally, the "there" of verse 7b most likely anticipates the reference to Gilead in the next verse.

With the arrival of verses 8-9, Hosea once again mentions place names. In verse 8 he levels this characterizing accusation against Gilead: "Gilead is a city of wrongdoers, tracked with bloody *footprints*" (NASB). Normally in the Old Testament Gilead indicated a geographical region, but here joined with the word "city" it may have been referring to Jabesh-Gilead east of the Jordan. Possibly, in view of the geographical expansions found in verses 8-10 and especially the commonly returning reference to Ephraim in verse 10, Gilead could be being used by metonymy as representative of the whole Northern Kingdom. Whatever the case, the people are identified as practitioners of iniquity with a murderous history.

The priests are once again singled out in verse 9.[179] Another analogy exposes their shocking perversities: "Like robbers who wait in ambush for someone, a band of priests murders on the road to Shechem. They commit atrocities" (HCSB). Ever since 1 Kings 12:1, wherein the first king of the north was installed, Shechem was notorious for all kinds of treachery. (See some background in Gen 34.) Herein, along the road to Shechem, the priests had shown themselves to be muggers and murderers. No wonder a paraphrasing of this indictment might read: "Indeed (or surely) they have acted infamously!"

Another recurrent theme, the primary one, lies at the heart of verse 10. It is the depiction that set this prophecy in motion, harlotry. Concerning "the house of Israel," most likely referring to the dynasties of the Northern Kingdom, Yahweh's x-ray eyes detest a hamartiological

---

178   Here in Hos 6:7 represented by the *abar* and *bagad* word groups. Furthermore, theologically Rom 5:12-14,20, among other important realities, develops the relationship of the one, Adam, to the many (i.e., the sinful race) and general sin made particular by specific laws (cf. the analogous "covenant" violation of Gen 2:17 on the part of Adam).

179   Cf., e.g., 5:1.

cancer, that is, "a horrible (or disgusting) thing."[180] What God revulses at is the whoredom of His people, which leads to only one irrefutable conclusion: "Israel is defiled."[181] She, being unclean, is radically separated from her most holy God.

At the outset of verse 11 there breaks in another one of those "and-I-have-not-forgotten-about-you, Judah" declarations: "Also for you, Judah, a harvest is appointed" (NIV). Judah, too, will reap in the judgment those evil things it has sown.[182]

The next line of text in the Hebrew Bible, along with the English versions which follow suit, is printed as verse 11b of chapter 6; however, logically it seems better to construe it with chapter 7. It marks yet another blessed intrusion of the magnificent mercy of God, in this context a future turning around of His people. The key Hebrew verbal of this line interestingly picks up on its last occurrence in 6:1 (i.e., "let us *return* to Yahweh"). There it involved the need for a repentant *turning* back to God on the part of the people. However, the obstinance of the people precluded this, and it will do so again in forthcoming contexts.[183] But in 6:11b the prophet reveals a time in the future when the LORD Himself will cause His people to turn back to Him. He must, however, take the initiative in such a restoration because of Israel's sinful resistance.[184]

Due to an idiomatic association of words,[185] this line might be taken in two possible ways as indicated by the following translations:

When I return my people from captivity ... (HCSB)
When I restore the fortunes of my people ... (ESV)

---

180 Cf. this and a similar word in Jer 5:30; 18:13; 23:14.

181 Cf. 5:3.

182 Cf. this biblical principle in the NT in Gal 6:7-8.

183 Cf., e.g., 6:4ff. with 7:1bff.

184 Cf. this reality displayed in the two usages of *shub* in Jer 31:18 and Lam 5:21.

185 This association is composed of two sound-alikes which should have intensified the punch power of Hosea's oracle.

The first would indicate *specifically* a return from exile to the Promised Land.[186] The second is more generic, referring to a re-establishment of blessings.

EXHORTATIONS

This chapter contains Israel's first recorded response to the heavy indictments, severe warnings, and predicted judgments that God has levied against His people. Their words take the form of a collective, national soliloquy in which they call each other to renewed spiritual fervor that is devoid of any contrite confession of sin, appropriate fear of God, or genuine, humble repentance. Instead, this articulation of their inner thoughts is characterized by disgusting self-pity and arrogant presumption in the grace of God. This passage looms as a sobering monument to the human heart's ability to stand convicted by the righteous standards of God's Word and to offer in response only false repentance.

THE MARKS OF FALSE REPENTANCE

Before examining what is glaringly absent from Israel's religious monologue, let us recognize what is at least orthodox about their words. They do, at least, express a corporate determination to "return to the LORD" and "to know the LORD" (vv. 1,3). They also acknowledge that the calamities that they have experienced were indeed from God's own hand: "He has torn us … He has wounded us" (v. 1). They do not fail to recognize the merciful character of God who will heal, bandage, revive, and raise them up (vv. 1-2). Further, the language of verse 3 indicates that the speech was offered with intensity and passion, "So let us know, let us press on to know the LORD" (v. 3). The repetition of the word "know" coupled with the concept of pursuing such knowledge of God like a hunter chasing down his prize, indicate that this communal speech was certainly not spoken in a detached manner. Since the people's desire to

---

186 Cf., e.g., Deut 30:3-5 (but in this context predicated on the people's repentance); Hos 11:10-11; etc.

return to God uses the key Old Testament word for repentance, at first glance it does appear that the people are sincerely repenting. God had repeatedly faulted Israel for being devoid of the knowledge of Himself, so this stated resolve to seek Him seems to be a significant change of heart.

Failure To Confess Specific Sin

However, despite these initial favorable impressions, what is conspicuously lacking in Israel's words is the very thing that God desired—an acknowledgment of their personal guilt (5:15). While the national conscience is more than willing to presume on the merciful and gracious character of God, there is utterly no confession of the people's contrasting wicked character. There is not even a veiled admission of their stiffnecked rebellion, hardened unfaithfulness, or cold indifference to God's loyal love. There is none of the penitent confession of the downcast publican crying out, "God be merciful to me, the sinner!" (Luke 18:13). Absent is any of the grief over sin commanded in James 4:9: "Be miserable and mourn and weep; let your laughter be turned into mourning and your joy to gloom." Nothing resembling humble confession is found anywhere in these words.

Since Israel will not own their sin, the LORD Himself must supply the catalog of iniquities which they should have confessed.

> But like Adam they have transgressed the covenant; there they have dealt treacherously against me. Gilead is a city of wrongdoers, tracked with bloody footprints. And as raiders wait for a man, so a band of priests murder on the way to Shechem; surely they have committed a crime. In the house of Israel I have seen a horrible thing; Ephraim's harlotry is there, Israel has defiled itself (vv. 7-10).

Failure To See Sin's Offensiveness to God

Not only does Israel fail to confess any specific sin, they also fail to acknowledge that their sin is an offence against a holy God and thus worthy of His severest condemnation. David exemplifies the correct, humble perspective regarding sin which Israel was missing when he wrote, "Against You, You only I have sinned and done what is evil in Your sight" (Ps 51:4). David is not denying that other people were affected by his sin; rather, his prayer reflects a genuine belief that the worst thing about his sin was that it was perpetrated against a holy God. In the light of the affront that his sin was to his God, David further admits, "You are justified when You speak and blameless when You judge" (v. 4). While David humbly sees his sins as justly deserving the judgment of God, Israel proudly perceives themselves as an unjust victim of God's wrath. In the light of the sins they had committed, the entire nation should have affirmed that God was perfectly righteous in coming to them like a lion to rip them to pieces (5:14-15). Instead, they complain of how keenly they feel the sting of God's tearing and wounding chastisements.

Presuming on the Grace of God

If the nation did feel any twinge of conscience about their sinful lives, they offered themselves false consolation by reminding themselves of God's gracious character. They glibly assumed, "He will heal us ... He will bandage us ... . He will revive us ... He will raise us up on the third day, that we may live before Him" (vv. 1-2). Indeed, God would do just such a healing and restoring work were they but to confess their sins and admit their need of it! But for Israel to imagine that without any admission of their adulterous idolatry and all of the wickedness that arose alongside it, that God would automatically forgive and quickly relent from promised calamity, was indeed the height of presumption! Had God's people simply prayed something like, "Though we don't deserve anything but Your wrath, could you find it in your heart to forgive us? Would you be so kind as to heal us? Could it be possible that we could ever be made to come to spiritual life?"—God would have heard their cry and abundantly forgiven them. But instead they acted as though God were somehow obligated to forgive them, as though bestowing grace was "God's job." Even without confession or contrition, Israel believed that God could be counted on to forgive, as mechanically and predictably as the sunrise or the changing of the seasons (v. 3). It is one thing for a needy sinner to have a robust faith in the promises and character of God; it is quite another for a calloused heart to presume on the forgiving nature of a just, yet gracious, God.

THE REJECTION OF FALSE REPENTANCE

The Lord expresses His sound rejection of Israel's false repentance with words which resemble the grieved exasperation of a parent of an incorrigible child: "What shall I do with you, O Ephraim? What shall I do with you, O Judah?" (v. 4). God is not impressed by His people's stated intentions to return and seek Him because He knows there is no substance behind their promises. The Lord likens the nation's flimsy profession of religious zeal to the impermanence of morning mist or disappearing dew at dawn (v. 4). In the face of Israel's unfounded optimism, the LORD provides a serious reality check. While they presume that God will gently heal and bandage them (v. 1), the LORD declares that He will slay them by the words of His mouth (v. 5). They imagine that God will deal with them tenderly "like the spring rain watering the earth" (v. 3); but in reality, He will rigorously judge them with the sudden fury of lightning storm (v. 5). The LORD proclaims that He delights in loyalty and intimate knowledge of Himself, not in perfunctory sacrifices or bogus burnt offerings (v. 6).

This passage serves as a template by which every believer can evaluate his own confession and repentance. Israel's sham attempt to reconcile with God exposes the characteristics of false repentance against which each of us must constantly be on guard. Quasi-confession avoids directly admitting specific sins and casually presumes that "God knows what I mean." Genuine confession humbly addresses particular sins to God. While false repentance hates the consequences of sin, true repentance has a growing hatred of sin itself. Counterfeit sorrow over sin is content to merely quiet the conscience, and at times, will even attempt to quiet it with religious activity. True sorrow over sin will not rest until the conscience is cleansed by the blood of Christ (Heb 9:11-14). Phony remorse makes premature commitments to change without admitting sinful patterns of the past. Authentic remorse seeks to repair the havoc created by their sins against God and others. False contrition is characterized by self-pity at God's chastening or anger at His unattainably high standards. True contrition possesses an abiding conviction that God is completely just when He disciplines His children, a conviction that enables a believer to patiently endure God's wise expression of parental discipline (Heb 12:4ff.). The New Testament parallels this teaching: "The sorrow that is according to the will of God produces a repentance without regret leading to salvation, but the sorrow of the world produces death" (2 Cor 7:10). Israel exemplifies the warning that must continually ring in our ears: God rejects false repentance!

7 HOSEA 7:1–16

EXPOSITION
(7:1–16) ISRAEL'S APOSTATE HEART

The rhetorically paralleled "when" or "whenever" of verses 6:11b and 7:1a are respectively related to God's coordinate exposures of the people's *iniquity* and their *wicked deeds*[187] in verses 7:1b and c. Then, according to common prophetic precedent, what follows is a list of evidences that document the LORD's just exposure of His perverse people.

First, in the remainder of 7:1 they have shown themselves to be doers of deceit, i.e., "they deal falsely" (NASB), they "practice deceit" (NIV), they "practice fraud" (HCSB). Less subtle and comparatively, "the thief breaks in, and bandits[188] raid outside" (ESV).

A reminder about the spiritual stupidity of all this lawless activity in 7:2 somberly interrupts further evidences and examples of it (i.e., in vv. 3ff.): "Now they (lit.) are not saying to their heart (i.e., they do not take to heart, bring to mind, etc.[189]) that all their wickedness I remember; now their deeds lie all around them; they are before My face." Whether

---

187 This Hebrew word group related to high-handed sin nuanced as wickedness or evil occurs four times in ch. 7 (i.e., vv. 1,2,3,15).

188 This Hebrew root also occurred as a descriptive in 6:9a.

189 Cf. the HCSB: "But they never consider … ."

internally or externally scrutinized, Yahweh's MRI sees with perfect acuity all their sinful heart attitudes and wicked deeds. Hiding anything from Yahweh is futile; just ask David (Pss 32; 51; 139)!

The string of indicting evidences of spiritual mutiny continues in verses 3ff. Although this section contains some imagery that is a bit obscure, verse 3 picks up, in order, the exposure of the general sins of wicked deeds and deceptions (cf. v. 1c,d): "They delight the king with their wickedness, the princes with their lies" (7:3, NIV). What is new in verses 3-7 is a special focus on the political scene. In these five verses "kings," "princes," and "judges" are mentioned six times in a setting brimming with political intrigue. The actual histories of the many vile goings on in the monarchies of the Northern Kingdom are painfully recorded in the books of Kings and Chronicles. Of course, the condemning oracles of many of God's prophets specifically supplement much of that dark history. Indeed, Hosea joins that company of Yahweh's mouthpieces, especially in this section.

These devious people of the kingdom with ambiguous agendas who *for the moment* make their rulers happy in verse 3 are now metaphorically described. Their first description is that old, common one of harlotry: "All of them are adulterous" (7:4a). Next begin the images of bakers, baking ovens, fire, heat, burning, etc. The first simile depicting these people with prostituting agendas[190] involves things common to a baker's vocation. An acceptable rendering of these challenging lines would be, "they are like a heated oven whose baker ceases to stir the fire, from the kneading of the dough until it is leavened" (7:4b-e, ESV). This language most likely indicates that they specialize in "cooking up conspiracies" which lead to coups.

Verse 5 is riddled with interpretive challenges. One of the more appealing ways of understanding it is to take these statements as a panning of the prophetic camera to the unwary king and his officials who, on a special royal occasion, are fully engaged in partying. This complacent king and members of his political hierarchy have no clue about the

---

190   I.e., most likely one of political ladder-climbing.

catastrophe that awaits them when "the baker gets up in the morning and stokes the coals."

In verse 6 the camera pans back to the conspirators who quite apparently can't wait to strike. The NASB's translation, utilizing one of its literal marginal options, helpfully reads, "For their hearts are like an oven as they approach their ambush; their anger smolders all night, in the morning it burns like a flaming fire." Concerning such historically recurrent episodes, verse 7 offers a tragic summary-conclusion: "All of them are as hot as an oven and they consume their rulers. All their kings fall; not one of them calls on Me!" (HCSB). These cycles of coups were one more indication that loyalty to Yahweh, the Great King and Caring Shepherd of Israel, was nonexistent.

In the remainder of chapter 7 (i.e., vv. 8-16) divine assessments of Israel's apostasy and pronouncements of judgments against the nation are enhanced by picturesque comparisons.[191] Verse 8b ties back into the baker-oven-heat imagery of vv. 4-7. But first in verse 8a Ephraim is emphatically identified[192] as mixing itself among the people or nations. This is the language of international politics and deal making. The LORD and His prophets repeatedly warned the people about both the hazard and the consequences of making an alliance with one international power in an attempt to protect themselves from another threatening nation. A primary passage with a quite direct application to this historical tendency of Israel is Isaiah 31:1-3:

> Woe to those who go down to Egypt for help
> and rely on horses,
> who trust in chariots because they are many
> and in horsemen because they are very strong,
> but do not look to the Holy One of Israel
> or consult the LORD!

---

191 Cf., e.g., the metaphor of v. 8 and the similes of vv. 11 and 16.

192 In the Hebrew text the independent pronouns along with the expressed subject of the verb put the full spotlight of culpability on the nation; there is no hiding from this indictment.

And yet he is wise and brings disaster;
he does not call back his words,
but will arise against the house of the evildoers
and against the helpers of those who work iniquity.
The Egyptians are man, and not God,
and their horses are flesh, and not spirit.
When the LORD stretches out his hand,
the helper will stumble, and he who is helped will fall,
and they will all perish together (ESV).

The metaphor of verse 8b literally reads, "Ephraim was [and by implication, *remains*] a bread-cake not turned over." They were like a tortilla not flipped. We might compare our usage of the phrase "half-baked." From Yahweh's perspective they were absolutely unpalatable. By abandoning the LORD and not trusting in His protection, the nation trashed the holy relationship previously established by divine covenant.

Some of the consequences of impenitence follow in verses 9-10. Verse 9 contains two jeopardizing realities in reference to which the nation had become responsibly blind.[193] First, they refused to acknowledge that their treaty-making was counterproductive. Foreigners were sapping the strength out of them. This was probably due to the inevitable result of the giving of tribute according to the demands of a superior international power. The ending revelation of Hosea 8:7 possibly dovetails into 7:9a. Furthermore,[194] in the second half of 7:9 the nation fails to recognize that "gray hair is sprinkled on it." This constitutes another indication of a weakened condition, this time one that comes with old age. Their national life span was coming to an end.

The arrogance of the apostate nation once again comes back to haunt it at the outset of verse 10 (cf. 5:5). Literally, "the pride of Israel answers (or responds) to its face," i.e., their self-exaltation testifies

---

193   Each line of the Hebrew text ends identically with the same divine exposure. Yahweh's wayward people refused to recognize or acknowledge their deteriorating condition.

194   This line in the Hebrew text begins with an adverbial connector which in this context would indicate "moreover, additionally, also," etc.

against them. This condemnatory witness is ignored since the verse goes on to declare, "but despite all this he[195] does not return to the LORD his[196] God or search for him" (NIV). By their pursuit of unholy alliances they turned their backs on Yahweh, their God, i.e., the only truly powerful Protector (cf. v. 10b). Their seekings or pursuits of security from finite and fallen sources cut off any movement toward the only Source of real help (cf. v. 10c).[197] Not only was the sanctity of the covenantal relationship with Yahweh violated, but also His sovereign Kingship was rejected.

Verses 11-12 are bound together by bird and hunter imagery. The simile of verse 11 reads, "So Ephraim has become like a silly, senseless[198] dove; they call to Egypt, and they go to Assyria" (HCSB). The first part of this verse anticipates the springing of a trapping net over the unwary birds as indicated in verse 12. The baiting of the bird in verse 11 makes the hungry creature focus on food alone and none of the dangers around it. For God's sinfully oblivious people this baiting apparently came from the offers of protection from two competing international powers. But, Yahweh, the supremely skillful Hunter, says, "As they go,[199] I will spread over them my net; I will bring them down like birds of the heavens" (v. 12a,b, ESV). They will not escape *His* judgment. The last line of verse 12 is most challenging. The central truth of it resides in God's discipline or chastisement of them.[200] However, the interpretation of the last prepositional phrase is disputed. Including this perplexing phrase the line reads,

---

195 I.e., the nation.

196 I.e., the nation's.

197 Such an indictment of refusing to seek the LORD extends beyond the nation and people of Hosea's day (cf. Pss 14:2-3; 53:2-3).

198 This renders a common Hebrew idiom, "without heart," i.e., lacking sense (cf. Prov 6:32; 10:13, 21; 11:12; etc.).

199 Applicationally, whether it be to Egypt or Assyria.

200 On this word group as expressing discipline, esp. that of the LORD, cf., e.g., Hos 10:10; Lev 26:18,28; Deut 4:36; 8:5; Ps 118:18; Prov 19:18; 29:17; etc.

"I will discipline them *according to a report to their congregation.*"[201] More
likely than not, this report was an announcement of God's impending
judgments delivered during Hosea's era. We cannot be sure, however, of
any specific historical occasion.

Verse 13 contains the prophecy's first explicitly designated "woe"
pronouncement.[202] Actually the first two lines of this verse contain two
parallel pronouncements: "Woe to them, for they have strayed from me!
Destruction to them, for they have rebelled against me!" (v. 13 a,b, ESV).
The first line brings woe because of their apostasy,[203] the second, devastation or ruin because of their rebellion.[204] The two parts of the last line
of the Hebrew text of verse 13 are contrastingly related by means of an
emphatic "now I"/"but they" construction: "Now I would redeem them,
but they have spoken lies against Me." Although the LORD was willing
to ransom them[205] from their apostasy and rebellion, they had a track
record of defaming Him. They were responsible for cutting themselves
off from their redeeming God. It was He who redeemed His chosen
people from the beginning (cf., e.g., Exod 15:13; Deut 7:8; 9:26; 21:8;
2 Sam 7:23; 1 Chron 17:21; Neh 1:10; Isa 29:22; Jer 31:11; Mic 6:4;
etc.). Yet, the LORD's merciful longsuffering[206] will come back as one
of those exceedingly amazingly mind-blowing reversals in that the questions about a divine "ransom" and "redemption" in 13:14a,b ultimately
will be answered "Yes!" in 14:4-7.

---

201 The italics indicate a literal translation of this challenging adverbial phrase. It is interesting
that the word for "report" (i.e., what is heard, i.e., a delivered message) here is the same term
found in Isa 53:1.

202 There is one more to come in the middle of 9:12.

203 Viewed as straying, departing, fleeing, wandering, etc., away from God.

204 This Hebrew root stands behind one of the most condemning word groups for high-
handed sin in the OT (cf., e.g., Hos 8:1; plus the last line of the last verse of the book
["transgressors": "the rebellious"]; 1 Kgs 8:50; Isa 1:2,28; 53:5,8,12; 59:12; Jer 2:29; 3:13;
5:6; Lam 3:42; Ezek 2:3; 18:31; 20:38; Amos 1:3,6,9,11,13; 2:1,4,6; 3:14; 5:12; Zeph
3:11; etc.).

205 This OT term and especially its NT counterpart often connote buying out of a slave market.

206 Cf. the tender compassion of Christ in a similarly climactic setting in Matt 23:37.

Verse 14 launches with another exposure of the insincerity of these people (cf. their feigned repentance in 6:1-3): "And they do not cry[207] to Me from their heart when they wail on their beds"[208] (v. 14a,b, NASB). They may have been crying out and howling, but it didn't come from the heart. Another external exhibition of crying out is coming shortly in the hypocritical declaration of 8:2. The third poetic part of verse 14 begins with a reminiscence of the tragic truth that was exposed in chapter 2, verses 5 and 8.[209] If (and it seems to be the case) they were prostituting themselves with pagan fertility gods, the verb herein probably comes from a root which means to cut or gash, rather than to assemble. This is captured in the respective renderings of the ESV and the HCSB: "for grain and wine they gash themselves"; "they slash themselves for grain and wine." This practice brings to mind the pagan practice of the Baal worshippers in 1 Kings 18:28. The final indictment of Hosea 7:14 is the quite familiar one of apostasy. The clause literally reads, "They turn aside (or depart) against Me." This represents a hostile departure from Yahweh, the only true God. Such a rejection is all the more culpable in view of God's perfect parental history with them. The LORD affirms that "although I trained and strengthened their arms, yet they devise evil against me" (ESV). Hosea will provide even more commentary in the first seven verses of chapter 11 on how God had faithfully fathered them from the beginning. But here at the end of 7:15 it reveals that the people had a habit of plotting evil against their loving heavenly parent. Fittingly, more exposures of their malignant heart follow, along with equitable divine judgments in the last verse of chapter 7.

In spite of some textual and hermeneutical challenges, the gist of verse 16 is clear enough:

---

207 This is one of two words used for strongly crying out in a time of acute need (cf., e.g., Exod 2:23; Jud 3:9; 6:6; 10:10; 1 Sam 12:8,10; 1 Kgs 22:32; Ps 107:13; Hab 1:2; etc.).

208 Cf. the linking of both crying out and wailing also in Jer 48:20 and Ezek 21:12 [v. 17, Hebrew].

209 Vv. 7 and 10 in Hebrew.

They turn, but not upwards, They are like a deceitful
bow; Their princes will fall by the sword because of the
insolence of their tongue. This will be their derision in
the land of Egypt (NASB).

Using the most theologically conspicuous verb for turning, returning, repenting, etc.,[210] herein indicates that these people were on the move
but not back to Yahweh the "Most High" God.[211] Another simile comes
along next in verse 16b, further depicting the apostate nation. They are
likened to "a bow of deceit" or "treachery" (cf. the same imagery in Ps
78:57), i.e., a faulty bow that prohibits its arrows from hitting the target,
or possibly a "slack bow" that is incapable of even firing off an arrow.

The predictive prophecy of verse 16c conveys a future downfall of
"their princes."[212] In this context these would obviously be the nation's
military officers. They will fall by the sword literally "because of a curse
(or the indignation) of their tongue." Since the nation's princes are insub-
ordinate to the great King-General, they are especially culpable as they
lead the people into rebellion (cf., e.g., v. 13). Verse 16 closes with these
chilling words, "This will be their mocking (or derision) (or ridicule)
in the land of Egypt."[213] In the ancient Near East this would be looked
upon as the worst imaginable judgment (cf. the thrust of the divine judgments of Ps 44:9-16). Egypt is most likely being used emblematically for
Assyria's subjugation of Israel, then farther down the road for Babylon
taking Judah captive.[214]

---

210 Cf. previous discussions relating to 3:5; 6:1; etc.

211 Interpreting the preposition translated "upward" in NASB as "Most High" (NIV) still
seems to be the most viable option for v. 16a.

212 Cf. the occurrences of this leadership designation as previously encountered (i.e., 3:4; 5:10;
7:3).

213 I.e., referring to the tauntings they will experience in an Egypt-like captivity (cf. the 400+
years of their ancient bondage).

214 Cf. "Egypt" in Hos 7:11; 8:13; 9:3,6; 11:1,5,11; 12:1,9; etc.

EXHORTATIONS

This chapter revisits the themes of chapter 5, namely the certainty of God's perfect knowledge of and chastisement for Israel's sin. However, in this second treatment of those twin certainties, there is a focus on the deceptive nature of all sin. Repeatedly sin is shown to create a blinding effect that renders the heart unable to see spiritual realities about ourselves, those around us, or, most dangerously, God Himself. Hosea's words expose the shameful tendency of the human heart not merely to believe profane lies about God but simultaneously to deny profoundly beautiful truths about His holy, merciful, and gracious nature. Israel succumbed to three deceptions which have been a fundamental part of the ultimate deceiver, Satan, since the beginning of time. Let us learn from them "so that no advantage would be taken of us by Satan, for we are not ignorant of his schemes" (2 Cor 2:11).

(7:1–7) DECEPTION #1:
SIN WILL NOT BE REMEMBERED BY GOD

Despite the earlier, definitive declaration of God's full awareness of His people's iniquitous lifestyle (5:3), Israel remains unconvinced. So the LORD charges, "they do not consider in their hearts that I remember all their wickedness. Now their deeds are all around them; they are before My face" (v. 2). Israel did not live with an abiding awareness that their multiplied sins were committed before God's face, right under His nose so to speak. Seen at close range, their sins cannot be missed! Yet they did not have a functional belief in God's omniscience that would cause them to refrain from or repent of their transgressions. But sin hoodwinked Israel into thinking there was nothing to fear because somehow they'd managed to sin without God's knowledge or consequence. They ignorantly believed that they had gotten away with murder, literally (v. 7)!

But nothing could be further from the truth as so many passages in the Scriptures remind us. Numbers 32:23 states, "Be sure your sin will find you out." Proverbs 5:21 reads, "The ways of a man are before the eyes of the LORD." The profound folly of believing that one can somehow conceal his sin from God is dramatically illustrated in the life and death of Achan in Joshua chapter 7. After covetously stealing forbidden contraband, Achan concealed it under his tent. What Achan tried to cover up with a thin layer of sand under a cloth shelter was seen by God as though in broad daylight. What was the result? Achan and his family were stoned and burned, and a heap of stones was raised over their charred remains as a memorial to the danger of attempting to fool an omniscient God! Further, the Bible teaches that God's enemies mock the thought of God's awareness of sin, taunting, "the LORD does not see, Nor does the God of Jacob pay heed," but in reality, God not only sees, He also "knows the thoughts of man, that they are a mere breath" (Ps 94:7,11). How sad that such unbelief and the subsequent absence of fear that was true of the pagan Canaanite nations should now be true of Israel as well!

In a similar vein, the apostle Peter writes of unbelievers' blasphemous denial of divine knowledge of sin and the resulting possibility of future judgment. Peter authoritatively predicts,

> Know this first of all, that in the last days mockers will come with their mocking, following after their own lusts, and saying, "Where is the promise of His coming? For ever since the fathers fell asleep, all continues just as it was from the beginning of creation." For when they maintain this, it escapes their notice that by the word of God the heavens existed long ago and the earth was formed out of water and by water, through which the world at that time was destroyed, being flooded with water. But by His word the present heavens and earth are being reserved for fire, kept for the day of judgment and destruction of ungodly men. (2 Peter 3:3-7)

In the case of the mockers of the last days, Peter likewise states that certain truths "escape their notice." What is it that escapes the notice of the end-time mocker? The fearful thought that God had observed the sin of Noah's day which brought a devastating global flood in judgment.

God can and will bring global judgment again, only this time it will be with fire!

The doctrine of God's omniscience is fundamental to an informed conscience. The Reformers encouraged the biblical mindset that every aspect of life is lived *Coram Deo*, that is, "before the face of God." Still today, we teach our children songs like "Oh, be careful little eyes what you see." The song's later verses encourage little ones to be careful of their little hands, feet, ears, and mouth as well! What is the motive for all this careful living? God's omniscience! "For the Father up above is looking down in love … ." We do well to literally indoctrinate our children with the truth of God's omniscience, a doctrine which Israel so easily cast aside.

What a pathetic irony that ultimately it is not Israel's sin that goes unnoticed, but rather, God's mercy which is ignored. Consumed with sinful desires, God's people rendered themselves completely oblivious to the LORD's unfathomable willingness to restore and heal His people (vv. 6:11b-7:1a).

(7:8–12) DECEPTION #2: SIN CAN BE EASILY CONTAINED

Once Israel lost sight of the fundamental reality that God possessed a flawless recall of every one of their sins, they soon discovered that their wicked desires raged into an inferno of iniquity. The imagery of a hot oven is used to describe Israel's sin and its increasingly high-handed rebellion (vv. 4,6-7). No longer content with merely lying and stealing, Israel now found herself determined to overthrow the very authority of God Himself. With smoldering anger and sinister strategies that would rival any espionage novel of today, Israel attempts to subsume God's unrivaled power and right to raise up and remove political leaders (v. 6). Their political schemes often included murderous assassinations that demonstrated a further attempt to usurp God's exclusive authority over life and death as well (v. 7)! Once sin deceives the heart into believing that the LORD will not observe or judge your sin, it will take its duped victim swiftly into the grossest expressions of hubris and rebellion.

Israel continues her determined pursuit of sin by seeking protection and prosperity through alliances with the powerful, surrounding nations (vv. 8-12). Such treaties were expressly forbidden by God, who had commanded His people to keep themselves utterly separated from the Canaanites. The LORD declares that there would be heavy consequences for seeking security from pagan rulers—penalties that Israel would not even perceive, due to the blinding effects of sin. Like the proverbial "frog in the kettle," Israel would not recognize the gradual, increasing danger in which these rebellious treaties would place them. Hosea reflects, "Strangers devour his strength, and he knows it not" (v. 9). Israel certainly would have anticipated the great financial cost of paying ongoing tributes to political rulers in exchange for military protection. But the LORD warns them that alongside the slow draining of their national wealth, there would also be an equally steady deterioration of their corporate strength, a decline so gradual that the people would not even recognize it was occurring.

The LORD describes another imperceptible penalty for Israel's political concessions, "Gray hairs are sprinkled upon him, and he knows it not" (v. 9). Typically in the Old Testament, gray hair was a symbol of maturity and made one worthy of honor (Lev 19:32; Prov 16:31; 20:29), but in this passage gray hair is speaking of premature aging. The nation's sin accelerates the inevitable, withering effect of aging, and sin's deception keeps Israel from discerning it. The rapid, unmistakable change in physical appearance that we have all observed in political leaders or prisoners of war would occur to Israel on a national, spiritual level. But sin-blinded Israel would look in the mirror and fancy herself as youthful and strong as ever. The adage is true: *sin will take you further than you want to go, keep you longer than you want to stay, and cost you more than you want to pay.* The last one to perceive sin's high price tag is the one deeply involved in it. The LORD uses the image of a senseless, silly dove to depict those who have succumbed to such unperceived spiritual diminishment, and as an unthinking bird is vulnerable to the hunter's net, so Israel will not escape the LORD's chastisement (v. 12).

(7:13–15) DECEPTION #3:
SIN WILL NOT LEAD TO JUDGMENT

Although some of the effects of Israel's sin might go undetected, God's active chastisement of His people would be dramatic and unmistakable. In verse 13, the LORD utters a pair of terrifying judgments: "Woe to them for they have strayed from Me! Destruction is theirs, for they have rebelled against Me" (v. 13). Prophetic oracles can be divided roughly into two types: "blessed" statements, which announce God's favor and plans to prosper, and "woe" statements, which predict furious, destructive judgment from God's hand. Here, in this verse, we have the first "woe" proclamation in Hosea which is paralleled directly with the pronouncement of violent devastation.

Yet even in the midst of such an intense prophetic condemnation, the LORD expresses His great desire to restore: "I would redeem them, but they speak lies against Me" (v. 13). Though Israel hears God express again His willingness to restore them, they refuse to repent and further harden their hearts. Having been completely deluded by sin's insipid lies, Israel herself now propagates further deception by speaking slanderous blasphemies against the LORD. God's people speak profane lies against the one who had redeemed them and would gladly redeem them again, but in their blind rage, they will have no part of it. Jesus would utter a similar frustrated cry centuries later: "Jerusalem, Jerusalem, who kills the prophets and stones those who are sent to her! How often I wanted to gather your children together, the way a hen gathers her chicks under her wings, and you were unwilling. Behold, your house is being left to you desolate!" (Matt 23:37-38).

While God's people do eventually cry out under the weight of their escalating afflictions, they don't cry to out to the LORD; "They turn, but not upward" (vv. 14,16). Speaking with parent-like pathos, the LORD bemoans, "Although I trained and strengthened their arms, yet they devise evil against Me" (v. 15). Israel responds to God's grace by devising not only evil words, but evil deeds as well. The chapter closes with the dark prediction that the shame and ridicule associated with Israel's former captivity and enslavement in Egypt would come upon them again, this time in the land of Assyria (v. 16). The exodus from Egypt, regarded as the centerpiece of God's redemption of His people, is now reversed, and a death march back into a land of slavery and ill-treatment has begun. Woes, destruction, derision, and death await all those who are taken captive by sin's crafty deceit.

Sin works with equally costly deception today. The Scriptures teach that the ultimate author of all deception is Satan. From the beginning the serpent was acknowledged as the craftiest of God's creatures (Gen 3:1). He deceived Eve in the Garden of Eden with twisted lies about the veracity of God's words and the trustworthiness of His character (Gen 3:1-5). Jesus describes Satan as one who "does not stand in the truth because there is no truth in him. Whenever he speaks a lie, he speaks from his own nature, for he is a liar and the father of lies" (John 8:44). This master deceiver has, for thousands of years, been spreading variations of the same lies he perpetrated in the Garden. He utilizes other "deceitful spirits" who teach the "doctrines of demons" to extend his falsehoods (1 Tim 4:1). The apostle Paul expresses his concern about Satanic deception in the church at Corinth stating, "But I am afraid that, as the serpent deceived Eve by his craftiness, your minds will be led astray from the simplicity and purity of devotion to Christ" (2 Cor 11:3). In addition to the active work of Satan and his forces, the New Testament warns of many sources of deception. We are all susceptible to being blinded by our own lusts (Eph 4:22), misled by men's empty words (Eph 5:6; Col 3:8), or utterly fooled by worldly wealth (Matt 13:22). With so many avenues for lies to lead the heart into temptation, little wonder that we are called to "encourage one another day after day, as long as it is still called 'Today,' so that none of you will be hardened by the deceitfulness of sin"! (Heb 3:12).

How consoling to know that the deception that characterizes Satan and fallen men is utterly foreign to God's nature! He has never lied (Num 23:19; 1 Sam 15:29), for "God is light and in Him there is no darkness at all" (1 John 1:5). His words are not only truthful, they are truth itself (Ps 119:142,151,160; John 17:17). Jesus affirmed that He was born and came to earth in order to testify to the truth (John 18:37), and further, He referred to Himself as "the truth" (John 14:6). The apostle John described Christ as one who was "full ... of truth" (John 1:14). Christ promised His disciples that He would send "the Spirit of truth" (John 14:17; 15:26), who would guide them into all the truth (John 16:13). With such an infallible source and guide, there is absolutely no reason for us ever to be "fooled" into committing sin. While we will all battle temptation and failure until our salvation is consummated in heaven, let us determine, by God's grace, to avoid any sinful act that is based on culpable, long-term deception!

8 HOSEA 8:1–14

EXPOSITION

(8:1–14) THE LORD AS EXECUTIONER ORDERS THE PUNISHMENTS OF HIS CRIMINAL PEOPLE (PART 1)

Hosea 8:1 literally reads, "To your palate a shofar! Like a vulture over the house of Yahweh, because they have transgressed My covenant, and against My instruction they have rebelled." Or, smoothing out the verse, "Set the trumpet to your lips! One like a vulture is over the house of the LORD, because they have transgressed My covenant and rebelled against My law." This kind of sarcastic taunt is reminiscent of the ones delivered by God through his prophet in chapter 5, verse 8. They are told to sound the alarm because divine judgment is on the horizon. Yahweh's instrument of judgment is compared to an eagle, or better, a carrion-eating buzzard.[215] This language brings to mind the warning recorded in Deuteronomy 28:49ff. about an attacking nation.[216] A twofold justification for such divine vengeance comes at the end of verse 1: the people had violated the covenant and had rebelled against inscripturated divine instructions.

---

215 Note that such ugly instruments will be used as a clean-up crew after the eschatological "battle" of Rev 19:11ff. (note esp. vv. 17-18).

216 Contrast the positive illustrations of Yahweh's care for the nation in Deut 32:11.

In verse 2, their hypocritical cryings out come back once again to haunt them (cf. 7:14). The people were claiming that they knew or acknowledged the only true God as their own. However, that is not the case, as indicated by the exposure of them in verse 3a: "Israel has spurned[217] the good" (ESV). They blatantly disregarded Moses' challenge recorded in Deuteronomy 30:15ff. Even beyond that, they turned their backs on the embodiment of all good (i.e., Yahweh God Himself, cf. Exod 33:19). As a consequence, Yahweh announces that "an enemy will pursue (or persecute) him" ("him" = Israel).

The first two lines of verse 4 are parallel and reveal Yahweh's strong disapproval of the leadership of the Northern Kingdom. He refused to be associated with their[218] installation of kings,[219] and He refused to acknowledge[220] their secondary rulers. Their unauthorized actions would ultimately prove to be fatal (cf. Hos 13:10).

The latter half of verse 4 introduces a typically prophetic anti-idolatry polemic, which continues through verse 7. Speaking about the masses of Israel, verse 4 c,d literally reads: "(With) their silver and their gold they [i.e., the people] made for themselves idols in order that (or with the result that) it [i.e., the nation] will be cut off."[221] Such fabrications of these objects that characterized pagan worship were not a new problem

---

217 The verb is rendered "to spurn, to reject"; another occurrence will follow quickly in v. 5, but from the divine side of things. Furthermore, this Hebrew verb sounds similar to the primary noun used for "prostitute" in this book.

218 The Hebrew text, with its introductory independent pronoun, emphasizes the fact that the people had taken these matters of installation into their own hands (ironically contrast, e.g., 1 Sam 16; Dan 2:20-21; 4:34-37; Rom 13:1-7; etc.)

219 Remember much earlier in the nation's history their craving for a king to rule over them *like all the other nations* (cf. 1 Sam 8). Therein, Samuel was jealous for the divine King of Israel. Yet we need to remember that one day in the future a truly repentant nation would "seek the LORD their God and David [i.e., the Greater David, the Christ] their king" (Hos 3:5, NASB).

220 There may be a play on the Hebrew verb "to know" in the sense of Yahweh's non-acknowledgement here with the nations' hypocritical "acknowledgement" of the LORD back in v. 2.

221 Note the irony: these makers of idols had benefit on their minds; however, their idolatrous labors would ultimately result in disaster.

to the nation. Unfortunately, the people had a track record of violating the first two commandments[222] over and over again. As a matter of fact, it was not long after their calling as a nation that the first golden calf incident occurred.[223]

Another "calf-idol" (NIV) immediately comes into view in verse 5 of Hosea 8. However, the leading verb in the Hebrew text is most challenging. The root of this opening verbal, conveying Israel's *rejection*[224] of good, is the same root that occurred in verse 3. The question about it here is textual. Should it be inflected as a passive (i.e., "your calf *is rejected*, Samaria"),[225] or as an imperative (i.e., "reject your calf, Samaria!"),[226] or as a third-person reference to God as subject, (i.e., "He has rejected your calf, O Samaria"),[227] or should the Hebrew text be emended according to the early Greek translation ("I have spurned your calf, O Samaria")?[228] Whatever the case, rejection is rejection, and it seems most likely contextually that God Himself is the Agent. This is substantiated by the very next line: "My [i.e., Yahweh's] anger burns against them." Rounding off the verse comes a probing rhetorical question: "How long will they be incapable of cleanness (or innocence)?" Their time for exercising radical repentance was running out.

Another installment about the stupidity of idolatry lies at the heart of verse 6. Remember that some similar exposures may be found, for example, in Isaiah 44:9-20; Jeremiah 10:1-16; Habakkuk 2:18-20; *et al*. Here in Hosea the Northern Kingdom was established virtually on a religious footing of idol-calf worship (cf. 1 Kgs 12:25-33, esp. v. 28). This is

---

222 Cf. Exod 20:2-6.

223 Cf. Exod 32.

224 Also remember that this Hebrew root sounds similar to the most frequently occurring root for a prostitute or prostituting.

225 Cf. HCSB.

226 Cf. NIV; this is the least likely option because of gender and other considerations.

227 Cf. NASB.

228 Cf. ESV.

the historical reality that stands behind the first line of Hosea 8:6: "For from Israel is even this!" (NASB). The rationale which follows is that since a human being made it, it cannot be God: "A craftsman made it, so it is not God" (NASB). Jeremiah also reminded his wayward audience that "our fathers inherited only lies, worthless idols of no benefit at all. Can one make gods for himself? But they are not gods" (Jer 16:19b-20, HCSB). Because of the calves[229] which were not God, the LORD's sure judgment will come: "It will be broken in pieces, that calf of Samaria" (Hos 8:6d, NIV).[230]

Another harbinger of coming divine judgments is couched in the proverbial saying[231] that launches verse 7: "For wind they sow[232] but whirlwind they will reap." Unless they truly repent, a tornado of divine retributions surely awaits them.[233] Among those impending judgments would be catastrophic agricultural disaster as the last part of verse 7 makes clear.[234] This should not have come as a surprise to Hosea's audience since the majority of the forecasted curses of Deuteronomy were designed to hit a disobedient nation hard at a most basic level—their food supply.[235]

The last line of verse 7 provides a word-bridge pun to the first line of verse 8 through its employment of verb forms denoting swallowing. Here Israel's judgment is depicted as being gobbled up among the nations, and furthermore, this divine announcement is strengthened by a temporal "now." Although yet future in its fulfillment of its proclamation, it is as

---

229 Remember that there were two sites in the Northern Kingdom (i.e., Bethel and Dan; 1 Kgs 12:29) where these calf-idols were set up for public worship. There may have also been a proliferation of diminutive household calf-idols (cf. Hos 13:2).

230 Concerning the other large idol-calf, it was carted off to Assyria (i.e., Hos 10:6).

231 For similar kinds of constructs, cf., e.g., Job 4:8; 15:31,35; Prov 22:8; Gal 6:7.

232 Remember, this is a Hebrew word group that carries along a verb-theme in Hosea (cf. 1:4,5,11, 2:22,23; 10:12).

233 Cf. similarly Isa 29:6 and Nah 1:3.

234 Cf., e.g., a similar disaster that would be brought on the Southern Kingdom as testified to by Habakkuk in 3:17.

235 Cf., e.g., Deut 8; 28:15ff.

good as done from the divine perspective.[236] There is also a dimension of *lex talionis* in this judgment since that nation had taken up a habit of making deals with international powerhouses by mixing itself up with them (cf. 7:8ff.). Returning to Hosea 8:8, its final line employs a derogatory simile; this doomed nation is "like a vessel in which no one delights" (NASB), i.e., "like discarded pottery" (HCSB).

Verses 9-10a return to yet another exposure of Israel in its futile attempts to protect itself through international alliances. Herein they are depicted as fleeing to Assyria for protection. In the process they are characterized as "a wild donkey wandering alone" (ESV);[237] they have "hired lovers." Verse 10a expands this defining and damning tendency beyond a singular symbiotic deal with one nation to many nations. But more importantly, the initial "Even" and/or "though" at the outset of this introductory line sets up Yahweh's impending intervention of judgment, i.e., "I will now round them up" (HCSB). The first stage of divine judgment would be the devastating effects of paying tribute. The most likely reading of this last part of verse 10 is: "And the king and princes shall soon writhe because of the tribute" (ESV).[238] Such payments will indeed prove to be painful!

Evidences of apostasy related to worship return to center stage in verses 11ff. The tautology of verse 11 would have captured the ears of those first hearing this oracle: "Since Ephraim has multiplied altars for sin, they have become altars of sinning for him" (NASB). Verse 12 interjects a statement which is designed to escalate the nation's culpability in view of its total disregard of Yahweh's plentiful, perspicuous instructions. The ESV captures the thrust of this verse well: "Were I to write for him my laws by the ten thousands they would be regarded as a strange thing."

Their hypocritical worship was a perennial problem, and in verse 13 Yahweh asserts that He has had enough of it. When it literally says, "Sacrifice of My gifts they sacrifice and flesh they eat," it may be best in

---

236 Cf. this "now" as a marker of real time or imminence in Hos 4:16; 5:7; 8:10,13; 10:2.

237 Cf. their depiction as a "silly dove" in a similar context in 7:11.

238 For other translation options see NASB, NIV, HCSB.

light of the context to render the second part of that observation "so that they might eat flesh." In other words, they might go through the motions of sacrificing to Yahweh, but their real motivation is to consume the meat. For that, or a similar reason, Hosea declares that "Yahweh does not take pleasure in them"; He "does not favorably accept them."[239]

The verse now advances from rejection to retribution: "Now He will remember[240] their iniquity, and punish[241] *them* for their sins; they[242] will return to Egypt" (8:13b, NASB). This would be a divinely-engineered and effectuated *return* to captivity. The LORD had brought them out of bondage originally (cf., e.g., Deut 7:8b), and now He would be the one who would send them back into slavery. The original bondage of Israel had been in literal Egypt; however, here "Egypt" is being employed typologically for the sake of impact. Their shortly-to-be-experienced captivity would actually be in Assyria (cf., e.g., 9:3).

The last verse of chapter 8 is quite comprehensive, leveling general indictments followed by an announcement of an appropriate divine intervention. First, following on the heels of God's *remembering* in verse 13 is the nation's *forgetting* of their Creator as mentioned at the outset of verse 14. This too is not amnesia but a culpably deliberate refusal to recognize and live in the light of the obvious theological reality.[243] Instead of paying attention to and relying upon their God, Israel built palaces.[244] Furthermore, and somewhat surprisingly, Judah comes back into this scene and is exposed as a nation that multiplies fortified cities. Those selfish and faithless activities against Yahweh God bring a fiery judgment

---

239 Remember the rejection of hypocritical offerings in Amos 5:22; Mic 6:7; Mal 1:10,13; etc.

240 Remember that "remember" does not intimate any kind of recovery from divine amnesia, but indicates a deliberate act of paying attention to something for the purpose of taking action.

241 The verb literally means "to visit," a frequently employed idiom used of God's visitations either to bless or, as here, to punish.

242 Another occurrence in the Hebrew text of the emphatic use of an independent personal pronoun: emphatically *they* will return to Egypt.

243 Cf. Hos 2:13; 4:6; 13:6.

244 Would that they would have paid heed to all the implications of Ps 127:1.

upon North and South alike. Their Maker announces this coming conflagration with these concluding words to chapter 8: "So I will send a fire upon his cities and it shall devour her strongholds" (ESV).

EXHORTATIONS

While Hosea's messages contain frequent predictions of the coming judgment facing Israel, chapter 8 begins and ends with the most urgent warnings we have encountered thus far. The opening warning is one of impending invasion (vv. 1-3). In it, the Lord commands "Put the trumpet to your lips" (v. 1a). The trumpet mentioned here is the shofar, an instrument made of a ram's horn that was used to call God's people to worship or to summon them for battle. With frightening sarcasm, the LORD demands that the shofar be sounded because He is about to wage war against His own people! The human means by which God would carry out His campaign would be the mighty Assyrian army, eerily depicted as circling vultures waiting to plummet from the heights in order to feast on their dead bodies. The cause of this divine declaration of war is summarized here as twofold. First is Israel's premeditated, rebellious disobedience to God's declared will (v. 1c). Second is their outright rejection of "the good" (v. 3a). Yet, despite their cold spurning of the LORD and His repeated declarations to the contrary (4:1,6; 5:4; 6:6), they still cry out, "My God, we of Israel know You" (v. 2).

The closing warning of the chapter alerts Israel of their imminent destruction. Though Israel has "forgotten his Maker," the LORD will "remember their iniquity and punish them for their sins" (vv. 13-14). This retribution would include reducing Israel's fortified cities and impressive palaces to a smoldering heap of ashes. As in the chapter's earlier announcement of coming catastrophe, Assyria would again be the human instrument used by God to bring about "Egypt 2.0," complete with captivity, humiliation, and enslavement. Between the chapter's two alarms, the LORD delineates the sin and guilt that brought on the forewarned invasion and destruction. A careful look at God's perspective of Israel's failures reveals various categories of sin that plague the human heart even today.

(8:4A) THE AUTONOMY OF SELF-APPOINTED LEADERS

The LORD declares that one of the causes for the approaching invasion was Israel's autonomous appointing of kings and princes (v. 4a). Israel's initial demand for an earthly king, centuries before, was itself a rebellious rejection of the LORD (1 Sam 8:7; 10:18-19). The LORD had warned Israel through Samuel that they would one day lament choosing a mortal monarch over His glorious sovereignty. But the people insisted, "No, but there shall be a king over us, that we also may be like all the nations, that our king may judge us and go out before us and fight our battles" (2 Sam 8:19-20). What adolescent and sinful reasoning! In order to "fit in with the crowd" of the surrounding pagan nations, Israel traded the quintessential Judge and ultimate Commander of the armies of heaven for a finite, human leader. So, the LORD gave them the earthly leader they clamored for, and Saul was anointed as Israel's first king. His outward appearance was impressive and appealed to the people's shallow desires. He was the most handsome man in the country and was literally head and shoulders above his countrymen (1 Sam 9:2). But his disastrous, ungodly leadership would prove that his inner character was unattractive and scrawny. Saul's unchecked pride and fear of man would eventually cost him the crown, and the LORD appointed David "a man after his own heart" as king in his place (1 Sam 13:13-14; 15:24). But now Israel autonomously chooses kings for themselves based on their own worldly evaluation. God's endorsement or blessing is neither sought nor required. It is in this sense that the LORD declared that Israel had kings, "but not by Me" and "princes, but I did not know it" (v. 4).

Imbedded in every temptation that you and I face today is a similar desire to make autonomous decisions about what is best for us—decisions independent of God and His Word. As Eve was deceived into ignoring God's perfect assessment of good and evil and foolishly trusting in her own limited appraisal of what was in her and Adam's best interest, so we are often guilty of disregarding Scripture's objective guidance and placing too much value on our subjective, personal endorsements. Oh, how much grievous sin and needless suffering could be avoided by a simple faith in the Word of God and a humble distrust of our personal perspective!

(8:4B–6) THE STUPIDITY OF SELF-CREATED DEITIES

A second reason for the swiftly approaching disaster facing Israel was their continual participation in idolatry. The LORD notes that "with silver and gold Israel has made idols for themselves" (v. 4b). The practice of gilding statues with precious metals was a reminder that true devotion to an idol was costly. Significant financial sacrifices had to be made in order to fund the nation's false religion. How does the Lord feel about His people's costly, traitorous worship? He declares, "My anger burns against them" (v. 5). He expresses dismay that His holy people have become as unclean as the nations around them; they have become "incapable of innocence" (vv. 5-6). Further, He is appalled at the folly of Israel's deification of inanimate objects, stating, "a craftsman made it, so it is not God" (v. 6). With these words the LORD is pointing out the obvious, that every artisan who possessed the necessary skills to craft an idol was infinitely superior to that which his talented hands had produced. But despite that clear reality, the idol maker and those who paid him to manufacture a "god" would bow down before such man-made objects and worship them. In so doing, they were ultimately praising the work of their own hands and trusting in what they could accomplish in their own strength.

The prophet Habakkuk also addresses the relationship between worship and trust through a simple, rhetorical question: "What profit is the idol when its maker has carved it ... ? For its maker trusts in his own handiwork when he fashions a speechless idol" (Hab 2:18). Notice that the idol maker is not depicted as merely praising his own handiwork; rather, he is *trusting* in his own accomplishment. Similarly, the psalmist states, "Their idols are silver and gold, the work of man's hands.... . Those who make them will become like them, everyone who *trusts* in them (Ps 115:4,8, emphasis added). The essence of idolatry is placing your trust in anything besides the LORD, and when the object of your trust is something that you have created or achieved, then, in the final analysis, you are worshipping yourself. You do not have to prostrate yourself before a visible carved statue to be guilty of self-worship. The fight against spiritual narcissism rages in the heart of man.

However, in this passage the LORD does more than merely declare His severe displeasure over the idolatry and self-worship, He announces specific retribution that would come from His hand as a result. He announces that while their false gods promised fertility and prosperity, Israel would find themselves completely cut off and destroyed by the only true God (v. 4). With the same vigor with which Israel had rejected the LORD's goodness (v. 3), the LORD now spurns Israel's current idol of choice, a Samarian calf, and determines to shatter it beyond recognition (vv. 5-6). Finally, the LORD proclaims that judgment would come upon them with the unexpected fury and devastation of a tornado: "They sow the wind and they reap the whirlwind" (v. 7). Israel would pay dearly for her tenacious worship/trust of herself that was lurking beneath the formal trappings of Canaanite idolatry.

(8:7-10) THE FUTILITY OF SELF-PROTECTIVE STRATEGIES

Prominent throughout Israel's history was a failure to trust the LORD for military and political protection. Such unbelief gave rise to fears and as a result, God's people frequently sought refuge from the larger countries around them. As was noted earlier, these faithless agreements, designed to minimize risk, were expressly prohibited by God and became yet another cause for the imminent invasion which the LORD was bringing. But Israel's plans to reduce danger by self-protective political maneuvering backfired. Having mixed themselves with the nations (7:8), Israel is now "swallowed up," subsumed and enveloped into a political machine that was more than happy to receive their financial payments for political defense, but which had no more regard for them than a piece of broken pottery (v. 8). What a humiliating state for a people who had panted like an animal in heat after the same foreign nations that now despised them (v. 9)! Indeed, Israel "hired lovers" to provide the safety and security that the LORD had always graciously provided without fee. Indeed, Israel finds themselves languishing under an unbearable financial burden of their international alliances (vv. 9-10). Though Israel is embedded with the Canaanites as to be virtually indistinguishable, the LORD assures them that He will have no difficulty identifying His wayward people and assembling them for judgment (v. 10).

Like Israel, our hearts also give way to sinful doubts about God's loving protection and provision for us. How deeply we dishonor the Lord when we harbor secret fears that the Lord will not shield us from danger. We devise self-protective "safety nets" to fall into, just in case the Lord doesn't come through for us as we wish. But these unbelieving schemes come at a high price. We sacrifice our joy when we spend our life trying to insulate ourselves from perceived danger. We often lose sleep, anxiously tossing and turning about our finances rather than praying, "Give us this day our daily bread" (Matt 6:11). Driven by the hope of avoiding disease or death, we are willing to neglect private Scripture reading and prayer while we spend inordinate time and attention on our health or physical appearance. We give up the profound comfort of Christ, our sympathetic high priest, when we fail to draw near to the throne of grace and settle instead for mere human empathy from family or friends (Heb 4:15-16).

(8:11-13A) THE HYPOCRISY OF SELF-STYLED WORSHIP

The LORD declares that Israel's pattern of corrupt worship was another reason for the fiery destruction that He was about to bring about. Though Israel could never have been accused of renouncing altogether the offerings commanded by the LORD, they were indeed guilty of failing to bring Him sincere and exclusive worship. Israel's proliferation of altars demonstrates that there was no lack of national religious fervor. But whether they offered hypocritical worship to the LORD or illicit pagan idolatry, every new "sacred" altar that Israel built was nothing more than a setting for yet further sin (v. 11). The word of the LORD, once warmly treasured within Israel's heart, was now coolly regarded from a distance and treated as an estranged friend that was once held dear (v. 12). The sacrificial gifts of God's people once gratefully given to the LORD were now being consumed by self-indulgent men, reminiscent of the wicked and immoral sons of Eli who took for themselves that which belonged to God (v. 13; cf. 1 Sam 2:12-17).

With altars that produced nothing but sin, divine revelation regarded as strangely foreign, and offerings that were meaningless tokens, why did the people of Israel continue to go through the motions of external worship? Perhaps it was just a comfortable ritual. Maybe it was a love of impressive palace-like nature of the temple building itself. It could have been fear of the consequences of breaking with multi-generational traditions. But the ultimate reason that Israel continued in their self-styled worship was because it made them feel better about themselves! This self-exaltation was at the heart of each of the sins for which the nation would soon experience the onslaught of God's fury. Israel valued their own opinion in choosing their civil leaders. They gloried in their own ability to create false gods. They smugly enjoyed their ability to reduce their vulnerability of being harmed by marauding enemies. And now, in the arena of worship, they supremely valued their feelings about what real worship should be.

Still today, those who love their sin and do not wish to be parted from it, those who want their conscience quieted but not cleansed, those who lack true faith in God's Word and are devoid of willingness to submit to or obey it, yes, for these sorts of people, going through the motions of sheer external worship rituals is the perfect means of propping up their sense of self-righteousness. Showing up on Sundays can provide just the fix that a feeling-addicted heart is looking for. While grand architecture, powerful music, or eloquent liturgy may trigger aesthetic or emotional experiences, true worship is induced only by transcendent truths which are in turn received by faith. Our worship gatherings should be filled with many feelings but not driven by them!

Israel's flagrant confidence in their own abilities is representative of various categories of self-sufficiency that plague the human heart even today. The Scriptures repeatedly call believers to avoid Israel's blatant self-trust and live in humble dependence on the Lord. Solomon pled with his sons, "Trust in the LORD with all your heart and do not lean on your own understanding" (Prov 3:5). John the Baptist's words, "He must increase, but I must decrease" are the very antithesis of self-promotion (John 3:30). Jesus instructed His disciples that "apart from Me you can do nothing" (John 15:5). Paul explained that true believers are marked by their commitment to "glory in Christ Jesus and put no confidence in the flesh" (Phil 3:3). The prophet Jeremiah appealed to Judah:

> Cursed is the man who trusts in mankind and makes flesh his strength, and whose heart turns away from the LORD. For he will be like a bush in the desert and will not see when prosperity comes, but will live in stony wastes in the wilderness, a land of salt without inhabitant. Blessed is the man who trusts in the LORD and whose trust is the LORD. For he will be like a tree planted by the water that extends its roots by a stream and will not fear when the heat comes; but its leaves will be green, and it will not be anxious in a year of drought nor cease to yield fruit. (Jer 17:5-8)

The curses that come upon the self-reliant and the blessings ensured for those whose exclusive trust is in the LORD, prove that there is no place in the Christian life for unfounded, foolish self-reliance.

9 HOSEA 9:1–17

EXPOSITION

(9:1–17) THE LORD AS EXECUTIONER ORDERS THE PUNISHMENTS OF HIS CRIMINAL PEOPLE (PART 2)

The opening verses of Chapter 9 reach back and weave together several key themes which occurred earlier in the book. For example, the major theme of prostitution and/or the "wages" of a prostitute picks up threads from 1:2; 2:5,12 [vv. 7,14, Hebrew]; and 4:12-15. These perverse realities constitute the reasons for the divine prohibitions which stand at the head of this chapter. Notice the connection:

> Rejoice not, O Israel!
> Exult not like the peoples;
> For you have played the whore, forsaking your God.
> You have loved a prostitute's wages[245]
> On all threshing floors.
> Threshing floor and wine vat shall not feed them,
> and the new wine shall fail them (Hos 9:1-2, ESV).

---

245 As background, call to mind again, e.g., Deut 23:18; Isa 23:17-18; Ezek 16:34; Mic 1:7.

Because of these spiritually heinous behaviors, God pronounces His sentence. They would be expelled from Yahweh's land (v. 3a). The nation too often had forgotten that the Promised Land belonged to Him and that they were to be responsible tenants (cf. Lev 25:23). Yahweh had brought the nation out of Egypt into Canaan, but since they had violated the 'lease agreement' (i.e., the many covenant stipulations), to Egypt they would return (cf. 3b; 8:13).[246] It is this verse, however, that informs us that this is metaphorical "Egypt" since they would be sent to Assyria (v. 3c). This will be reconfirmed in Hosea 11:5. Furthermore, ironically, Israel had tried to broker protective alliances with both of these international powers (cf. Hos 12:1).

Furthermore, when they would be sent into Assyrian captivity they would eat unclean food. Since they indeed would be expelled from the "Holy Land" to an *unclean* land (cf. Amos 7:17), their food would be nothing but unclean, and that is unacceptable to a *holy* God. As verses 4 and 5 go on to implicate, this would make any acceptable worship of Yahweh impossible. As a matter of fact, in this pervasively unclean environment the captives themselves would become "defiled," i.e., unclean (cf. v. 4d). Therefore, unholy offerings must not enter "the house of Yahweh."[247] As the rhetorical questions of verse 5 painfully reveal, this would leave them without any options for celebrating the appointed feast days established by divine mandate through Moses.

The central judgment being an Egypt-like captivity (cf. v. 3) is borne along by the language of verse 6: "For behold, they are going[248] away from destruction; but Egypt shall gather them; Memphis shall bury them. Nettles shall possess their precious things of silver; thorns shall be in their tents" (ESV). The movement in the first part of verse 6 basically

---

246 There is another sound-alike noun in the original Hebrew text between the verbs of v. 3a (i.e., rendered "remain" in NASB) and v. 3b (i.e., rendered "return" in NASB).

247 In this context a reference to the Holy Land of promise.

248 In Hebrew another verb functioning as a prophetic perfect (i.e., in God's book this is as good as done).

parallels, in its significance, our saying "Out of the frying pan into the fire." They were going to leave a devastated homeland only to end up in the bondage of an international powerhouse. Back "home" in a land once manicured by the blessing of God, thistles and thorns[249] would engulf their former wealth and domiciles.

The imminence of divine judgment is emphatically affirmed in verse 7 with the arrival of two more prophetic perfect verbs in Hebrew: "the days of punishment[250] have come; the days of retribution[251] have come" (v. 7a,b, HCSB). Both the time of punishment and of retribution are viewed as having begun. The next short line comes with a textual variant,[252] and it also is viewed as the point of departure for a variety of interpretations concerning the remainder of verse 7 and verse 8.

This brief line could be translated, based upon the Hebrew text, in various ways: "Let Israel know!" (most literal[253]); "Let Israel know *this*!" (NASB); "Israel shall know it"(HCSB); etc. This challenge for the people of the nation to acknowledge or to recognize something could refer to the impending judgment that was on their doorstep (i.e., v. 7a,b), or to what follows concerning the prophet or prophets (i.e., vv. 7d-8), or even both to what precedes and to what follows. Now coming to the most difficult interpretive issue which involves the rest of verse 7 and verse 8, among all the options it seems best to view Hosea, as Yahweh's true prophet, herein exposing the lying cult and court prophets of Israel.[254] The causal

---

249 Thistles and/or thorns are often used to convey the aftermath of divine judgment, i.e., a ghost-town kind of imagery (cf. both nouns in Isa 34:13).

250 The verb forms standing behind this noun denote to "visit," i.e., in the sense of to "punish" in negative settings such as here (cf. 1:4; 2:13 [v. 15, Hebrew]; 4:9,14; 8:13; 12:2 [v. 3, Hebrew]). On a "day of punishment," cf. Isa 10:3.

251 Cf. "a day of recompense" or "retribution" in Isa 34:8. Remember that Yahweh owns the exclusive rights to exercise retribution (i.e., Deut 32:35).

252 This variant comes from the LXX's reading, which was apparently based on a verb meaning to "cry out" instead of the Hebrew text's verb form denoting to "know."

253 I.e., there is no object attached in the original.

254 A similar scenario was Micaiah's exposure of Ahab's ear-tickling prophets in 1 Kgs 22. Cf., Jeremiah's conveyances of divine judgment while many people were chanting, "Peace! Peace!"

statements (i.e., v. 7f,g) that follow the parallel and fittingly derogatory
characterizations of the false prophets (i.e., v. 7d,e) apply either directly
or indirectly to those frauds. They themselves are so labeled "because of
the magnitude of your [i.e., the false prophets being spoken to directly
by Hosea] guilt and hostility" (v. 7f,g, HCSB), or this could refer to the
people constituted as an exceedingly sinful nation, the masses of Israel
toward whom these prophets were turning a blind eye. Obviously there
was plenty of culpability that Hosea could spread around.

As already noted, translational[255] and interpretive challenges move on
into verse 8. It seems most likely that the first line is an affirmation about
a true prophet. He as the "watchman"[256] was the one who was to warn
the people of all kinds of impending danger. If he proved to be faithful in
respect to his duties he, like Hosea, would stand in an intimate relationship with his God.[257] However, the false prophet stands in stark contrast
with the true prophet as the next line of verse 8 indicates. He is graphi-
cally depicted by Hosea not as protecting the people but as setting snares
and traps for them. These words expose his nefarious *modus operandi*.
Finally, Hosea reveals that resident in the "house" of the false god of the
false prophet is "enmity" or "animosity," "hatred," "hostility," *et al.*[258]

The first part of verse 9 returns to the thoroughly sinful state of the
people, but possibly in this context viewed as catalyzed by the prophets of
perversity. Actually there are two verbs placed side by side at the outset of
verse 9. Literally these perfect tense verbs of description would translate:
"They have made deep"; "They have dealt corruptly."[259] Most modern ver-

---

255 E.g., "Ephraim *was* a watchman with my God, a prophet" (NASB); "The prophet is the
     watchman of Ephraim with my God" (ESV); "The prophet, along with my God, is the
     watchman over Ephraim" (NIV); "Ephraim's watchman is with my God. The prophet ..."
     (HCSB).

256 Cf., illustratively, 2 Sam 18:24-27; Isa 52:8; Jer 6:17; Ezek 3:17; 33:2ff.; Mic 7:4,7; etc.

257 Called "my God" by Hosea, our watcher-prophet.

258 Cf. the previous occurrence of this noun in v. 7. For verbal occurrences from this Hebrew
     root, see Gen 27:41; 49:23; 50:15; Job 16:9; 30:21; and Ps 55:3 (v. 4, Hebrew.)

259 For two very theologically significant occurrences of this Hebrew root in verb forms, see
     respectively Gen 6:11,12. Also note the golden calf episode in Exod 32:7ff.

sions merge the two verbs in some fashion; for example, "They have deeply corrupted themselves" (ESV); "They have sunk deep into corruption" (NIV); etc. To these indictments is added a heinous historical illustration. The words "as in the days of Gibeah" likely refer to Judges 19-20, the shocking episode that chronicles the rape and murder of a Levite's concubine wherein also he dismembered her body to muster the tribes to deal with the perpetrators.[260] In view of the people of Israel diving so deeply into depravity the twin pronouncements of divine retribution return (cf. Hos 8:13): Yahweh God "will remember their iniquity; He will punish their sins."

The next section of chapter 9 begins with a divine reminiscence: "Like grapes in the wilderness, I found Israel.[261] Like the first fruit on the fig tree in its first season, I saw your fathers" (v. 10a,b). But it didn't take long for them[262] to display rotten fruit as Yahweh goes on to attest. The reference to the dark historical episode at Baal-peor is found in Numbers 25, especially as identified succinctly in the first three verses. Here in Hosea 9:10 it characterizes those people as having dedicated themselves to shame. Hosea's audience was replicating that kind of gross apostasy. The last line of verse 10 points to the analogous result of such idolatry: "And they became as detestable as that which they loved" (NASB). The word group conveying what is abominable or detestable has various applications in the Old Testament, the two primary ones being references to unclean food and to idolatrous worship as here.

Verses 11 and 12 conceptually interrelate as documented by the departure references of verse 11a and 12c. This inclusio about the flying away[263] of Ephraim's (i.e., the people's) glory stands in a parallel relationship with Yahweh's leaving them.[264] More actively, regarding the inner lines of verses 11-12, Yahweh is depicted as implementing a program of

---

260   Judg 19:30 calls special attention to the notoriety of this episode.

261   Cf., e.g., Deut 32:10.

262   This next line begins with an emphatic "they," which sets up the logical antithesis.

263   Cf. the bird-in-flight imagery.

264   This foreboding prophecy reminds one of other "*Ichabod*" passages such as 1 Sam 4:10-22 and Ezek 10:18-19; 11:22-23.

genocide! He is going to prevent conceptions, gestations, and births.[265] Furthermore, He is also going to wipe out their older children. No wonder these two verses end on the low note of an exclamatory "woe!"

The central theme of childlessness from verses 11 and 12 is picked up in verses 13 and 14.[266] Although verse 13 exhibits some of the most difficult textual and interpretive challenges yet encountered in this book, several things are relatively clear. In the first half of this verse Ephraim is being compared with notorious Tyre (cf., e.g., Isa 23:1ff., and Amos 1:9-10). What is particularly compared is the original place of privilege and blessing of both this pagan city-state and God's chosen nation. What stands in stark contrast with their blessed beginnings will be their similar, destructive ends. In the case of the Northern Kingdom of Israel, that could involve the leading out or bringing forth of their own sons (i.e., children) to a murderer (i.e., an executioner).[267]

Now in verse 14, the prophet, apparently being overcome with an acute need for divine justice,[268] bursts out with an imprecation: "Give them, O LORD—what will you give? Give them a miscarrying womb and dry breasts" (ESV). Hosea, in specifying a divine judgment of an aborting womb and non-lactating breasts, quite likely had in mind Jacob's final prophecies and blessings as recorded in Genesis 49. In verse 25 of Genesis 49, concerning Joseph's inheritance, which would be divided between *Ephraim* and Manasseh, the dying patriarch mentions

---

265 The text actually reverses the order, accentuating a divine reversal of the mandate to multiply in Gen 1:28.

266 As it will again return in v. 16 wherein Yahweh will be depicted as a post-partum slayer of any children that might be born.

267 As an interesting side note, the last words of the two lines constituting v. 13 end with soundalikes which would have catalyzed the heavy impact of this somber piece of revelation.

268 Notice how quick Hosea is to inform Yahweh on what would be appropriate for Him to give to this rebellious nation.

"blessings of the breasts and of the womb" (Gen 49:25). What a reversal Hosea's suggested judgment would be![269]

Gilgal was obviously a buzz-location associated with evil, especially with idolatrous worship (cf. 4:15 and its parallelism with Beth-aven; 12:11; Amos 4:4; 5:5; etc.). "Because of the wickedness of their deeds" (v. 15c), especially as exhibited at Gilgal,[270] Yahweh's hatred has been kindled (v. 15b). Due to such rampant wickedness (i.e., v. 15a,c), the LORD pronounces His judgment: "I will drive them out of My house" (v. 15d).[271] Like a double-barreled blast that kills a relationship, the first barrel's blast of hatred (v. 15b) is quickly followed by one of the love cancelled (v. 15e). The last line of verse 15 once again singles out members of the nation's leadership with an indictment of rebellion.

Verse 16, although employing some new imagery, is essentially a recapitulation of verses 10ff. The verse begins with a comprehensive description of their sure judgment: "Ephraim is stricken" (v. 16a, NASB). In view of the plant metaphors from the immediate[272] and larger[273] circles of context, some versions render this lead-off verb "blighted" (cf. NIV, HCSB). Once stricken and "their root is dried up" (v. 16b, ESV), the possibility of bearing fruit is gone (i.e., v. 16c). As the next line is revealed, the referents of these metaphors become clear: the fruit is speaking of children. Now this is where God was headed with these kinds of word

---

269 This language about wombs and breasts also quite likely would have related to manifestations of the nation's idolatrous apostasy. Much literature and statuary along with the commonality of temple prostitution in the ANE linked these objects and practices with a desire for agrarian fertility and productivity. God's professing people all too often accepted this idolatrous outlook and jumped on the bandwagon of pagan nations.

270 Note the locative adverb translated "there" in v. 15b.

271 Notice how this picks up on the separation already announced in vv. 11a and 12c. The verb used here in v. 15 is the same one that Sarah used for the "kicking out" of Hagar and Ishmael (cf. Gen 21:10).

272 E.g., v. 16 a,b.

273 E.g., 9:10; 10:1; 14:5ff.

pictures: "Even if they bear children, I will kill the precious offspring of their wombs" (v. 16 d,e, HCSB).

Hosea, in verse 17, steps back in with a summation and interpretation of such shocking revelations of Yahweh's judgments. First he concludes, "My God will reject them" (v. 17a, ESV).[274] The justification for this divine action immediately follows: the people refused to heed their God.[275] Finally, he refers to their imminent exile (v. 17c). Dark days were ahead for unrepentant Israel. They surely will become wanderers because of their disobedience (cf. Deut 28:64ff.).

EXHORTATIONS

If chapter 8 could be characterized by urgency, then chapter 9 is characterized by severity. It contains the harshest and most definitive statements of God's wrath and judgment that we've yet encountered in this book. While many passages of Scripture, particularly in the book of Psalms, call God's people to rejoice, the opening command of this section is striking: "Do not rejoice, O Israel, with exultation like the nations" (v. 1). The reason for the boycott on celebration follows as the LORD reproaches in turn the nation as a whole, the prophets of the land, and the political leaders. After delivering an undeniable catalogue of shameful charges against each group, God then pronounces the punishments that He has tailor made to fit their crimes.

As a result of the nation's unrepentant idolatry, Israel will be completely banished from "the LORD's land"—the very land which He had promised to give to Abraham, the father of their nation. Further they will be "gathered up" and made slaves as they once had been in Egypt, now in the land of Assyria (vv. 1-6). The stated reason the LORD brought His people out of Egypt was that they might worship Him (Exod 3:12; 5:1-3). Israel's inexcusable idolatry struck at the very heart of the purpose of

274 Note two occurrences of this verb for rejection in Hos 4:6, where it speaks about their highly culpable rejection of the knowledge about Yahweh.

275 Cf., e.g., their non-responses to the commands to heed found in Hos 4:1; 5:1; etc.

their redemption from Pharaoh's tyranny: worship! As they had returned to false gods, so the LORD would return them to the land of slavery. As false gods had made lavish promises of fertility of agriculture and livestock, so the only true God would remove Israel from the very land which made prosperity possible. Similarly, because of the prophets' deep depravity, the LORD would bring "days of punishment and retribution" (vv. 7-9). God assures the phony prophets that their gross iniquity and bitter hostility have not gone unnoticed and that He will be careful to mete out punishment that fits their crimes. Addressing the nation as a whole a second time, the LORD declared that as a consequence of their ingratitude for the lavish spiritual privileges the LORD had bestowed on them, the legacy of an entire generation of children would be lost (vv. 10-14). As the people had sinned against God since the moment of their "birth" as a nation, so the LORD will punish them with "no birth, no pregnancy and no conception! ... a miscarrying womb and dry breasts" (vv. 10-14). The wicked rebellion of the royal leadership of Israel would draw the most disturbing predictions of the entire chapter. For their evil deeds, they would reap the LORD's hatred (v. 15). God's animosity toward them would give rise to the violent slaughter of their infants (v. 16), and being cast away as wanderers among the nations (v. 17).

Studying passages like these is important and necessary since few pulpits today deliver sermons on universal accountability, divine judgment, or an eternal hell. Such doctrines were, in large measure, jettisoned generations ago in an attempt to create a church in which unbelievers would feel comfortable. As a result, most evangelicals' "fear-of-God-meter" is in serious need of recalibrating. Unaccustomed to hard-hitting passages like the one before us, readers might be tempted to object to God's unapologetic, terrifying expressions of His wrath or attempt to "edit" or "domesticate" His words. Statements like, "I came to hate them ... I will love them no more ... I will slay the precious ones of their womb" (vv. 15-16) are admittedly hard to read. Let me suggest four interrelated reasons why we are tempted to avoid passages like this one and are generally uncomfortable with the doctrine of God's wrath altogether.

A SHALLOW VIEW OF GOD'S RIGHTEOUSNESS

A clear view of the incomparable righteousness of God is the necessary foundation for affirming His equally unrivaled right to judge. Yet, because sin has corrupted everything and everyone that we have ever known, we find it exceedingly difficult to conceive of a God whose heart is perfectly pure, untouched by evil, and incapable of committing sin (Job 34:10; Ps 5:4; 11:7; 92:15; 1 John 1:5; James 1:13). But the Scriptures are definitive that God can neither participate in sin, nor ignore even the slightest sin in others. Habakkuk testifies, "Your eyes are too pure to approve evil, and You cannot look on wickedness with favor" (Hab 1:13). Because the LORD loves righteousness (Ps 11:7), He justly hates sin, and that unrelenting hatred culminates in the righteous judgment of all sinners. An anemic view of God's righteousness will lead sinners, who themselves are worthy of condemnation, to shake their fists in protest at the perfections of God's just judgments.

A SHALLOW VIEW OF SIN

A superficial understanding of sin also contributes to our unfounded resistance to affirm His right to universal judgment. Every sin is a frontal assault on the veracity of God's Word and the trustworthiness of His character (Gen 3:4-5; 1 John 3:4). Knowing that the Lord declared that the penalty for such treasonous rebellion is death should be sufficient to permanently inform our understanding of how abhorrent a thing sin is to Him (Gen 2:16-17; Ezek 18:4; Rom 3:23). Yet we salve our accusing consciences by subjectively categorizing sins into minor infractions and weightier sins. But the Bible teaches that just one infraction of the law of God carries the same sentence as breaking each and every one of them (James 2:10). In the words of J. I. Packer, "There are no small sins against a great God" (*God's Plans for You*, Wheaton: Crossway Books, 2001, p. 44). Perhaps the greatest proof of the truly awful nature of sin is the fact that nothing less than the violent death of the God-Man, Jesus Christ, could pay the penalty for sin (Heb 9:13-14; 10:10,14; 1 Peter 2:24). The cross of Christ stands as a monument not only to the magnitude of

God's love for sinners, but also to the heinous nature of sin itself. Sin is grievous (Gen 6:6-7), wearisome (Isa 43:24), provoking (Deut 32:19; 1 Kgs 14:22), and detestable to the Lord (Prov 6:18-19; Luke 16:15; Rev 2:6). Trivializing sin's detestable nature and presuming on God's abundant mercy result in a heart that stands in arrogant opposition to the unbending justice of God.

A SHALLOW VIEW OF LOVE

Being shocked or offended by the severity with which God chastises His people belies a dreadfully inadequate understanding of God's love. The willingness of God to severely chastise His people doesn't meet with the expectations of easy-going, indulgent affection, created by a feeble definition of love. Only a weak, overly tolerant love would allow a rebellious nation to flourish in their sin. God's committed love could not prosper His people with wine, and wheat, and livestock, and progeny while they remain unrepentant. Rather, driven by genuine love, the LORD would go to any length to separate His people from their idols and bring them home to Himself. That's ultimate love. Knowing how little human love resembles God's discriminating love, the apostle Paul prayed "that your love may abound still more and more in real knowledge and all discernment, so that you may approve the things that are excellent" (Phil 1:9).

A SHALLOW VIEW OF JUDGMENT ITSELF

The denial of the reality of wrath and judgment runs deep; it has existed from the beginning of time. Genesis 3 records that the first assault against truth was an attack on God's declaration that death would be the consequence of sin. The defiant, blasphemous claim from Satan, "You surely shall not die" has been used to deceive men into believing that they can sin without consequence or judgment ever since. As a result, we really shouldn't be surprised when something inside us recoils at the thought of accountability to God and joins in the age-old, contradictory cry, "I surely shall not die." Yet, to struggle to accept the future judgment of every man is to chafe against one of the most clearly attested doctrines in

Scripture. The author of Hebrews states definitively, "it is appointed for men to die once and after this comes judgment" (Heb 9:27). Paul corroborates that "every mouth may be closed and all the world may become accountable to God" (Rom 3:19; see also Acts 10:42; Rom 3:6; 1 Peter 1:17; 2:23).That God the Father has delegated judgment to His Son is equally uncontested: "[God] has fixed a day in which He will judge the world in righteousness through a Man whom He has appointed, having furnished proof by raising Him from the dead" (Acts 17:31; see also John 5:22-24; 9:39; Rom 2:16; 2 Tim 4:1,8; Rev 19:11-16).

Those who possess a robust faith in this important doctrine do not merely concede the fact of God's right to exercise judgment; their lives, convictions, and even their emotions are shaped by it. The souls of faithful martyrs in heaven express a visceral longing for the Lord to judge their assassins. They cry out at full volume, "How long, O Lord, holy and true, will You refrain from judging and avenging our blood on those who dwell on the earth?" (Rev 6:10; see also Isa 35:4). Believers are motivated to forbear patiently with the sins and idiosyncrasies of one another, remembering that "the coming of the Lord is near" and that "the Judge is standing right at the door" (James 5:8-9). Those who rejected Christ and remained composed in their self-assured cynicism at the thought of personal accountability to God will in the last day tremble in terror as they anticipate an omniscient Judge's just verdict and sentencing (Heb 10:26-31).

Far from offering a detached acknowledgement of God's judicial rights, the psalmists call all creation to rejoice in God's pure and equitable judgments: "Let the heavens be glad, and let the earth rejoice; let the sea roar, and all it contains; Let the field exult, and all that is in it. Then the trees of the forest will sing for joy before the LORD, for He is coming, for He is coming to judge the earth. He will judge the world in righteousness and the peoples in His faithfulness" (Ps 96:11-13; see also Ps 97:1-2; 98:9). Those who have suffered greatly for the sake of the gospel, those who are jealous for God's glory, those who are weary of hearing His name blasphemed by the lips of arrogant men do indeed long for God to "set the record straight" and put his glorious reputation on global display. Christians do not contest the truth of divine judgment and retribution; they call others to join them in rejoicing in it.

Of course, only those who possess complete confidence that Jesus has absorbed God's fierce wrath and unrelenting justice that they deserve can dare to join the psalmist in exuberant singing at the thought of coming judgment. The apostle John taught that an ever-maturing knowledge of and robust faith in God's redeeming love eliminates cringing fears of God's just judgment.

> Now little children, abide in Him, so that when He appears, we may have confidence and not shrink away from Him in shame at His coming. (1 John 2:28)

> We have come to know and have believed the love which God has for us. God is love, and the one who abides in love abides in God, and God abides in him. By this, love is perfected with us, so that we may have confidence in the day of judgment; because as He is, so also are we in this world. There is no fear in love; but perfect love casts out fear, because fear involves punishment, and the one who fears is not perfected in love. (1 John 4:16-18)

Of course, the strength of a believer's confidence in God's love is constantly being matured or "made perfect." Augustus Toplady, an Anglican minister who was contemporary with the Wesleys, Whitefield, and Newton, is best known for his hymn "Rock of Ages." He wrote another profound hymn which models how believers must battle any remaining fearful doubts about condemnation in the day of judgment by rehearsing the glorious sufficiency of Christ's atoning work.

From Whence This Fear and Unbelief
By Augustus Toplady (alt. by Todd Murray)

From whence this fear and unbelief?
Hath not the Father put to grief
His spotless Son for me?
And will the righteous Judge of men
Condemn me for that debt of sin
Which, Lord, was charged on Thee?
Complete atonement Thou hast made,
And to the utmost Thou hast paid
Whate'er Thy people owed;
How then can wrath on me take place,
If sheltered in Thy righteousness,
And sprinkled with Thy blood?
If thou hast my discharge procured,
And freely in my [place] endured
The whole of wrath divine;
Payment God cannot twice demand,
First at my bleeding Surety's hand,
And then again at mine.
Turn then, my soul, unto thy rest!
The merits of thy great High Priest
Have bought thy liberty;
Trust in His efficacious blood,
Nor fear thy banishment from God,
Since Jesus died for thee.

10 HOSEA 10:1–15

EXPOSITION

(10:1–15) THE LORD AS EXECUTIONER ORDERS THE PUNISHMENTS OF HIS CRIMINAL PEOPLE (PART 3)

Agrarian word pictures continue with the arrival of chapter 10. Just eight verses earlier Israel was compared via a simile to grapes. Now in 10:1 she becomes a vine.[276] The "vine" is a common symbol throughout the Bible.[277] Its portrayal often, especially in the prophets, emphasizes the coming of divine judgment. The history of the nation is one that began with God's choice and care for the nation-vine followed by its own sin-fertilizer leading to morally rotten fruit. Yet, amazingly, Yahweh, the merciful farmer, will return to care for it that it might again flourish (cf. Hos 14:7).

With these things in mind listen to the tragic irony of Hosea 10:1: "Israel is a lush vine; it yields fruit for itself. The more his fruit increased, the more he increased the altars.[278] The better his land produced, the

---

276 Later she will be depicted as a cow (cf. 10:11).

277 Cf. in figurative contexts, e.g., Gen 49:11; Deut 32:32; Judg 9:12-13; 1 Kgs 4:25; Job 15:33; Ps 80:8,14; Isa 5:1-2; 17:10-11; 32:12-13; Jer 2:21; 5:10; 6:9; 8:13; Ezek 15:6; Joel 1:7,12; John 15:1,4 (of Christ); etc.

278 Cf. Hos 8:11.

better they made the sacred pillars" (HCSB). Among other things, the
nation obviously paid no attention to the warnings of Deuteronomy 8.
The ultimate cause of this ungrateful track record is recorded in the first
line of v. 2: "Their heart" was "slippery," that is, "deceptive, devious," possibly even "duplicitous."[279]

The verdict is delivered in verse 2b, and the sentence is pronounced
in 2c,d. That verdict is succinct: "Now they must bear their guilt" (10:2b,
NASB). Yahweh Himself will step in to execute the sentence: "The LORD
will break down their altars and demolish their sacred pillars" (10:2 c,d,
HCSB). Interestingly, the verb used for the *breaking down* of these altars
is not the normal one Moses used to command the people to do so, but
it is a special term connoting the breaking of an animal's neck. Such
vocabulary may indicate another preference for agrarian terminology.

The "now" of verse 3 is concurrent with Yahweh's judgment "now"
of verse 2. When God would carry out that righteous punishment, the
people's belated (i.e., as far as true repentance is concerned) response is:
"'We have no king,[280] because (or since) we have not feared Yahweh, and
the king [i.e., indeed, even if we had another human king] what would
he do for us?'" This would be an important, though non-redeeming,
recognition on the part of the judged nation, especially in view of its
kingship history.[281]

Verse 4a brings forth more condemnatory evidence substantiating
the LORD's pronounced judgments: "They speak [mere] words, taking
false oaths while making covenants" (HCSB). This represents a con-
crete manifestation of the people's devious heart (v. 2). Ancient Near
Eastern covenant making, which was quite standardized, was deviously
being abused by them. When they dealt like this with nations such as

---

279 Cf. the LXX rendering of this Hebrew root both here and in Ps 55:21 [v. 22, Heb]. Although
     the adjective that describes the sinful heart in Jer 17:9a comes from a different Hebrew root,
     there is much conceptual congruity.

280 A negated possessive idiom in the Hebrew text.

281 Recall some of the important milestones of this history, noting both warnings, violations
     and consequences, e.g., Deut 17:14ff.; 28:36; Judg 21:25; 1 Sam 8:4ff.; 10:19; 12:1; etc.;
     internally, cf. esp. Hos 3:3,4; 5:1; 7:3-7; 8:10; 11:5; 13:10-11.

Assyria (cf. 12:1) they were playing with fire. The consequences of such an under-handed flouting of political protocol are picked up in the second half of verse 4 along with those which follow. Once again another agrarian image launches this section: "So judgment springs up like poisonous[282] weeds in the furrows of the field" (v. 4b, ESV). Similar imagery appears in Deuteronomy 32:32 and Amos 6:12b.

As previously noted, chapter 10, verses 5 and 6 climactically capstone the sarcastic exposures relating to the location of the centerpiece of Israel's idolatry (cf. Hos 4:15; 5:8; 8:5-6), "the calf-idol[283] of Beth-aven" (v. 5b, NIV). As far as Yahweh was concerned, Bethel (i.e., "house of God") was no longer Bethel but had become "Beth-aven" (i.e., "house of iniquity") because of the worship of this calf-idol at that previously sacred site. The departure[284] of this calf-idol as tribute to the great king (cf. 5:13) of Assyria (10:6a) will occasion the intense responses of dread and grief on the people's part (10:5a,c), mourning on the part of the idolatrous priests (10:5d), and consuming shame[285] on the part of the whole nation (10:6b,c).

Verse 7 picks up the "king"-thread from verse 3. Using a good-as-done verb form,[286] the opening line literally reads: "Samaria—her king has been cut off."[287] Cessation stands at the core of this Hebrew root. A

---

282 I.e., bitter.

283 The Hebrew reads feminine plural (i.e., calves). The LXX takes this word as a singular, and all subsequent pronoun references to it are masculine singular. Nonetheless, this eye-catching feminine *plural* was most likely employed by Hosea as a plural of majesty which would heighten the people's accountability since they regarded this to be the supreme object of their worship.

284 Interestingly, the same verb for departure or being taken away into exile was used along with a reference to an object's "glory" is found in 1 Sam 4:22, the account of an earlier generation's forfeiture of the ark in battle.

285 Shame is the most grievous of all judgments in the ANE.

286 I.e., a prophetic perfect.

287 Cf. 10:15.

graphic simile shows how quick his disappearance will be; it will be like
a splinter upon the surface of water.[288]

Although the calf of Aven (v. 5) was the chief center for idolatrous
worship, it was not the exclusive place. "High places" were unfortunately
prevalent throughout the dark chapters of Israel's history. Here these
iniquitous high places, i.e., "the high places of Aven," standing in apposition with the words "the sin of Israel," are doomed to destruction. This
would furthermore lead to a memorial of desolation as indicated by the
thorns and thistles[289] which would grow up and cover any remnants of
those ignominious altars.

The last part of verse 8 chronicles the desperation of the people on
that day of Yahweh's judgment: "Then they will say[290] to the mountains,
'Cover us!' and to the hills, 'Fall on us!'" (v. 8b, ESV). Their perception
of such a catastrophic judgment elicits this desperate desire for their own
personal demise (cf. Luke 23:30; Rev 6:16).

Hosea 10:9 picks up a loud echo from 9:9, which in turn had picked
up a fainter one from 5:8. Once again, although we cannot be certain
about what the historical episode at Gibeah involved, it obviously had
come to stand for an especially heinous exhibition of Israel's sinfulness.
As a matter of fact, it's as if that dark picture from the past had become
freeze-framed, therefore characterizing the errant nation in all of its subsequent history up to the very present (i.e., v. 9b): "There they stand!"
(NASB); or, "They have taken their stand there" (HCBS); or, "There they
have continued" (ESV); or, "And there you have remained" (NIV). Quite
a pronouncement of incorrigibility!

The last part of verse 9 is more challenging. Although a Hebrew interrogative particle does not stand at the head of this line, these words obviously express a rhetorical question meant to be answered with a "yes."
Indeed, warfare was standing at the doorstep of their location in prophetic "Gibeah," and it will defeat them. The "them," the sinning people

---

288 In Hosea's mind, this was probably *rapidly* moving water.

289 Interestingly, compare this combination of words in the curse of Gen 3:18.

290 Contextually, this "say" probably indicates a crying out.

of Israel, are further described by the phrase "sons of iniquity (or wickedness) (or injustice)."[291] The "sons of" idiom is common throughout the Bible, herein conveying people characterized by wickedness.

Verse 10 begins with a reminder that these assessments and judgments are all emanating from Yahweh God Himself. The two "when" statements[292] coordinate, indicating that the nation's forthcoming punishment (v. 10b,c) will be executed according to the LORD's sovereign pleasure and timing (v. 10a). When it says "peoples (or nations) will be gathered against them," the passive verb, although calling attention to the instruments of chastisement, has divine implementation in view. Furthermore, the very last phrase speaking of "double iniquity (or guilt)"[293] emphasizes the fact that God's retributive justice is always proportionally and perfectly meted out.[294] The wayward nation would painfully come to know that the impartial Judge (cf. Deut 7:9-10; Rom 2:11; *et al.*) operates on the principle of "to whom much is given much is required" (e.g., Luke 12:47-48).

As we move into verses 11ff., the agrarian imagery returns initially with Ephraim being labeled a "trained[295] heifer" (NASB, NIV). A state of being verb needs to be added to constitute a clause, and the ESV is probably correct in rendering it as past tense: "Ephraim was a trained calf … ." Once again, the good old days are in view. Unfortunately, over time she had become "a stubborn cow" (4:16), but back then when Yahweh first selected her, she is depicted as having been compliant, as further evidenced by the modifying participle, "who loved to thresh."

---

291 This renders the key descriptive based upon credible manuscript variants. That noun will occur again shortly in the first line of 10:13. Cf. the whole phrase in 2 Sam 3:34 and 7:10.

292 Translating the infinitives absolute of v. 10a and 10c.

293 The *Qere* reading is undoubtedly correct.

294 Speaking about Jerusalem from an aftermath perspective Isa 40:2c reads, "she has received from the LORD's hand double for her sins" (ESV).

295 Interestingly, this word comes from a Hebrew root that speaks of *learning* in one stem and of *teaching* in another stem. It most often speaks of the two sides of discipleship in the OT.

The next line is especially challenging. How it begins[296] is no problem since it obviously reintroduces Yahweh God, her Owner-Farmer. It is the remainder of the line that presents the challenge. Literally the Hebrew text reads: "And I passed by her good neck." However, many translations appropriate a textual emendation involving both a changing of the very stem and the adding of the noun object "yoke" (cf. NASB, NIV, HCSB). On the other hand, the ESV renders the line "and I spared her fine neck." So this passing by without yoking her seems to be tied back into her earlier obedience; however, as the next line will reveal, historically she would become progressively more stubborn and therefore would need more gear to control her.

Because of that growing resistance, the LORD says, "I will harness (or yoke) Ephraim." This judgment will be implemented not only against the Northern Kingdom, but also against the Southern Kingdom[297] as the final words of verse 11 indicate: "Judah must plow; Jacob must harrow for himself" (ESV). The "for himself" most likely signifies that the nation will be on their own; they have separated themselves from the divine Owner-Farmer. The judgment once again is perfectly equitable: "You have resisted Me; I will deliver you over to your own desires and demise."[298]

In spite of this prophesied judgment, Yahweh longsufferingly exhorts this "stubborn cow" nation (4:16) to repent in 10:12. Verse 12's commands are based on a proverbial principle, one which also finds its way into the New Testament: "Do not be deceived, God is not mocked; for *whatever a man sows, this he will also reap*" (Gal 6:7, NASB, emphasis added). Therefore, God passionately challenges the people to "sow

---

296 I.e., with the emphatic "and I" (or "but I") (or "now I").

297 This whole nation's inclusion occurs elsewhere (cf., e.g., Hos 5:5; 8:14; etc.)

298 This scenario revisits the principle of judgment that might well be labeled "You want it; you got it!" (cf. "God delivering [sinners] over to … " in Rom 1:24,26,28).

for yourselves[299] righteousness; reap steadfast love; break up your fallow ground" (10:12a, ESV). They were guilty of violating the Character and commands of God in unrighteousness; therefore, they were being urged to live righteously[300] as measured by Yahweh's Person and precepts. This kind of sowing[301] assumes a commensurate harvest. So the second line of verse 12 might be looked upon as a command mixed with a consequence: "Reap in accordance with (or in proportion) to loyal love.[302]" The third command basically involves the ploughing of new ground (cf. Jer 4:3). They needed to quit ploughing the old ground of sin and rebellion, and to start out fresh by ploughing a new field of undivided loyalty and obedience to Yahweh.

These commands needed to be put into action quickly as the last part of verse 12 makes clear: "For (or now) it is time to seek (or pursue) Yahweh." This is one of those 2 Corinthians 6:2 urgencies: "Behold, now is 'THE ACCEPTABLE TIME,' behold, now is 'THE DAY OF SALVATION'" (2 Cor 6:2b, NASB). Such decisive actions on the part of God's wayward people would ultimately lead to His sending of abundant rains, downpours of righteousness, upon them.

However, verses 13-15 bring us back to the sad reality of no repentance, as the first three lines of verse 13 make crystal clear. Instead of ploughing the new ground of righteousness, they continued preparing the old ground of wickedness.[303] Instead of reaping loyal love, they were

---

299 A couple notations are in order: 1) these plural designations are aimed at all the people who constitute the nation which was previously identified and addressed with singular verbs and pronouns; and 2) the close proximity of "for himself" (v. 11) with the "for yourselves" (v. 12) heightens human responsibility when it comes to waking up to sin, recognizing it as an affront to Yahweh, repenting and producing fruit commensurate with repentance.

300 Righteousness is a communicable attribute; cf., e.g., a theological chain such as the following one: Gen 15:6>Hab 2:4>Titus 2:12.

301 I.e., the kind that James is referring to when he speaks of "the seed whose fruit is righteousness" (3:18).

302 This foundational attribute exhibited gloriously in God is also to be an observable communicable attribute among His people.

303 This term for wickedness is a common term for high-handed sin throughout the OT. It most often connotes spiritual criminality.

bent on a harvest of injustice.[304] In addition, God addresses them with yet another indictment: "You have eaten (or devoured) the fruit of lying."

Between the third and fourth lines of verse 13 the imagery shifts from agriculture to warfare. The causal abuse that stands at the end of verse 13 provides the preeminent reason for the divinely directed military and political judgments of verses 14-15. As so often, sinful nations and sinful people[305] have faith or confidence in the wrong object(s). The nation of Israel and its people over and over again had trusted in anything, everything, and anyone except their God. Here they are called out for trusting in their "way" and in big armies. This tragic, core sin is biblically exposed not just throughout Israel's history but also via the dark history of all humanity (cf., e.g., Isa 31:1,3; Jer 17:5; etc.) This foundational sin at heart entails a flagrant refusal to rely on God; it is often evidenced by disobeying warnings such as Psalm 146:3: "Put not your trust in princes, in a son of man,[306] in whom there is no salvation" (ESV). It tragically substitutes self for the only true Savior.

The consequences of the nation's defiance are sketched out in verses 14-15. Furthermore, verses 14a, 15 summarize the devastating judgment which was to come upon Israel while verse 14b provides an international illustration of it. If they had read those "headlines," they should have been trembling in fear.

The prospect of an imminent, devastating attack is conveyed with these words: "Therefore, a tumult will arise among your people, and all your fortresses will be destroyed" (v. 14a, NASB). The word "tumult" conveys loud noise. It is most frequently used in the context of a deafening battle as is the case here (cf., e.g., Amos 2:2).[307] The outcome of this prophesied war is not left open to the imagination; all the nation's strongholds or fortresses

---

304 Or, "iniquity, wickedness" (cf. Hos 10:9).

305 The singular referents to the nation return in vv. 13b-14, then the plurals come in v. 15.

306 I.e., in any finite and fallen human being.

307 Note that many versions supply a descriptive phrase because of the context (e.g., HCSB, "the roar of battle").

would be destroyed. These are the facts concerning what will happen. Now the blood-curdling illustration immediately follows.

This "as" or "like" historical event (v. 14b) sets up the "thus" application which follows (v. 15): "As Shalman destroyed Beth-arbel on the day of battle, *when* mothers were dashed to pieces with *their* children" (NASB). Although several historical candidates have been proposed in an attempt to identify "Shalman,"[308] and there have been conjectures regarding the location of "Beth-arbel,"[309] we cannot be sure about the king-general involved nor about the destroyed city-state. However, for Hosea's audience that referenced episode would be comparable to our remembrance of Osama bin Laden and 9/11.

The terrorizing analogy is now revealed: "So it will be done to you, Bethel, because of your extreme evil. At dawn the king of Israel will be totally destroyed" (v. 15, HCSB). The Hebrew text exhibits several features that magnify the gravity of this predicted outcome. For example, more of those prophetic perfect tenses occur (i.e., those 'good-as-already-accomplished' usages). The verb translated "will be done" is already a done deal from God's perspective, as is the case with the cutting off or destruction of the king. In addition, there are two repetitions of Hebrew roots that are used to convey a to-the-max emphasis. The first pertains to the extent of the nation's depravity. Literally, the cause of such devastating judgment is stated literally as "because of the evil of your evil." The second doublet is applied to the doom of Israel's monarchy; it literally says of the king of Israel, "being cut off he will be cut off." The point is that the nation's king "shall be utterly cut off" (ESV).

Before moving on, it must be noted in verse 15 that the noun of direct address is "Bethel."[310] But remember in Yahweh's eyes "Bethel" was no longer "Bethel" ("house of God"); it had become "Beth-aven," house of iniquity! What had been a special place of Yahweh worship

---

308 Often suggested is one of the Shalmanesers who ruled Assyria.

309 One of which is in the region of central Gilead.

310 On taking a vocative function herein, cf. ESV, NIV, HCSB.

in the foundational years of Israel's recognition of the only true God[311] ended up as chief city for idolatry, a desecrated place where calf worship prevailed.[312]

EXHORTATIONS

Hosea did not have an enviable ministry. To be the voice that continually spoke out against the same shameful sins without seeing any real conviction of sin must have been profoundly discouraging. How grieved he must have been to preach year after year and watch his own people reject God's Word and descend into greater degrees of wickedness. How frightening to repeatedly describe the destruction and death of the impending Assyrian invasion in graphic detail. Little wonder that the Hebrew often translated "oracle" in the prophetic books could also be translated "burden" (Hab 1:1; Nah 1:1; Mal 1:1; *et al.*). Sadly, this chapter delivers nothing new. Israel's shameless idolatry, insincere words of remorse, and false trust in military might for security are heard once again like a broken record. The LORD's anger over His people's sin and plans for their national deportation are reiterated *ad nauseum*. If you find yourself fed up with Israel's hard-heartedness when merely reading such words, put yourself in Hosea's sandals and imagine delivering such messages publicly! But of course, the LORD Himself would experience the most intense grief and the deepest provocation. And yet, here in the midst of Israel's calloused sin, the LORD once again mercifully reminds His obstinate people that all hope is not lost if they will but repent. Sadly, as we have come to anticipate, they do not.

(10:1-2) CONTINUED IDOLATRY

The LORD exposes the inverse relationship between Israel's increase in physical riches and their decline into spiritual poverty. Centuries before

---

311   Once again cf., e.g., Gen 12:8; 28:18-19; 31:13; 35:1,15; Hos 12:4; etc.

312   Remember esp. Hos 10:5.

Hosea, the LORD had explicitly warned Israel through Moses that along with the material blessings that He would provide them, there would also be an intense temptation to praise themselves or false gods for those very blessings (Deut 8:11-18). The LORD had stated, "It shall come about that if you … go after other gods and serve them and worship them, I testify against you today that you will surely perish" (Deut 8:19). But despite the warnings throughout Israel's history right up until Hosea's time, the more they prospered, the more idolatrous they became (v. 1, cf. 8:11). The excessive production of altars and sacred pillars was the result of the bogus belief that idols had provided their riches. As a result, the LORD declares, "Now they must bear their guilt" (v. 2). Intolerant of their continued false worship, God Himself will violently destroy their sacred shrines, break their obelisks into pieces, and conceal any remaining ruins under a shroud of thorns and thistles (v. 8).

(10:3-10) Continued False Repentance

But even in the day when the LORD destroys the very trappings of false worship, Israel will still not genuinely repent but remain steadfast in their rebellion (v. 9). Perceiving that they were vulnerable without a king's protection, the nation will admit that they had not feared the LORD (v. 3). However, they will not humbly seek forgiveness for such sinful irreverence. The LORD will see through the thin veneer of their remorse and declare that Israel's words are empty, their oaths are worthless, and their promises meaningless (v. 4). "There they stand," as stiff-necked as ever, proclaims the LORD (v. 9). In contrast to their dispassionate acknowledgement of their lack of fearing God, Israel will be highly expressive as they suffer the results of their sin. The people will greatly mourn the removal of their idols, but they will not shed tears over their own wickedness. The priests will cry aloud, mourning over the departure of the "glory" of their false god (v. 5), but will not grieve when the genuine glory of God departs from His people (9:11-12). Israel will feel stinging shame when their calf-idol is given as a tribute to a foreign ruler, but experience none over their sin (v. 6). In the face of such misdirected sorrow, both the nation and their earthly king will be cut off as swiftly as a broken twig is swept away by whitewater rapids (v. 7). At the LORD's appointed time, Israel will be "bound for their double guilt" and carried into captivity to Assyria (v. 10).

False repentance like Israel's is typically marked by deep sorrow over the painful consequences of sin, but not over sin itself. As a warning to avoid phony penitence, the Scriptures record others whose misplaced sadness left them unforgiven and ultimately condemned by God. Esau, despite copious tears and deep regret, was soundly rejected by God (Heb 12:15-17). Judas felt real grief when he saw Jesus condemned and even attempted to make restitution by returning the 30 pieces of silver, yet he was certainly not reconciled to God, for Jesus said "It would have been good for that man if he had not been born" (Matt 26:24; 27:3-5). Obviously, not all tears are created equal.

A tremendous depth of feeling may indeed be a part of confession and repentance, but they are never the essence of it. King David exemplifies this principle. Though he was tortured by his emotions and even suffered physical weakness prior to confessing his notorious adultery and murderous cover-up scheme, David did not focus merely on his subjective *feelings of guilt in his heart*; he also squarely faced the objective *fact of his guilt before God*. When he stopped hiding the depths of his moral twistedness, gave a full disclosure of his secret sin, and confessed that his lawless rebellion was against the LORD, then he was finally forgiven (Pss 32:3-5; 51:1-4). David proved that profound emotional sensations must be accompanied by equally deep theological convictions. Otherwise, such feelings are nothing more than evidence of worldly sorrow (2 Cor 7:10).

While many intense emotions may follow your own sinful failures, it is not wise to automatically equate all troubled feelings with genuine repentance. On closer examination of your heart, you may discover the real causes of your agitation are not Spirit-wrought conviction of sin at all. Sometimes the source of agitation is simply the proud frustration that you haven't lived up to your own expectations. At other times you may find that you are primarily disturbed by the fact that your sins might have damaged your reputation in the eyes of others. While self-pity is admittedly upsetting, it should never be mistaken for true humility. You may even find that underneath deep angst over your sin lurks an ugly anger toward God for His seemingly unattainable standards of righteousness (e.g., Cain in Gen 4:5-7). Clearly, it is possible to be filled with all kinds of grievous, disquieting emotions and yet be devoid of any serious concern that you have "sinned and fallen short of the glory of God" (Rom 3:23).

The primary evidence of genuine repentance is not subjective displays of emotion, but objective acts of submissive obedience. Seeing the Pharisees and Sadducees coming to be baptized, John demanded that they abandon their self-deceiving religious pretense and "bring forth fruit in keeping with repentance" (Matt 3:8; 21:32). To the crowds made up of tax collectors, prostitutes, and ruffian soldiers, John preached with great clarity that repentance is utterly forsaking their old way of life (Luke 3:10-14). The essence of Paul's evangelistic preaching was that Jew and Gentile alike should "repent and turn to God, performing deeds appropriate to repentance" (Acts 26:20). Let Israel serve as a warning to your soul. Neither their glib acknowledgment of sin nor their deep sorrow over the consequences of their sin were received by the LORD as sincere repentance. Solomon reminds us that "He who confesses and forsakes [his transgressions] will find compassion" (Prov 28:13).

(10:11–12) CONTINUED OPPORTUNITY TO REPENT

Israel had not always been so resolute in their sin. Once, they had been yielding in their service to God as a well-trained, compliant heifer, but they have become unyielding and must be harnessed to perform unwilling toil (vv. 11). However, despite their persistent stubbornness, the LORD mercifully summons Israel to genuine repentance with these poetic and memorable words: "Sow with a view to righteousness, reap in accordance with kindness; break up your fallow ground, for it is time to seek the LORD until He comes to rain righteousness on you" (vv. 12). With incredible generosity the LORD assures His people that while time is running short, it is not too late to repent! If they would willingly sow the seeds of righteousness, the LORD assures them that He would grant an abundant harvest of His loyal lovingkindness. But in order to reap such glorious fruit, they must, without delay, plunge the plowshare of repentance deep into their stony hearts.

(10:13–15) CONTINUED FALSE TRUST

But tragically, Israel spurned the gracious invitation and continued to plow wickedness and feasted from the inevitable harvest of deception. Frequently condemned for their trust in themselves or in idols, Israel is now specifically judged for their false confidence in the protection of their human armies. Israel's psalmists sometimes expressed praise in terms of abandoning all hope in military might and relying wholly on the LORD. David proclaimed, "Some boast in chariots and some in horses, but we will boast in the name of the LORD, our God" (Ps 20:7). Israel may have sung together, "The king is not saved by a mighty army; a warrior is not delivered by great strength. A horse is a false hope for victory; nor does it deliver anyone by its great strength" (Ps 33:16-17), but they certainly didn't live in the light of it! And now the LORD warns of a tumultuous invasion that would leave their fortresses demolished, their women and children slaughtered, and their kingship abolished (vv. 14-15). Such a poignant and just punishment for a people who had rejected the LORD's rule over them and sought their deliverance in earthly kings and soldiers.

11 HOSEA 11:1–12

EXPOSITION

(11:1–12) THE LORD AS LOVER
RESTORES HIS CRIMINAL PEOPLE (PART 1)

Chapter 11 launches with yet another emotional flashback[313] with God unashamedly expressing his paternal love for Israel (vv. 1,3,4). This historical reminiscence is conveyed by the opening temporal clause "When Israel was a youth." The Hebrew term for "youth" exhibits a wide referential spectrum with Old Testament examples ranging from three months old (Exod 2:3,6) to seventeen years old (Gen 37:2). The point of the imagery however is to frame up historically the time of Yahweh's initial acts of grace in calling the nation to Himself.[314] The first mentioned exhibition of God's intervening grace nationally was his *love* as corroborated by the Exodus. In verse 1 this is signaled by the words "and from Egypt I called my son." For both His love and the grand demonstration of it recall Deuteronomy 7:7-8: "The LORD did not set His love on you nor choose you because you were more in number than any of the peoples, for you were the fewest of all the peoples, but because the

---

313 Most recently, cf. 10:11.

314 I.e., in their infancy as a nation. Concerning this being a much, much, better time of the tender relationship, cf. also Hos 2:15; Jer 2:2; Ezek 16:22,43,60.

LORD loved you and kept the oath which He swore to your forefathers, the LORD brought you out by a mighty hand and redeemed you from the house of slavery, from the hand of Pharaoh king of Egypt" (NASB). Concerning Israel being identified as "my son," remember Exodus 4:22-23: "Then you[315] shall say to Pharaoh, 'Thus says the LORD, Israel is my firstborn son, and I say to you, "Let my son go that he may serve me." If you refuse to let him go, behold, I will kill your firstborn son'" (ESV). So the "My son" of Hosea 11:1 and the "my firstborn son" refer to the nation of Israel constituted of its *many* people (cf. the plural "sons" in v. 10 and the "them" in the next verse). So the references entail both the one and the many, a common biblical motif. This recognition is the place to begin when considering Matthew's utilization of Hosea 11:1 in his gospel (i.e., in 2:15). The One he speaks of analogously is of course Christ who was brought out of Egypt after Herod's death. Jesus, however, was always perfectly obedient in stark contrast with Israel, the incorrigible son.

Although verse 2 presents some textual and interpretive challenges, the gist of it is evident. It is a synopsis of Israel's subsequent history. After God delivered them from Egyptian bondage, they kept on evidencing their rebellion against Yahweh. Taking off with another occurrence of the verb to call, verse 2a literally reads "they called them." The most satisfactory explanation of the plural verb, "*they* called," is God's utilization of his mouthpieces, the prophets.[316]

The next part of the verse indicates that verse 2a is to be taken as the complementary part of a couplet of comparison; compare, for example, the HCSB: "[the more] they called them, [the more] they departed from Me."[317] As usual, the evidence for such a summarizing indictment immediately follows. The verbs especially emphasize the habit of their

---

315 I.e., Moses.

316 The other acceptable way of handling this lead-off verb is to treat it as an implied passive with Yahweh the entrusted caller (cf. ESV).

317 Actually the Hebrew text literally reads "they walked away from *their* presence," i.e., from the true prophets who had always faithfully spoken for Yahweh.

blasphemous idolatry: "They kept sacrificing to the Baals and burning offerings[318] to idols"[319] (v. 2b, ESV).

So, chapter 11 began with a beautiful picture of their loving Father (v. 1) while verse 2 reviewed how terrible and insolent His sons were. Now in verses 3 and 4 snapshots of their longsuffering God return. These snapshots are mostly paternal pictures; however, part of verse 4 reverts back to agrarian imagery.

Verse 3 begins with another mind-blowing reversal of emphatic contrast: "It was I who taught Ephraim to walk, taking them by the arms" (NIV).[320] Immediately, another evidence of their ingratitude stains this precious portrait: "But they never knew that I healed them" (HCSB). This constitutes another non-acknowledgment, another non-recognition of the LORD's tender kindnesses. The people characteristically turned a deaf ear to the so-called Song of Moses found in Deuteronomy 32, especially verse 39: "See now that I, even I, am he, and there is no god beside Me; I kill and I make alive; I wound and I heal; and there is none that can deliver out of my hand" (ESV).

Verse 4, in spite of their refusal to recognize the LORD as the only true God, presents more evidence of His unflinching TLC. The first part of the verse reads literally, "With cords of a man I have led them, with ties of love." The first instrument of God's leadership of the people was "by means of human, or fitted to the husbandry imagery, 'humane' cords." The reference to ties or ropes of love may have been an allusion to Yahweh's leadership referenced in Jeremiah 31:3b,c: "I have loved you with an everlasting love; therefore I have drawn you with lovingkindness" (NASB). The kind treatment of a beast of burden continues in verse 4b (cf. an analogous one at 10:11): "And I became to them

---

318   For these terms for sacrificing, see 4:13.

319   Explicitly, carved images.

320   The Hebrew is quite challenging as exemplified by various attempts at translation, which also lead to different interpretations. However, all of these preserve the benevolent, parental imagery of God.

as one who eases the yoke on their jaws" (ESV).[321] The singular pronoun[322] referring to the nation returns in the last line of verse 4, and it becomes part of the substantive translational and interpretive perplexities of these final three words of the original text. Tentatively, I'm proposing the following rendering: "And I turned unto him [i.e., the nation]; I fed [him]." The LORD God had habitually and beneficently gone to Israel to provide for them.

Another reversal to a prophetic pronouncement of judgment comes on the scene with the arrival of verses 5-7. This particular one-eighty will set up the superlative one to come in verses 8ff. wherein the amazing Gospel of God will shine forth with its glorious brilliance. Verse 5 clarifies the book's Egyptian bondage motif (cf. 7:16; 8:13; 9:3,6). Their future Egypt-like bondage would actually be located in Assyria: "He [i.e., the nation of Israel] will not return to the land of Egypt, but Assyria will be his [i.e., its] king" (v. 5a,b). The occurrence of the "return" triggers a word play in connection with verse 5c and then it is picked up again in verse 7a. Besides denoting "to turn," "to return," etc., call to mind that this is the workhorse Hebrew root for repentance in the Old Testament. So at the core of this section is the common thread of the nation's historical refusal to repent.

Verses 5c and 6c summarize the reasons for God's predicted judgments (i.e., v. 6a,b). The cities of Israel will be attacked by armies who will penetrate their defenses since the people refused to repent (v. 5c)[323] and because of their notorious scheming (v. 6c).[324] By combining the Hebrew verbal's root connotation with a contemporary idiom, the opening words of verse 7 could be rendered: "Now (or So) (or Indeed) My people are 'hung up ones' (with the intention of) turning away from Me."

---

321 On the background picture of the humane treatment of beasts of burden, cf. Deut 25:4; Prov 12:10a. For a case of a harsh treatment of the gentile nations under God's judgment utilizing the similar imagery of harnessing, cf. Isa 30:28.

322 I.e., in the Hebrew text.

323 Remember the repentance mentioned in 6:1 was a feigned repentance.

324 Cf. those treaties they made with other nations for protection (e.g., 7:11).

The NIV dynamically captures the intent of this challenging Hebrew line with "My people are determined to turn from me." That is, they are characteristically bent on apostatizing.

The last line of verse 7 also comes with puzzling constructions. Two *general* ways of handling this last part of verse 7 are exhibited in the modern translations. For example, the NASB regards the subject of the leading verb to be another implied reference to God's true prophets;[325] it reads, "Though they [i.e., the prophets] call them [actually him, a reference to the nation, with its people] to *the One* on high, none at all exalts *Him*." On the other hand, several modern translations assume the subject of that lead off verb refers to the people of Israel. For example, the HCSB reads, "Though they [i.e., the nation's people] call to Him on high, He [i.e., Yahweh God] will not exalt them at all." This interpretive reading obviously assumes that this calling out to God by Israel's people is also as vacuous as the feigned repentance of Hosea 6:1ff. Both conceptions are possible, but the latter rendering would seem to weaken just a bit the *unbridled* apostasy of verses 5c and 7a. It might also potentially distract one from the shocking power of the greatest of all mind-blowing reversals which immediately follows in verses 8ff.

Hosea 11:8-9 is *most holy* ground indeed. It's hard to imagine any other location in the Old Testament that reveals God's longsuffering so succinctly and transparently. The opening interrogatives when heard or read by finite people who personally have never been sinless[326] but who have a relativistic sense of righteousness and holiness and of right and wrong,[327] would answer these questions in the light of over eleven chapters of background, "Easily!" Men, upon hearing these questions, would immediately give a thumbs down to this wicked nation, but not their mysteriously gracious yet holy and righteous God. Consequently, the shock power of these two verses, once we review them, should shake us

---

325 Cf. 11:2.

326 I.e., *ala* Rom 3:23; 1 John 1:8,10; *et al.*

327 Cf., e.g., even unbelievers who boo the guys in the black hats and cheer for the guys in the white hats.

into worship mode as much as Paul's statement about the same God who justifies the ungodly in Romans 4:5.

Now, resisting any impulse to respond with *our* hair-trigger answers, listen to these four questions which God poses to Himself, obviously with the ultimate goal of teaching us about Himself:[328]

> How can I give you up, Ephraim?
> (How)[329] can I deliver you over, Israel?
> How can I make you[329] like Admah?
> (How)[329] can I make you[330] like Zeboiim?

The mention of the cities of Admah and Zeboiim brings into the picture the historical destruction of Sodom and Gomorrah along with such surrounding cities as these. Of course, the absolute destruction of the more familiar cities is mentioned as a fact of history and as an object lesson throughout the Bible.[331] A very telling reference linking Sodom and Gomorrah with the two neighboring cities, illustratively named here in Hosea, is Deuteronomy 29:23:[332] "All its land is brimstone and salt, a burning waste, unsown and unproductive, and no grass grows in it, like the overthrow of Sodom and Gomorrah, Admah and Zeboiim, which the LORD overthrew in His anger and in His wrath" (NASB). Now we

---

328 The translation attempts to capture by its layout the Hebrew's perfectly balanced lines of poetic couplets in v. 8a,b,c,d. This poetic pattern persists in the last line of v. 8, i.e., the couplet of v. 8e,f. Often when this kind of poetic precision is encountered, its purpose is to magnify the content of the revelation, like a crystal vase would do for a beautiful bouquet or like a handsome frame would do for a piece of great art.

329 The interrogative particle is implied by contextual extension.

330 The same Hebrew verb is used in lines one and three, but the second occurrence is rendered "make" in view of the inseparable preposition that introduces a simile, i.e., the comparison "like Admah." Although the Hebrew verb of the fourth line is different from the one mentioned above, it conceptually is also rendered "make" because of its collocation with the simile that complements it.

331 Cf., e.g., Gen 10:19; 13:10; 14:10; 18:20; 19:24; Isa 13:19; Jer 49:18; 50:40; Amos 4:11; Matt 10:15; 2 Peter 2:6; Jude 7; *et al.*

332 V. 22 in the Hebrew text.

should applicationally be able to perceive the continuity and discontinuity of the similes of verse 8c,d. Although Yahweh would eventually follow through in a disciplinary fashion by placing the nation of Israel under the heavy hand of Assyrian domination, He would *not exterminate* His chosen people. He would not renege on His covenant promises.

Furthermore, in keeping with the faithful, loving husband motif in Hosea, the remainder of verse 8 anthropopathically expresses God's intense emotions: "My heart is turned over within Me, all my compassions are kindled" (NASB). Yahweh transparently shares with us this MRI of His own "heart," His rational, volitional, and emotional core of being. It is probable that a pun is being employed via the verb "turned over" or "overturned." The same Hebrew verb was used to chronicle the historical *overthrow* of Sodom and Gomorrah (cf., e.g., Gen 19:25,29 and again Deut 29:23). Here it indicates an emotional upheaval within the heart of God.[333] This revelation is followed by these reinforcing words: "In unison my compassions grow warm and tender." The noun for "compassions" derives from a verb that often means "to comfort," "to console." It is all of these feelings of compassion that are stoking up in Yahweh's heart.

These are the emotional goings on that relate to the "I will not's" of verse 9a,b.[334] Yahweh shockingly announces that He would not unleash His wrath and thereby annihilate the sinful nation:

> I will not execute My burning anger;
> I will not turn[335] to destroy Ephraim.

Once again, these affirmations do not deny a disciplinary judgment to come. However, because of Yahweh's inviolable covenant promises to

---

333   Another emotional usage on the human level is evidenced in Lam 1:20c.

334   The objective negations of the Hebrew text are rendered in the LXX by the strong combination of the two main negative particles in Greek.

335   Most versions take the verb "to turn" adverbially, i.e., "again"; however, taking it with what appears to be a complementary infinitive makes good sense (cf., e.g., HCSB).

the patriarchs (e.g., Gen 12:1ff.),[336] He would not exterminate all the people. Leviticus 26:44[337] never runs out of applicational relevance: "Yet for all that,[338] when they are in the land of their enemies, I will not spurn them, neither will I abhor them so as to destroy them utterly and break my covenant with them, for I am the LORD their God" (ESV).

That "for" clause from Leviticus about Yahweh being their God seems to be a natural parallel for one of the most mind-blowing causal clauses in all Scripture. Hosea 11:9c is the reason offered by God Himself as to why He would not annihilate such an apparently incorrigibly wicked nation: "For (or Because) I am God[339] and not man,[340] the Holy One in your midst." At its heart, this is an affirmation about how transcendently different Yahweh God is in comparison with finite and fallen human beings. Similar passages emphasize this radical difference in nature, actions, and reactions (cf., e.g., Num 23:19; 1 Sam 15:29; Isa 55:8-9; Ezek 28:2; etc.), but our present text in its context seems to be the most shocking and amazing one of them all. Because He is divine, His actions and reactions are perfectly balanced; ours are imbalanced, being driven by imperfect perspectives on righteousness and holiness. He indeed is the Holy One as Isaiah had personally discovered (cf. Isa 6:1ff.).

In view of who God uniquely *is*,[341] He returns to a reaffirmation (cf. v. 9a,b) of His determination *not* to wipe this rebellious nation off the face of the earth: "And I will not come into a city" (v. 9e, trans., Hebrew text).[342] If the Hebrew text is left to stand as it is, then, although God's instruments of chastisement would eventually come against the

---

336 Remember also what the author of Hebrews says about this inviolability in 6:17-18.

337 And in a NT context see passages like Rom 9-11.

338 I.e., referring to their history of iniquity.

339 In Hebrew, *'el*, the shortened form of *'elohim*.

340 In Hebrew, the masculine noun *'ish*.

341 Cf., e.g., the unlimited breadth and magnitude of His self-identification and designation, in Exod 3:14, "I AM who I AM."

342 The LXX also reads "city."

cities of Israel (cf. v. 6), Yahweh, who was still by grace "in their midst" (v. 9d), would preserve a remnant. He would not do what His Assyrian instrument would have loved to do (cf. Isa 10:5-19). A word needs to be said about how most modern versions render this last line of Hosea 11:9. Instead of "city" they accept a slight emendation of the Hebrew text thereby rendering v. 9e "and I will not come in wrath" (NASB; cf. ESV, NIV; "rage," HCSB, etc.). Whatever the translational preference, because of Yahweh's gloriously balanced attributes in harmony with His covenant promises,[343] discipline would come, but not to the point of ethnic demise.

Verses 10 and 11 look beyond the yet future discipline of the nation[344] to a time when Yahweh would round up His people[344] and re-establish them in the Promised Land. The opening line of verse 10 will document in general terms a future repentance on the part of the people: "They will walk after Yahweh." This, of course, would be a 180-degree about face when compared with their previous walkings after false gods. More detail on what would stand behind such a turnaround immediately follows in verses 10b-11b. It was in response to Yahweh's call, poetically described as the powerful roar of a lion (i.e., v. 10b,c; cf. Hos 5:14; 13:7; Amos 1:2), that the people would return in fear from captivity.[345] It is obvious that this "trembling" (vv. 10d, 11a)[346] is that healthy fear of God that is essential in salvation and sanctification.

God again speaks personally as this grandest of sections comes to an end: "And I will cause them to dwell in their houses—the utterance (or

---

343 Cf., e.g., the implications of such passages as Exod 34:6-7 and Deut 7:9-10.

344 Note another one of those shifts in number from the singular nation (vv. 8-9) to the plural designations in vv. 10-11. In v. 10 also notice the shift from God speaking in the first person to third-person references, a phenomenon often observed in the prophets, but especially in Hosea.

345 Notice again the parallels not only between the nation's past historical bondage in Egypt (cf., e.g., 7:16; 8:13; 9:3,6; 11:5) and the forthcoming bondage under Assyrian control, but also a future exodus patterned after the initial exodus at the time of the nation's birth (cf., e.g. 2:15; 12:9; 13:4).

346 Remember a synonym for this kind of fear, noticing the contextual parallelism of Hos 11:10-11 with 3:5.

declaration) of Yahweh" (v. 11c). This divine promise and its ironclad punctuation mark are reassurances that beyond a future time of certain chastisement there would be a time of restoration. Yahweh God would not go back on the promises He had made to Abraham and had reiterated to other patriarchs; for example, in Genesis 17:8 He affirmed, "And to you and your offspring after you I will give the land where you are residing—all the land of Canaan—as an eternal possession, and I will be their God" (HCSB).

One of the most unfortunate chapter breaks in our English Bibles occurs between Hosea chapters 11 and 12. Chapter 11, verse 12 should really be chapter 12, verse 1, as it is in the Hebrew Bible, the early Greek translation (i.e., the LXX), etc. Therefore, Hosea 11:12 (Eng.) most assuredly introduces a new section.[347] The first two lines of 11:12 level a parallel divine indictment against Israel.

Like the Patriarch Jacob, who was renamed "Israel" by Yahweh God (cf. Gen 32:27-28), the nation all too consistently demonstrated that its heart also was deceitful (cf. Hos 4:2; 7:3; 10:13; 12:7).[348] The history of Ephraim, via parallelism, Israel, had indeed clearly displayed the wicked craftiness of the Northern Kingdom.[349]

It is, however, the last two lines of 11:12 (i.e., about the Southern Kingdom) that present translational and interpretive challenges. Some translate these lines positively while others cast them in a negative light. Contrast the treatment of 11:12c,d in the ESV and NIV, respectively:

> but Judah still walks with God and is faithful to the Holy One (ESV).

> And Judah is unruly against God, even against the faithful Holy One (NIV).

---

347 The English versification will be followed through the remainder of chapter 12.

348 Of course, such deceit is found in the hearts of all the sons of Adam (cf., e.g., the Hebrew root for the name Jacob occurring as an adjective in Jer 17:9).

349 Interestingly, the verb "to surround" in v. 11a picks up the imagery of Yahweh in their midst in v. 9.

Besides a positive rendering's more inductive handling of the Hebrew text, there is corroborative evidence for this preference in that the Northern Kingdom would suffer God's judgment about 135 years sooner than its Southern counterpart. Although Judah *would also experience* God's retributive justice in time, space, and history (cf., e.g., 5:5,10,14; 8:14; 12:2), she would, at the time of the delivery of these oracles, be protected by God's grace a bit longer (cf., e.g., 1:7; 4:15).

EXHORTATIONS

After ten chapters detailing Israel's unwillingness and inability to repent and predictions of the horrific judgments they would suffer, chapter 11 marks the beginning of the final section of the book, which focuses on the LORD's future, loving restoration of Israel. While threats of the judgments necessitated by their rebellion still rumble in the background, the final four chapters of Hosea magnify God's unfailingly loyal love and gloriously irrevocable promises as the certain grounds for Israel's hope. Just as a mountain climber is rewarded for his strenuous efforts by the view from a summit, so the reading of the incomprehensible grace of God in these moving, climactic chapters is the payoff for trekking through the darker sections of the anthology of Hosea's prophetic ministry.

This particular transitional chapter focuses on two attributes of God as the basis for His gracious plans for Israel. The LORD's love is the focus of the first section (vv. 1-7), while His holiness is highlighted in the second section (vv. 8-11).

(11:1–7) HOPE IS GROUNDED IN GOD'S LONGSUFFERING LOVE

Love's Tenderness Recalled (vv. 1-4)

As in the early chapters of this book, Hosea again employs a familial image to communicate truth about the character of God and His people. Rather than the metaphor of a marriage, this chapter utilizes the tenderness of a parent-child relationship. In a father-like soliloquy, the LORD recalls the love He has had for Israel from their earliest days as a nation. He evidenced the depth of his affection for "His son" by delivering him from cruel Egyptian bondage. "When Israel was a youth I loved him, and out of Egypt I called My son" (v. 1). When writing his gospel account, Matthew would quote this verse as applicable to Jesus as the ultimate and perfect Son of God also delivered safely out of Egypt (Matt 2:15). Yet despite this act of merciful deliverance, Israel responded like an ungrateful teenage rebel. The more prophetic voices that God sent to call His people back to Himself, the further Israel went in pursuit of idols (Mark 12:1-11). The previous chapter ended with Israel's unthinkable refusal of God's urgent appeal for them to repent at the eleventh hour. This chapter reminds us that this obstinate pride has been typical of Israel from the very beginning.

Continuing to muse on the tender nature of His love for His people, the LORD recalls, "Yet it was I who taught Ephraim to walk, I took them in my arms" (v. 3). The LORD likens His care of Israel to that of an affectionate father helping an unsteady little child take his first steps and walking close behind him to catch him when he falls. What *pathos*-filled language! If God hadn't placed this image in His Word, I would almost think it sacrilegious to depict His love in such phenomenally gentle terms. But God is unashamed to portray His love for His own in the imagery of kind, fatherly affection. Once again, Israel fails to recognize such undeserved love appropriately: "But they did not know that I healed them" (v. 3). This clueless ingratitude harkens back to an earlier passage in which the LORD says of Gomer that she "[did] not know that it was I who gave her the grain, the new wine and the oil, and lavished on her silver and gold, which they used for Baal" (2:8).

The LORD concludes His recollection of His longsuffering love for Israel with an additional image—that of an owner's kind treatment of a favorite animal. Upon completion of its labor each day, the laborer carefully unyokes the beast of burden and kneels to feed by hand the animal of which he is so fond. Like the affection of the animal's owner, the LORD's love for Israel is *more* than humane. Israel's gross indifference and outright rejection of such over-the-top affection is magnified as a truly monstrous evil.

As you survey your own life, can you see that the Lord has dealt as tenderly with you as He did the ancient Israelites? Long before you were aware of His divine protection and provision, the Lord loved you with a father-like patience and watch-care. How the love of God is magnified by His longsuffering with rebellious "sons" like Israel, and you and me!

Love's Severity Predicted (vv. 5-7)

I once heard wise parents recount that they often had to warn their disobedient children, "I love you, please don't make me do what love requires!" In essence that is the message of the next few verses. Having reminded Israel of His longstanding record of initiating tender love toward them, the LORD now warns them that because they refused to return to the LORD, they will now face captivity. As they had once been enslaved by Pharaoh, Assyria will be their new merciless master. Because of their rebellious counsels against such a loving LORD, the Assyrian forces would violently burst through Israel's supposedly impenetrable city gates and rush upon people and possessions alike to utterly consume them (v. 6). Citing again His repeated call to be reconciled to Himself, the LORD declares that "My people are bent on turning from Me" (v. 7, cf. v. 2). In the face of the mercy offered through prophetic messengers, the nation stubbornly refused to depart from their chosen path of apostasy.

How could our souls not fear for ourselves when we read of what Israel suffered in consequence of spurning the love of God? Our souls must be sobered to face the spiritual reality that to transform the hearts that are bent on turning away from Him, the LORD will indeed do whatever love requires.

(11:8–11) HOPE IS GROUNDED IN GOD'S INCOMPARABLE HOLINESS

Shocking Questions (vv. 8-9)

Not only is Israel's hope of future restoration based on God's tender love, but it is also grounded in His incomparable holiness. While Hosea contains many abrupt contrasts between God's promises of disciplinary catastrophe and pledges of unconditional compassion, these two verses contain the most dramatic and emotionally-laden reversal of the entire book. In the earlier section of this chapter the LORD unashamedly depicts His love for Israel in parental terms; in the next few verses, He proclaims that His faithful compassion reaches a depth that exceeds any category of human love. God declares that His love for such a detestable people can be comprehended only in terms of His transcendent holiness.

These astonishing verses take the form of another soliloquy designed to teach us about the LORD's character and plans. It opens with four shocking questions: "How can I give you up, O Ephraim? How can I surrender you, O Israel? How can I make you like Admah? How can I treat you like Zeboiim?" (v. 8). I can vividly recall, in my early study of these verses, pushing back from my desk in amazement and saying under my breath to myself, "Lord, how could you not, give them up?" After slogging through 11 chapters detailing Israel's despicable unfaithfulness and compulsive rebellion, my all-too-human impatience was more than ready for God to wipe them out! But in contrast to the limits of my finite mercy, the LORD speaks of recoiling at even the thought of destroying His people as He had once annihilated Sodom, Gomorrah, and their surrounding cities. In an interesting play on words, the verb which describes God's heart as being "turned over" (v. 8b) is used by Moses to describe the LORD's "overthrow" of these same intensely wicked cities (Gen 19:25; Deut 29:23). The LORD's rhetorical questions essentially reiterate that He will not—indeed, cannot—permanently reject and destroy His people. Rather, all of God's compassions for wayward and rebellious Israel grew even warmer and more tender. The word "kindled," used in verse 9 to describe LORD's profound emotions toward His people, is also used to depict Joseph as being "deeply stirred" at the sight of his younger brother Benjamin after years of painful separation (Gen 43:30). Similarly, it expresses the overwhelming panic of the genuine mother's heart when King Solomon proposed cutting her son in half as a manner of settling a maternity dispute (1 Kgs 3:26). While a close examination of Israel's sin kindles my anger, those same circumstances stoke the infinitely deep compassions of God. What radical, forgiving love and grace!

The LORD's next statements, "I will not execute My fierce anger; I will not destroy Ephraim again" (v. 9) should not be read as a contradiction of His earlier vow, "The sword will whirl ... and will demolish ... and consume them" (v. 6). Rather, as we have seen in the earlier assurances of a gracious future for Israel (1:10-2:1; 2:14-23; 3:5; 6:11-7:1), God's temporary chastisement of Israel by the Assyrian invasion, destruction, and captivity does not indicate that He will permanently reject or utterly annihilate His people.

The LORD follows these intensely emotional consolations with this profound explanation: "For I am God and not man, the Holy One in your midst, and I will not come in wrath" (v. 9). The reason for the LORD's inexplicable mercy is His supremacy over created humanity. Because He is not merely a man, He is not limited by the confines of meager human compassion. Through the prophet Isaiah, God offered a similar explanation for His unparalleled compassion, "For as the heavens are higher than the earth, so are My ways higher than your ways and My thoughts than your thoughts" (55:9). The LORD's phenomenal capacity to extend eternally loyal love, far beyond human ability or comprehension, is intrinsic to His deity. God's mercy is grounded in His character—an essential part of what it means to *be* God.

Further distinguishing Himself from finite and corrupt men, the LORD refers to Himself as the "Holy One." In reminding Israel of His holiness, God is emphasizing His apartness, separateness, or distinction from all that is commonplace, profane, corrupt, or in this context, human. Other passages scattered throughout Hosea's prophecies in which the LORD guarantees a glorious future for Israel pointed out various attributes of God: His righteousness, lovingkindness, justice, faithfulness (2:19-20), His compassion (2:23), His goodness (3:5). But here, all the goodness of God's character is majestically summarized in one phrase, "the Holy One in your midst." Typically in Scripture, the holiness of God causes fearful humility and overwhelmed contrition in men's hearts. When Isaiah saw the LORD in His unveiled glory and holiness, he announced a prophetic "woe" upon himself and confessed that he was a man of unclean lips (Isa 6:1-5). When Peter saw Christ's power over creation, he similarly pled, "Go away from me Lord, for I am a sinful man!" (Luke 5:8; see also Gen 28:16-18). But in this passage, the LORD's holiness, while no less transcendent, is not presented as a source of spiritual intimidation, but rather as the sole foundation for the astonishing, unconditional love of God.

Why does the LORD find the thought of giving up on His ungrateful children so reprehensible when any human parent would have easily given way to vengeful anger? Why is God's heart utterly in anguish at the thought of the extinction of His chosen, yet wayward nation? Why do God's compassions surge toward Israel even while they spurn His lovingkindness? Why will His righteous wrath for rebels not be the end of the story? Because He is God. Because He is not man. Because He is the ever-present Holy One.

Staggering Promises (vv. 10-11)

In the previous verses, the LORD has declared what He would not do. But the chapter ends with the LORD's irrevocable decree of the spiritual restoration that He will accomplish for His people. The first declaration is that Israel, who had routinely followed after other lovers (2:5,13; 3:1) and turned away from God (7:13-14,16), will finally walk after the LORD (v. 10). The Lord Himself will initiate the nation's unprecedented obedience by His own unmistakable call, issued forth as loudly and unmistakably as a lion's roar. Israel had once disregarded God's terrifying warning:

> For I will be like a lion to Ephraim and like a young lion to the house of Judah. I, even I, will tear them in pieces and go away, I will carry away and there will be none to deliver. I will go away and return to My place until they acknowledge their guilt and seek My face; in their affliction they will earnestly seek me. (5:14-15)

Having felt the teeth of God's chastisement before, now no Israelite would dare to ignore the lion's roar a second time. They would respond to the demand to return from captivity and follow the LORD with appropriate trembling.

The LORD additionally promises to settle His people once again as residents in the land He had promised to give them. This assurance is most likely intended as a beautiful reversal of the name of Hosea's son, Jezreel, whose name stems from the word for sowing or scattering. The people who had been captured and scattered throughout Assyria as captive slaves are assured by the LORD Himself that they will be graciously "re-sown" in the land promised to Abraham as an everlasting possession (Gen 17:8).

God makes His own character, specifically His limitless love and infinite holiness, the certain foundation for every oath ever made to Israel. One hardly knows what to say in the light such hope of Israel, since those same attributes are also the unfailing guarantee of His promises to us today as well. What greater confidence could we desire? Who can adequately worship a God whose Person is so utterly perfect that it forms the certain basis for the supreme reliability of His words? Since God can ensure His promises by no one greater than Himself, He guarantees His pledges by His own personal attributes (Heb 6:13). Indeed, as my dear friend and mentor Dr. Carl Wenger used to say regarding the Lord's faithfulness, "We have nothing but precedence for trust."

12 HOSEA 12:1–14

EXPOSITION

(12:1–14) THE LORD AS LOVER RESTORES HIS CRIMINAL PEOPLE (PART 2)

The spotlight quickly swings back to the Northern Kingdom in 12:1. The opening word picture about Ephraim feeding or grazing on the wind sets up the sure futility of their efforts at covenant making with surrounding international powers. Yahweh, the only loyal covenant Maker and Keeper, to use the words of the preacher in Ecclesiastes, places all such endeavors in the category of "vanity of vanities."[350] Furthermore, yet another[351] indictment of deception or falsehood returns at the very core of 12:1 along with a second involving their violence. Finally, in their deal making with opposing superpowers, they were apparently blinded by their sin of self-protection in that playing both ends against the middle would surely lead to their own demise.[352]

As already intimated in the comments above on 11:12, the focus once again abruptly returns to Judah in 12:2-6. Yet, after the divine promise to punish Judah (v. 2), there is a brief historical flashback to Yahweh's

---

350 Cf., esp., the references to wind both here and in Eccl 1:14.

351 Cf. the immediately preceding context at 11:12.

352 Cf. Hos 2:11.

establishment of the nation He had derived from Jacob (vv. 3-5)[353] along with a final exhortation to repent (v. 6). Now moving back to v. 2, the LORD once again assumes His role of Prosecuting Attorney (cf. 4:1). His charges are incontestable as Judah's ways and deeds[354] are entered into evidence. They will not escape the guilty verdict, and beyond that, the Prosecutor will become the sentencing Judge (cf., e.g., Deut 7:10).

The historical snippets from Jacob's life seem to be for the primary purpose of challenging the nation of Hosea's day to remember its inception in the grace of God's dealings with its ancestral patriarch. These three verses briefly summarize key episodes from the patriarch's life as excerpted from the Genesis accounts. Beginning with his birth (cf. Gen 25:19-26, esp. v. 26), he is noted to have grasped his twin brother by the heel. The Hebrew verbal root used both in Genesis and here in Hosea introduces an exceedingly significant word play. He attempted to "supplant" his brother, who was the firstborn. Later on in the same chapter (i.e., Gen 25:27-34) he bribed his hungry brother to surrender his birthright with a lunch. Furthermore, in Genesis 27 Jacob stole his father's primary blessing from Esau. In verses 35-36a of Genesis 27 this pun shows up in a threefold occurrence of this Hebrew root: "And he [i.e., Isaac] said, 'Your brother came deceitfully[355] and has taken away your blessing.' Then he [i.e., Esau] said, 'Is he not rightly named Jacob,[355] for he has supplanted[355] me these two times?'"[356]

Hosea 12:3b-4a,b highlights a later episode chronicled in Genesis 32. And, once again, another word play becomes obvious. This time it relates to the patriarch's newly-given name by God, i.e., "Israel." Hosea

---

353 V. 12 will allude to another episode in the life of the patriarch Jacob, i.e., Israel.

354 These nouns are in synonymous parallelism along with the verbs to punish and to repay. Incidentally, the verb to repay is literally "to cause to return"; their deeds would come back upon them like a boomerang.

355 That same Hebrew root.

356 Just a reminder that this Hebrew root most often emphasizes deceit, craftiness, deviousness, etc. (cf. once again God's analysis of the fallen human heart in Jer 17:9).

12:3b-4a reads, "and in his manhood he strove[357] with God. He strove[357] with the angel and prevailed" (ESV). Now notice Genesis 32:28: "Then he [the man/angel] said, 'Your name shall no longer be called Jacob, but Israel,[357] for you have striven[357] with God and with man, and have prevailed'" (ESV).[358] The reference to the seeking of grace or favor in Hosea 12:4b is paralleled conceptually in the historical account of Genesis 32:26b.

Hosea 12:4c most likely introduces twin episodes in the life of Jacob/ Israel (cf. both Gen 28:11-22 and 35:6-15). Although there has been some ambivalence on the identities standing behind the "he" and the "him" of this line, the best option is that the introductory "He" refers to "Yahweh, the God of hosts" (v. 5a), the same divine personage who "spoke with us" in verse 4d.[359] This view also preserves the precedent of the LORD's gracious pursuit of those who belong to Him.

Uncertainties about the identity of the angel in verse 4a are greatly eased by the appositions of verse 5: "Even Yahweh, the God of hosts;[360] Yahweh is His memorial (Name)."[361] Therefore, the patriarch, directly connected with the nation's establishment, wrestled with Yahweh God. He beheld the face of *God* (i.e., "Peniel," Gen 32:30 [v. 31, Hebrew]) and did not die. This divine personage had also chosen a special place to manifest Himself to Jacob/Israel, namely, Bethel (i.e., "house of God"; cf. Gen 28:19; 31:13; 35:1,3,6,15). Those were much better days in view of where Israel's descendants were standing during Hosea's ministry.

---

357 The Hebrew root undergirding this pun.

358 By putting the pieces together from the Genesis account and the Hosean account, this personage with whom Jacob/Israel wrestled was in all probability the Angel of the LORD, i.e., a pre-incarnate appearance of Christ.

359 NASB and ESV follow the Hebrew text with the translation "us"; other modern versions like the NIV and HCSB follow a variant and render the pronominal suffix as "him," which seems to be more logical. However, the plural may represent a designed emphasis on corporate solidarity, a Semitic association of the one with the many. This section indeed is heading toward the challenge of national responsibility (v. 6.).

360 Or, "armies."

361 Cf. the parallelism with "name" in Exod 3:15; Isa 26:8; Ps 135:13.

Indeed, as previously noted, the nation's apostasy had become so great that Bethel, "house of God," was now rightly dubbed Beth-aven, "house of iniquity."

These historical realities, both past and present, set up the call to repentance in verse 6. The first line of this verse contains the most familiar verb for repentance; however, its form and the preposition which links it to God are anything but standard for such a contextually apparent demand. It might be rendered, "So (or But) you,[362] in (or by means of) your God[363] should (or must) turn (or return)."[364] The remaining two lines of this verse each contain a direct imperative: "Maintain love and justice, and wait for your God always" (v. 6b,c, NIV). Because of the influence of these last two lines, most translations render the first line in such a manner like this, "Therefore return to your God" (v. 6a, NASB). So, yet another call to repentance goes forth.

However, their pride and wicked practices resist all such calls to repentance as 12:7ff. indicates. Verse 7 commences with an additional cycle of the signs of a nation in rebellion as contrasted with Yahweh's past long-suffering dealings with its people (vv. 9-10). Then, not surprisingly, yet another cycle follows with a current assessment of their sinful state (v. 11) contrasted with God's kind providence toward Jacob (v. 12) and later His rescue of the whole nation out of Egyptian bondage (v. 13). Then chapter 12 will conclude with the fact that, in spite of all these kindnesses of God, Ephraim remains incorrigibly resistant to God's gracious overtures (v. 14).

Somewhat strangely, an unethical *illustration* (v. 7) precedes the divine indictment brought against Ephraim in verse 8. The opening illustration of verse 7 represents someone who, according to God's law (e.g., Lev

---

362 A second-person singular pronoun referring emphatically to the nation as a whole.

363 Cf. ESV: "by the help of your God."

364 Possibly the idea is what Jeremiah expresses in 31:18-19 and in Lam 5:21 when he uses the same stock vocabulary for repentance: "Turn us that we may turn (or return) to You."

19:35-36), engages in an abominable practice[365]: "A tradesman[366]—in his hand are scales (or balances) of deception[367]—he loves[368] to oppress." In such a context this oppression is explicitly extortion.

That this exposing illustration of a crooked businessman pertains to Ephraim is clear in view of the nation's boasts in verse 8: "Ephraim has said, 'Ah, but I am rich; I have found[369] wealth for myself; in all my labors they cannot find in me iniquity or sin'" (Hos 12:8, ESV). The particle that stands at the head of the quote could also be nuanced, "How rich I have become!", thus conveying even more transparently the nation's audacious arrogance. Quite obviously, God's warnings about living during periods of prosperity[370] had no effect on their unbridled ego and behavior. Whomever or whatever the "they" in the "they cannot not find" refers to, the nation is obviously self-deceived in thinking that *they* will escape guiltlessly, because God surely sees what's going on and will judge accordingly.

In verse 9, the LORD answers the nation's revelings in their supposed state of success with a flashback reminder about their utter dependence upon Him from the days of Egyptian bondage through the wilderness wanderings, and, as they should have realized, throughout all their history and into the future. There is an echo from the foundational words of God's covenant originally established with the people (e.g., Exod 20:20; Deut 5:6): "But I am[371] Yahweh, Your God ... "! And, as already intimated, that relationship, established by sovereign grace, had its national inception as He was building them into a great people while

---

365 Cf., e.g., Prov 11:1; 20:23; etc.

366 For this particular meaning, cf. Isa 23:8; Zeph 1:11. Interestingly, the Hebrew noun more frequently means "Canaan"; if this were a planned association, it certainly would intensify this illustration of Israel's behavior.

367 I.e., deceptive scales; cf. the noun "deceit" employed most recently in 11:12.

368 A characterizing participle.

369 I.e., "found" in the sense of "gained." The same verb is used in the next line in the sense of not *discovering*.

370 E.g., Deut 8:11ff.; in the NT, cf. the preemptive warning of James 4:13-17.

371 Very emphatic.

they were living under Egyptian bondage. The LORD God nevertheless was protecting and caring for them during that period of more than 400 years. The same was true during the wilderness wanderings, and that 40 years included both punishment and protection.

These historical reminders become a harbinger of what lay ahead of them, another 'wilderness[372] wandering': "Again[373] I will cause you to live in tents as in the days of (the) appointed festival." In the future they will be leaving their perceived, self-attained wealth behind (cf. v. 8a,b). They are going to be placed by God in a dependent position. Israel needed to learn their lesson and repent, then they could celebrate the remembrance of not only God's judgment but also His sustaining care. Celebrations of the festivals, especially that of Tabernacles (cf. v. 9c with Lev 23:2,34-43) intimate that beyond Yahweh's future judgment would be occasions to remember His care while in it and His preservation through it.

Next God brings to bear a historical reminder about His gracious sending of prophet after prophet with their messages about the nation's sin and the people's need to repent.[374] Consequently, the first line of verse 10 continues the history of verse 9a,b until the time of Hosea's ministry and, by implication, beyond it.[375] In verse 11b Yahweh literally says that "I[376] multiplied vision," that is, He channeled through His selected mouth-pieces many visions. A vision was one of the many terms used for a prophecy (cf., e.g., Isa 1:1; Obad 1; Hab 2:2-3; etc.). Often a text will say that the prophet "saw" what was revealed to him by God and what he must relay to the people. However, it does connote in many settings simply the substance of what was revealed by Yahweh. It is the last line of verse 10 that beckons special interest. It reads literally, "and by the hand

---

372 Contra. the reference to Israel in the wilderness in Hos 2:14.

373 The adverb stands first in this line.

374 Cf. Hos 12:10 with the statements about special revelation through the prophets in Heb 1:1.

375 Note that the Moses of the Exodus and the wilderness sojourn will also be labeled a prophet in 12:13.

376 An emphatic "I."

of the prophets I liken," i.e., "and through the prophets I gave parables" (NASB). Their messages contained analogies and comparisons which we learn especially from the New Testament that this means of divine revelation both reveals and conceals.[377]

Verse 12:11 indicates that their message was still falling upon deaf ears. This verse begins with a conditional particle normally translated "if," but in this contextual setting there is an assumption of certainty. Compare the HCSB's rendering of this particle along with a different one in the second line, emphasizing the logical certainty of the outcome: "Since Gilead[378] is full of evil, they will certainly[379] come to nothing" (12:11a,b). The second part of the verse shows that their hypocritical, syncretistic worship will also come to naught under the judgment of Yahweh: "They sacrifice bulls in Gilgal;[380] even their altars will be like heaps of rocks on the furrows of a field" (v. 11c,d,e, HCSB).[381] Israel's altars will be torn apart and scattered like rocks on a ploughed field.

With the arrival of verses 12-13 more pleasant historical reminiscences return to contrast the bad days of the present with better days of the distant past. Verse 12 picks up the story of Jacob-Laban-Leah- and finally, Rachel (i.e., Gen 28-30) and how the LORD had providentially protected the nation's patriarch and had blessed him richly. Verse 13 jumps ahead more than 400 years to the Exodus accomplished by God through His instrument, Moses.[382] These excerpted pieces from the history of Israel are virtually self-explanatory:

---

377 Cf., e.g., Matt 13:34-35; 21:45; Mark 4:1-13; etc.

378 Cf. Hos 6:8.

379 I.e., "surely, indeed," etc.

380 Cf. 4:15; 9:15

381 It is noteworthy that the Hebrew text of this verse exhibits sound-alikes plus a pun on the place names and the word translated "heaps."

382 Cf. Exod 32:7.

> Jacob fled to the land of Aram; there Israel served for a
> wife, and for a wife he guarded sheep. By a prophet[383] the
> LORD brought Israel up from Egypt, and by a prophet
> he[384] was guarded (Hos 12:12-13, ESV).

The light from the memory of the good old days is once again quickly eclipsed by the darkness of Ephraim's current condition as Hosea 12:14 intimates. Verse 14a is a condensed summary of the multiple offences of the nation in the form of effect: "Ephraim has provoked to bitter anger" (NASB). Whom this nation has caused to be bitterly angry is not left to the imagination; it is "his Lord," the Sovereign One.[385] Although in the Hebrew text this identification of God as the Sovereign One comes at the very end of this verse, its position makes the two pronouncements of sentencing all the more authoritative. This Chief Justice of the universe "will leave his bloodguilt[386] on him and repay[387] him for his contempt" (v. 14b,c, HCSB).

EXHORTATIONS

Throughout the collection of Hosea's prophecies we have come to expect a kaleidoscopic blending of certain themes: the LORD's piercing indictments of Israel's sins, His urgent calls to repentance, His dismal warnings of the judgment necessary to bring the nation back to Himself, and His promises of the ultimate, glorious future restoration of Israel based on His indefatigable love. Though this chapter also contains those familiar themes, it is distinct in its use of a series of reminders from Israel's history as an impetus for repentance. In particular, several scenes from Jacob's

---

383 Cf. Moses' recognition of this function in Deut 18:15.

384 I.e., the "he" standing for the *many*, the nation having come from the *one*, Jacob/Israel.

385 I.e., not LORD, Yahweh, but *adonai*, "Lord."

386 Lit. "his bloods," or "bloodshed"; however, as nuanced in contexts like this "his bloodguiltiness" (cf., e.g., Exod 22:2; Lev 20:9,11,13; Ezek 18:13).

387 Lit. "cause to return, come back"; cf. this word and its boomerang effect in Hos 12:2.

past are presented as parallel to Israel and Judah's present sinful ways. Additionally, the LORD's pursuant mercy shown toward the patriarch serves as a compelling reminder of God's longsuffering with Israel and Judah as well.

The center of this chapter is found in verse 6, "Therefore, return to your God, observe kindness and justice, and wait for your God continually." Though warnings of judgment abound in this passage (vv. 2,9,11,14), an additional motivation for obeying the trio of imperatives "return," "observe," and "wait," is the humbling recollection of the persistent goodness of God in His loving pursuit of a disobedient and deceitful people. The word translated "return" is a word that has been used many times throughout this book. It is the primary Hebrew word for repentance—to "do a 180." At times it describes Israel's sinful turning away from God, and at other times, as in this passage, it is a call to repent, i.e., to return to Yahweh.

The second command, "to observe kindness and justice" is a call to keep/maintain or guard/protect the unconditional love of God which has been the theme of the entire book. It's a call for Israel to shower on others the quality of love which the LORD had lavished on them. Such love in horizontal, human relationships would show itself in just dealings and through interpersonal integrity. The observance of such justice is the polar opposite of the unfair merchant who makes himself rich by unscrupulous dealings with others (vv. 7-8).

The final imperative is a call to wait continually for God. While in English we tend to think of waiting in terms of passively measuring time with clocks and calendars, the Hebrew concept is synonymous with submissive trust and expectant hope *while* one is waiting. As part of their repentance, Israel is being called to *continually* exercise active faith in the character and the veracity of God's Word during any perceived gap between His promises and their fulfillment. These three interrelated commands constitute what should characterize Israel's repentance. This chapter uniquely reaches back into Israel's formative history as the spiritual stimulus for obeying these commands.

MOTIVATING MEMORIES

Recalling the LORD's Remarkable Grace (11:12-12:6)

Hosea's recollection of Jacob's ungodly practice of trickery and conniving should help Israel to see the folly of their own deceptive, scheming political alliances with foreign nations (11:12-12:2). The specific reminder that Jacob was born grasping the heel of his brother Esau was shorthand for Jacob's bribery and deception used to usurp the birthright that rightly belonged to his twin (Gen 25). Jacob's infamous, daring wrestling match with the pre-incarnate Christ is also recalled by Hosea. After this "contest" or "match," the LORD fittingly changed his name to "Israel," which means "one who strives with God" (Gen 32:24ff.). Every time the nation heard themselves addressed as "the sons of Israel," it should have reminded them of their legacy of contention in the very relationships that ought to have been characterized by integrity and love. Seeing their unfortunate similarities to Jacob was intended to induce national humility, contrition, and repentance in Israel.

Fortunately these negative attributes of Jacob are not the sole focus of the similarities between the nation and their forefather. Remembering the LORD's display of faithfulness, even in the wake of Jacob's failures, is an even greater incentive to "return ... observe ... and wait" (v. 6). Though Jacob's devious words and actions made him a cowering fugitive from his family, the LORD graciously "found him at Bethel" (v. 4c). Even while Jacob was sleeping away his fear and shame at Bethel, the LORD pursued him in mercy, assuring Him that the unconditional promises of blessings offered to his father Isaac and his grandfather Abraham were still equally true for him. God's original pledges had not been annulled through Jacob's sin! Surely Jacob was tempted to assume himself forsaken by God. But the LORD specifically assured Jacob, "I am with you and will keep you wherever you go, and will bring you back to this land; for I will not leave you until I have done what I have promised you" (Gen 28:15). God's unexpected mercy shown to Jacob gives Israel hope that if they would return to the LORD, they too would find forgiveness and full restoration.

Recalling the LORD's Powerful Deliverance (vv. 7-9,13)

In the next few verses the LORD indicts Israel of two specific sins: first, the nation's sinful practice of the accumulation of wealth by oppression and second, their unfounded delusion of spiritual innocence (vv. 7-8). As an incentive to repent, God reminds, "But I have been the LORD your God since the land of Egypt" (v. 9a). The recollection of God's active involvement from the very inception of Israel as a nation was intended to bring about repentance from the proud illusion of self-sufficiency. Verse 13 contains a related reminder of God's faithfulness, "But by a prophet the LORD brought Israel from Egypt, and by a prophet he was kept" (v. 13). Specifically remembering the LORD's appointment of Moses as a prophetic leader, the plagues He inflicted upon Egypt, which included the death of all the firstborn of Egypt and the sparing of the Israelites, God's mighty parting of the Red Sea, and His drowning of Pharaoh and his armies were to be seen as motivators of real repentance.

Recalling the LORD's Continual Revelation to Israel (v. 10)

God's people are called to turn from sin to the LORD by remembering His ongoing communication of truth. "I have also spoken to the prophets, and I gave numerous visions, and through the prophets I gave parables" (v. 10). Even words which the LORD spoke directly to Jacob at Bethel were received as truth spoken collectively to the nation. Knowing that the LORD had chosen to make Himself known to His people throughout their history by the oracles delivered through the prophets should have been reason enough for Israel to return to their LORD.

Recalling the LORD's Perfect Providence (v. 12)

Israel is provided additional motivation for obedience in the memorable way in which the LORD ultimately provided Jacob's wife, Rachel. But as we know from Genesis 28-30, God had painful lessons for Jacob to learn before marrying the woman he loved. With tremendous irony, the LORD allows Jacob, the usurper and trickster, to be deceived into marrying the wrong woman by his treacherous Uncle Laban. After agreeing to work an additional seven years, Jacob finally received Rachel as his wife. Recalling the wisdom of God in both the bitter and sweet providences of Jacob's life constrains Israel to trust that the LORD would ultimately bestow the same kind of unmerited kindness that Jacob had received.

The New Testament also speaks of the importance of intentionally bringing to mind the reality of our own Jacob-like depravity and God's persistent, unmerited care. There are grave spiritual dangers in forgetting either truth, since both are catalysts for repentance and change in a believer's life. Jesus warned the church in Ephesus, "Remember from where you have fallen and repent and do the deeds you did at first; or else I am coming to you and will remove your lampstand out if its place—unless you repent" (Rev 2:5). The church in Laodicea is likewise admonished,

> Because you say, "I am rich, and have become wealthy, and have need of nothing," and you do not know that you are wretched and miserable and poor and blind and naked, I advise you to buy from Me gold refined by fire so that you may become rich, and white garments so that you may clothe yourself, and that the shame of your nakedness will not be revealed; and eye salve to anoint your eyes so that you may see. (Rev 3:17-18)

The apostle Peter describes a believer who fails to diligently pursue holy living as being spiritually forgetful. He writes, "For he who lacks these qualities is blind or shortsighted, having forgotten his purification from his former sins" (2 Peter 1:7). None of us as believers can afford to forget the former sinful life from which we have been cleansed. We must never lose sight of who we were when mercy found us—not even for a moment. Rather, we must imitate Paul, who never forgot that he was once a blasphemer, a persecutor, and a violent aggressor who was shown mercy because he acted ignorantly in unbelief (1 Tim 1:13). We can all admit that "we also were once foolish ourselves, disobedient, deceived, enslaved to various lusts and pleasures, spending our life in malice and envy, hateful, hating one another" (Titus 3:3).

Likewise, we must never forget God's mercy and love for the undeserving. Certain truths must never be far from our minds. "But God demonstrates His own love toward us, in that while we were still sinners, Christ died for us" (Rom 5:8). "But God being rich in mercy, because of the great love with which he loved us, even when we were dead in our transgressions, made us alive together with Christ" (Eph 2:4-5). "But when the kindness of God our Savior and His love for mankind appeared, He saved us, not on the basis of deeds which we have done in righteousness, but according to His mercy" (Titus 3:5). Finally, Paul's rhetorical question stands as a warning to us all: "Do you think lightly of the riches of His kindness and tolerance and patience, not knowing that the kindness of God leads you to repentance?" (Rom 2:4).

Hosea's preaching jogged the spiritual memories of Israel, reminding them that however deep the abyss of their national and personal sin, God's love was deeper still.

13 HOSEA 13:1–16

EXPOSITION

(13:1–16) THE LORD AS LOVER RESTORES HIS CRIMINAL PEOPLE (PART 3)

Chapter 13 begins with more evidences concerning the depths of depravity into which Ephraim[388] had sunk and was continuing to sink more deeply. The opening two lines of verse 1 set up the connection between position and pride and the inevitable divine judgment that incurs: "When Ephraim spoke, there was trembling; he was exalted in Israel, but he incurred guilt through Baal and died" (Hos 13:1, ESV). Baal worship[389] was especially abominable to Yahweh, therefore the nation "died." They were in God's book as good as dead, being in gross violation of the covenant (cf., e.g., Deut 30:17-18a). Because of this heinous apostasy, their future captivity was signed and sealed, but yet to be delivered. Like the fulfillment of Habakkuk's vision, the judgment was on the horizon; it would come to pass (see Hab 1:5; 2:2-3).

---

388 There is some ambivalence concerning the designation "Ephraim" at the head of this section. Is it again, according to Hosean precedent, standing for the whole Northern Kingdom, or is it more restrictive, standing for that tribe of the central hill country? Probably the best way to answer this question is to recognize the historical prominence of this tribe (cf., e.g., Num 2:18-24), which led to an intense pride that characterized both it and the whole nation it came to represent.

389 Cf. Hos 2:8; 11:2.

Similar to the phenomenon that the apostle Paul references concerning his day and our day (i.e., 2 Tim 3:13), things in Hosea's day were going from bad to worse: "And now they sin more and more,[390] and make for themselves metal images, idols skillfully made of their silver, all of them the work of craftsmen" (v. 2a,b,c, ESV).[391] All such idol crafting was explicitly prohibited by divine mandate (cf., e.g., Exod 34:17; Lev 19:4; Deut 27:15). The last line of verse 2 is particularly challenging. Literally rendered the Hebrew text reads, "To them they are saying, 'Sacrificers of mankind, calves they will kiss.'" Here are two representative English renderings of verse 2d:[392]

> They say of them, "Let the men who sacrifice kiss the calves!" (NASB).

> It is said of them, "Those who offer human sacrifice kiss calves!" (ESV).

No matter whether the current situation of Hosea's day involved human sacrifices[393] or men who were sacrificing whatever to idols, it was an exceedingly abominable affront to God and deserving of the most severe judgment.

And that judgment is poetically captured by the four similes of verse 3. The common denominator of these comparisons is transience, things that are here today and gone tomorrow, or here now and gone in a moment. Yahweh's judgment of this idolatrous nation would be one of their quick passing from prominence to obscurity in captivity as illustrated by the disappearance of clouds in the morning, of the vanishing

---

390 A good idiomatic rendering of the Hebrew which reads literally, "And now they are adding to sin."

391 V. 2 contains a veritable catalog of Hebrew words and roots pertaining to idolatry.

392 It is not inappropriate to mention again the futility and stupidity of idolatry as it is often cast in the OT (cf., e.g., Hos 8:5-6; Isa 44:9ff.).

393 Note, e.g., Ps 106:37.

of early morning dew under the sun's heat,[394] of chaff driven away by the wind,[395] and of smoke out of a window.

A verbatim echo of Hosea 12:9a[396] is heard loud and clear in 13:4a: "Yet I have been the LORD your God since the land of Egypt" (NASB). Yahweh will disperse them in judgment; nevertheless, He has remained faithful even in the face of their unfaithfulness. This mini-section of Hosea as in the case of multiple sections throughout this book is conspicuously exemplary of the Pauline maxim in 2 Timothy 2:13, "If we are faithless, He remains faithful, for He cannot deny Himself" (NASB). His unflinching loyalty was historically documented in the Exodus event (cf. Exod 20:2).

Because of who Yahweh is and what He has accomplished with great power, "You shall have no[397] other gods before me" (Exod 20:3, ESV). This exclusivity of the one and only true God is borne along in the last two lines of Hosea 12:4 by the words translated "but" or "besides" or "except."[398] There was no other god who made himself known to Israel and was to be known by Israel, especially as a savior. Verses 4b,c,5 are bound together largely by a word play on the verb "to know."[399] God knew His people intimately in elective (cf., e.g., Gen 18:19; Amos 3:2; *et al.*) and protective ways.[400] Yet repeatedly His people did not acknowledge[401] Him.[402]

---

394   Cf. Hos 6:4 on the first two similes, but there applied to the nation's feigned loyalty to covenant.

395   For an application of this judgment on an individual level, remember Ps 1:4.

396   Remember this is 12:10 in Hebrew.

397   In Hebrew this prominent commandment was stated negatively, and those following it might better be rendered as imperatives; cf. "Do not have other gods besides Me" (Exod 20:3, HCSB).

398   Cf. the language of Isa 45:5,21.

399   Cf. the ESV, which retains the Hebrew verb's basic meaning in vv. 4b-5.

400   Note how the NASB and NIV nuance the knowing of v. 5a with caring.

401   Another contextually rendered meaning of the Hebrew verb "to know" as to *recognize* or *acknowledge* (cf., e.g. the Pharaoh of Exod 1:8).

402   Quite obviously, Hos 13:5 (cf. 9:10) refers to Yahweh's protective care during the nation's wilderness wanderings.

The tragic evidence that they did not respond the way they should have is brought forth in verse 6: "According to their pasture they became satisfied; they were satiated and their heart was lifted up; consequently, they forgot Me." The dynamic, more interpretive rendering of the NIV helps to capture the sequence of their sin as it and they plummet downward: "When I fed them, they were satisfied; when they were satisfied, they became proud; then they forgot me." The warnings, even the specific vocabulary of Deuteronomy 8:11-20, rise up to leave them without excuse and in jeopardy of severe punishment. And that is exactly what Yahweh God reveals through Hosea in the two following verses.

Indeed God casts Himself as vicious beasts in verses 7-8.[403] Four more similes[404] return, plus an inferential one in the last line, which characterizes them all as terrorizing, wild animals. The first and the last of these specifically listed wild beasts, i.e., the "lion" (v. 7a) and the devouring "lioness" (v. 8c) need no explanation except that according to subsequent reputation these designations refer to none other than the "king of beasts" (cf. also Hos 5:14). The leopard is characterized as lurking by the wayside in order to pounce upon its prey. The third beast that depicts Yahweh is especially aggressive. It is "a bear robbed of her cubs" (cf., e.g., 2 Sam 17:8; Prov 17:12). Appropriating this imagery, God says that He is going to "tear open the enclosure of their heart."

It is hard to imagine a more contrasting characterization of the LORD God in that Hosea 13:4-6 is immediately followed by verses 7-8. Indeed the protecting Shepherd has become, in judgment, the Predator of His high-handedly disobedient sheep. Yet, once again, what is said in these last two verses does not signal the total extermination of the people. Inexplicably (except for the astounding revelation of Hos 11:8-9), the longsuffering Shepherd will have mercy upon His wayward sheep (cf. esp. 14:4ff.)

Verse 9 seems to function both as an indicting recapitulation of what precedes it and as a preview of more condemning evidences to follow. The

403 In application, explicitly to the Southern Kingdom, cf. Jer 5:6.

404 Cf. Hos 13:3.

text literally reads, "He (or it[405]) has spoiled (or ruined) (or destroyed) you, Israel, that (or because) against Me, against your help." Obviously, in translation, words need to be supplied; compare the NASB: "*It is your destruction, O Israel, that you are against Me, against your help.*" However this verse is rendered, its message is that Yahweh's impending judgment would be their own fault. They had resisted and were resisting their true Helper (cf., e.g., 2 Chron 14:11).

The taunting interrogations of Hosea 13:10 expose the futility of any hope for help outside of Yahweh, the King-Helper-Savior. The monarchy in Hosea's day was in declension and it would finally be cut off when Assyria no longer allowed Israel to have puppet leaders. Therefore, God's tauntings through Hosea were particularly apropos. The first line of verse 10 actually has two terms that pose the piercing question; consequently, it has the force of "Where, O where, is your king ... ?"! Their original hope which was progressively being shown to be false was that a national king would be able to protect all their various cities. Other officials, like "judges" or "rulers" (v. 10c; cf. 7:7) and "princes" (v. 10d) would also show themselves to be impotent in the face of an instrument of international power in the hands of Sovereign Yahweh.[406] That these human officials were what Israel wanted from early on is verified by the reminder of their clamoring cry (cf. Hos 13:10d with 1 Sam 8:4ff.).

Because of that explicit cry for a king and human rulers, which also implicitly constitutes a rejection of King Yahweh, God says in verse 11, "I give you[407] a king in My anger[408] and take away[407] [a king] in My wrath[408] (HCSB). This is the principle of "you want it; you got it" (cf.,

---

405   Some translations accept a first-person singular variant i.e., "I will destroy you." (cf. NIV, HCSB).

406   Remember the exposure of merely human leadership already brought to light in Hos 7:3-7; 8:4; 10:3; etc. Israel throughout its history should have heeded the warnings of passages like Ps 146:3.

407   The verbs are both imperfects and should be considered to have a customary force (i.e., not just in the case of Saul, but throughout the history of Israel's monarchy). Also, on God's sovereignty concerning His giving and taking in general, it is appropriate to remember Job's panoramic perspective in Job 1:21.

408   Notice Yahweh's speaking in wrath to the kings of the earth in Ps 2:5.

once again, God giving sinful people over to what they long for and strive after in Rom 1:24,26,28). But this comes with a solemn reminder of the price tag, the burning wrath of Yahweh. Nevertheless, after the course of the LORD's judgment, He will in the future install and establish His Son in Jerusalem as King over the whole planet (cf. Ps 2:6-9 with Hos 1:11; 3:5).

Verse 12 seems to function as another[409] recapitulation of the nation's cumulative guilt which has brought the people up to the very brink of their day of judgment. Nevertheless more condemning assessments pile on in verses 12 and 13. The parallel assertions of verse 12 indicate that Ephraim's iniquity[410] is wrapped up in a package, and their sin[411] is kept in store ready to be unwrapped and uncovered by God in judgment. The imagery of a past-due birth due to an uncooperative baby escalates the nation's accountability in verse 13. The metaphors of this verse seem to mix especially in reference to the labor pains universally experienced by a mother but here are attributed also to the baby. The dynamic rendering of the NIV seems to capture this facet of Ephraim's culpability: "Pains as of a woman in childbirth come to him, but he is a child without wisdom;[412] when the time arrives, he does not come to the opening of the womb."

The first two lines of verse 14 release another undeserved dose of divine mercy.[413] Although some versions render these lines as questions,[414] that understanding is imposed upon the Hebrew text, which is best rendered, "I will ransom them from the power of Sheol. I will redeem them

---

409 Cf. v. 9.

410 Cf. Hos 4:8; 5:5; 7:1; 8:13; 9:7,9; 12:8; 14:1,2. It is important to note that what they denied in 12:8 is all bundled up and ready to be unwrapped, exposing all its ugliness here in 13:12.

411 Cf. Hos 4:8; 8:13; 9:9; 10:8.

412 Conceptually, cf. the "silly dove without sense" simile in Hos 7:11.

413 Cf., esp., the quintessential mind-blowing reversal in 11:8-9.

414 Cf., e.g., NASB, ESV.

from death" (HCSB).[415] These synonymous lines rival the ones recently observed in verse 12. Here in verse 14 two crucial words for redemption reinforce each other.[416] The first soteric term frequently conveys a ransoming from slavery (note, esp., Deut 7:8),[417] and the second usually brings in the idea that it is a near kinsman who is doing the purchasing (cf., e.g., Ruth 2:20; 3:9,12,13; 4:4,6 with Exod 6:6; 15:13; *et al.*).

The next two lines of verse 14 are cast as questions and are linked to the previous couplet chiastically:

> A Sheol (14a)
>   B death (14b)
>   B' death (14c)
> A' Sheol (14d)

Because the LORD God would *ultimately* redeem His people Israel (cf., e.g., Lev 26:44), Sheol and death are here taunted.[418] However, that gracious, but distant, salvation and restoration (i.e., as will be seen in 14:4ff.) would not cancel the divine judgment that would be coming around the corner. At that time of heavy-duty divine discipline, Yahweh makes this somber announcement, "Compassion[419] is hidden from my eyes" (v. 14e, ESV), i.e., "I will have no compassion" (NIV). Indeed, the next two verses will concentrate on that coming judgment from Yahweh.

---

415 Cf. the NIV: "I will ransom them from the power of the grave; I will redeem them from death." These renderings help better to explain Paul's utilization of the next lines in 1 Cor 15:55.

416 Cf. this pair, e.g., in Jer 31:11.

417 This OT word group paves the way for its counterpart in the NT, which focuses upon the riches of redemption in the Person and work of Christ.

418 For the absolutely final disposal of these threatening things see Rev 20:14; 21:4.

419 This is a new form of a quite common and significant Hebrew root. One of the most characteristic denotations of this root is "relenting, a changing of the mind." Both spheres of usage, "to have compassion" or "pity" and "to relent," when used of God, are most likely anthropopathically freighted. Or, in the short run, God will not change His mind; He will not exercise compassion or comfort while He is meting out their deserved discipline.

The first line of verse 15, complicated by the emendations of the LXX, is quite challenging. However, whether one takes the introductory conjunction as "because" or "since," or better, as "although," the Hebrew text is intelligible, especially in view of subtle contextual and canonical associations. Literally it reads, "Although he—a son of brothers—exhibits fruitfulness— … ."[420] The reference to a "son of brothers" pertaining to Ephraim quite likely refers back to Jacob/Israel's prophetic pronouncements and blessings of the twelve tribes with Joseph's two sons inheriting alongside of their uncles (cf. Gen 49:22-26 with 48:8-22).[421] Therefore, the "he" of verse 15a speaks of "Ephraim" (cf. v. 12) in its more restrictive, tribal sense.[422] Also in the first line of the Hebrew text there is another one of Hosea's puns. The core of the verb meaning "to be fruitful" not only seems to sound like the proper name Ephraim, but this association was also intended when Joseph named his son (as recorded in Gen 41:52).

As already mentioned, the concessive observation of verse 15a, which summarizes the good times of Ephraim, introduces the terrorizing prospect of really bad times on the horizon. Probably with 'intentional irony' in comparison with 12:1a,b, the next line of 13:15 promises that "an east wind will come, the wind of Yahweh." For making covenants with Assyria and Egypt (i.e., 12:1c,d), supposedly but vainly for self-protection, God is going to use Assyria against the Northern Kingdom. The "wind *of* the LORD" makes it clear that this formidable superpower would be God's instrument of discipline (again, cf. Isa 10[423]). This political and military sirocco in the hands of God would desiccate the rebellious nation; Israel's "fountain shall dry up; his spring shall be parched" (v. 15c,d,

---

420 This historical picture of ongoing fruitfulness was one that was soon to change in view of the certainty of coming judgment (cf. a similar setup for an imminent disaster in 13:1a,b).

421 Note even the *déjà-vu* scenario of the second-born being elevated to preeminence by their usurping grandfather!

422 Yet remember this designation most often refers to the whole Northern Kingdom (cf., e.g., the triple parallelism in 7:1).

423 Even in Isa 10, notice that after severe punishment, God, in His mercy, promises a remnant that He would again grow it into a great nation.

ESV). Furthermore, the insatiable instrument "will plunder the treasury of every precious item" (v. 15e, HCSB).

It's hard to imagine a worst case scenario of judgment, but verse 16[424] continues with a summary of Yahweh's primary charge against Israel, followed by the assured coming of the most viciously cruel atrocities known to the ancient Near East. And indeed Assyria was the historical master when it came to employing these military means of conquest. Concerning the perfect divine justice undergirding the activation of those most severe punishments, Yahweh God posts this reminder through Hosea in 13:16a: "The people of Samaria[425] must bear their guilt, because they have rebelled[426] against their God" (v. 16a,b, NIV). Now comes the bloodcurdling revelation of God's impending retribution via voracious Assyria: "They [i.e., the people of the Northern Kingdom] will fall by the sword, Their little ones will be dashed in pieces,[427] And their pregnant women will be ripped open[428]" (v. 16c,d,e, NASB).[429] Although it sounds like total genocide was about to occur, that would not be the case in view of the higher note of revelation found in the last chapter of Hosea.

EXHORTATIONS

As the darkest hours precede the dawn, so this chapter's grim descriptions of Israel's iniquity and God's violent judgments are strategically placed just prior to the hope-filled final chapter of the book. Following a now familiar "crime and punishment" pattern, these verses review the

---

424 I.e., 14:1 in the Hebrew Bible.

425 A metonymy for the whole nation (cf., again, e.g., the parallelisms of 7:1). Also notice this same guilt applied to the whole nation and its people in 5:15; 10:2; 13:1.

426 This verb all too often characterized the gross defiance of the people (cf., e.g., Deut 1:26; 9:23; 31:27; Pss 5:10 [v. 11, Hebrew.]; 78:8,17,40,56; 106:7,43; Isa 63:10; Jer 4:17; 5:23; Ezek 20:8,13,21; etc.).

427 Cf. Hos 10:14; also, Ps 137:9; Isa 13:16; Nah 3:10.

428 Cf. 2 Kgs 15:16.

429 On all three of these horrendous acts of brutality, cf. 2 Kgs 8:12.

anticipated list of Israel's well-attested failures. However, the descriptions of the coming resultant suffering, which have been steadily becoming more graphic since chapter 4, reach their terrifying zenith in these verses. Yet even in the midst of these vivid predictions of His severest judgment, the LORD provides a brief assurance of Israel's final salvation that will be the entire focus of the next chapter.

(13:1–3) THE IDOLATRY OF SELF-WORSHIP

Once again, Israel's invisible, private practice of self-exaltation inevitably led them to visible public involvement in idolatry—another reminder of the inextricable link between self-love and false worship. Behind the thin veneer of gold or silver which covers the face of an idol is the image of the worshipper himself. The Israelites brought costly offerings to the Canaanite deities not out of sincere adoration, but because they craved the prosperity, pleasure, and protection which they "promised"—blessings only the LORD Himself could provide. This combination of pride and idolatry became the portal which led the nation to "sin more and more" (v. 2a). The LORD declares that the consequence of their vain self-glorification would be the loss of their perceived prominence through deportation to Assyria. Israel's so-called stability would be as momentary as a morning cloud and disappearing dew and as unsubstantial as chaff and smoke.

(13:4–8) FORGETTING THE LORD

While the previous chapter emphasized the positive role of spiritual memory in *repenting* from sin, these verses demonstrate the dangerous role of spiritual forgetfulness *leading* to sin. Depicting Himself as a caring, tender shepherd, the LORD exposes Israel's ingratitude for His provision. "As they had their pasture, they became satisfied, and being satisfied, their heart became proud; therefore, they forgot Me" (v. 6). Physical prosperity acts like a spiritual head injury that causes Israel to forget the very existence of the one true God. Earlier in the book the Lord also accused His people of disregarding Him, stating, "I will punish her for the days of the Baals when she used to offer sacrifices to them and adorn herself with earrings and jewelry, and follow her lovers so that *she forgot me*" (2:13, emphasis added). Israel's grotesque practice of enjoying her Shepherd's caring provision and then in turn forgetting Him altogether is sadly true of every fallen man. Paul, the apostle, writes, "For even though they knew God, they did not honor Him as God or give thanks … . [They] exchanged the truth of God for a lie, and worshipped and served the creature, rather than the Creator, who is blessed forever. Amen" (Rom 1:21,25).

In stark contrast, Psalm 119 speaks often of the psalmist's determination to *never* forget God or His words: "I delight in Your statutes; I shall not forget your word" (v. 16). "I have remembered Your ordinances from of old, O LORD, and comfort myself" (v. 49). "O LORD, I will remember Your name in the night, and keep Your law" (v. 55). "Though I have become like a wineskin in the smoke, I do not forget Your statutes" (v. 83). "I will never forget Your precepts, for by them You have revived me" (v. 93). "Look upon my affliction and rescue me, for I do not forget Your law" (v. 153). "I have gone astray like a lost sheep; seek Your servant, for I do not forget Your commandments" (v. 176). As a catalyst for submissive obedience and true faith, all believers must intentionally stimulate and cultivate their spiritual memory banks. Such recollections are strengthened by combining meditation on Scripture with thankful recollection of the unique ways in which the LORD has displayed His faithfulness in their personal lives.

The price that Israel will pay for forgetting God would be severe! The LORD chose four images of ferocious, deadly animals to describe the violent retribution He would bring on those who summarily dismissed Him from their memory. God would punish Israel with the ferocity of a hungry lion, the stealth of a leopard crouching in readiness to attack its prey, the fury a mother bear attacking those who stole her cubs, and with the determination of a lioness ready to devour her prey. The ominous picture of God coming in holy wrath to tear Israel to pieces, ripping open their chests, and devouring them as a meal is truly horrifying! What a contrast to the earlier image of the tender Savior-Shepherd who would provide protection and pasture for His flock!

(13:9–11) REJECTING THE LORD

Having forgotten her LORD, Israel descends yet further into iniquity by rejecting God altogether. "It is your destruction, O Israel, that you are against Me, against your help" (v. 9). The LORD declared that Israel was their own worst enemy. Through their rejection of God, they would bring upon themselves their own calamity. Having been warned by God of the consequences of their sin, when the Assyrian army did finally arrive to plunder the people, they would have no one but themselves to blame.

Who will come to the aid of a people who reject the only source of help? Will help come from an earthly king? Certainly not! The LORD exposes the nation's completely vulnerable position, with these taunting words, "Where now is your king that he may save you in all your cities, and your judges of whom you requested, 'Give me a king and princes'? I gave you your king in My anger, and took him away in my wrath" (vv. 10-11). The nation is forced to recall that their original request for an earthly king was the result of rejecting the LORD as their divine ruler (1 Sam 8:5-6). Having rejected their divine king, Israel now finds themselves without an earthly king as well. They will have to face the tsunami of violence at the hand of the Assyrians, completely defenseless and exposed.

(13:12–14) PRIZING THE PRACTICE OF SIN

While the LORD's people have jettisoned their God, they certainly have not parted with their sin. Rather than abandoning their morally evil perversions in repentance or seeking to have their iniquity lifted off their shoulders through forgiveness, Israel carefully wraps up their iniquity in order to guard and protect it as one would a treasured possession (v. 12). Earlier Israel is described as "directing their desire toward their iniquity" (4:8). Israel's value system is so twisted that they guard as precious that which the LORD refers to as grotesque (9:7).

This warped sense of right and wrong is further reflected in the LORD's concise understatement concerning Israel that "He is not a wise son" (v. 13). The wisdom that will be commended as the only hope of escaping calamity in the final verse of this book is completely lacking in His chosen people. Similar indictments of distorted spiritual perception are leveled throughout the book: "So Ephraim has become like a silly dove, without sense" (7:11). "Harlotry, wine and new wine take away the understanding" (4:11). "So the people without understanding are ruined" (4:14).

Rather than recording the commensurate justice that typically follows the LORD's charges against His people, the LORD rather shockingly expresses a compassionate desire to ransom and redeem Israel from the enslaving power of death and the grave (v. 14). The concept of ransom emphasizes the payment price involved in purchasing freedom for a slave. Redemption alludes to God's intention to assume the role of a kinsman-redeemer demonstrating loyalty to a family member who is in distress. Seeing their plight, a loving kinsman-redeemer assumes the responsibility to provide whatever their relative may need.

In inexplicable mercy, the LORD assures His people that He will both pay the ransom price and come to their aid with the love and loyalty of a close family member. Further, with rhetorical questions, He mocks death's power to ultimately defeat His people: "O Death, where are your thorns? O Sheol, where is your sting?" (v. 14). Though Israel would be animalistically slaughtered by the Assyrian forces, the LORD's benevolent desire to purchase His people back from death and the grave is more than merely a spiritual metaphor. As has been noted before, the announcement of ultimate liberation from death does not revoke the prophecies of the coming enemy invasion with all of its cruelty, but rather assures that Israel will not be completely wiped from the face of the earth.

(13:15–16) REBELLING AGAINST THE LORD

Closely related to Israel's sinful rejection of God was their willful rebellion against Him. This sin is often spoken of in relationship to commandments from the LORD and as a result, is sometimes translated "disobedience." Sadly, such flagrant disregard for the LORD and His Word had always characterized the people of God, "You have been rebellious against the LORD from the day I knew you" (Deut 9:24). The 40 years between the Exodus from Egypt and entering the Promised Land were filled with rebellion. Asaph describes Israel during this period as:

> A stubborn and rebellious generation, a generation that did not prepare its heart and whose spirit was not faithful to God.... They still continued to sin against Him, to rebel against the Most High in the desert.... How often they rebelled against Him in the wilderness and grieved Him in the desert! ... They tempted and rebelled against the Most High God and did not keep His testimonies. (Ps 78:8,17,40,56; cf. Num 20:10,24)

The judgments which the LORD describes would be the result of such patterned rebellion, and they are certainly the severest in the entire book. Following the Assyrians' plunder of Israel's treasury of material goods, there would be the greater loss of human life. The predicted cruel murder of children and the vicious slaughter of expectant mothers by the sword would prove that the earlier imagery of an overpowering beast ripping open its victims was more than a mere metaphor.

The reluctance of our hearts to embrace the wrath of God expressed in such intensely violent terms exposes an anemic understanding of the nature of God's holy hatred of all that is evil. We must come to grips with the reality that God cannot be trifled with. It is no small thing to sin against a holy God. Those who ignore His call to repent with warnings of judgment do so to their own peril.

14 HOSEA 14:1–9

EXPOSITION

(14:1–9) HOPE ARISES FROM THE INEXPLICABLE MERCY OF THE LORD

Chapter 14 launches with a passionate plea urging the nation[430] to repent in contrast with the pseudo-repentance of ch. 6.[431] The legitimacy of Hosea's plea[432] is quite obviously, but not presumptuously, built upon his understanding of the longsuffering attributes of his God (cf. Exod 33:19; 34:5-6). His invitation to Israel is therefore to "return[433] to" Yahweh their God. It is interesting that the preposition that follows the command is not the usual directional one that would point in God's direction (cf., v. 2a), but one that normally stresses arrival or contact. The idea seems to be 'Please come all the way home to God.' The nation's desperate need for true repentance is given in verse 1b. This statement could be looked

---

430 The command, another verb, and the pronouns are all singular in v. 1 referring to Israel as an entity. They will switch to plurals in v. 2, putting all its people individually under the spotlight.

431 Compare the opening verses of ch. 6.

432 Exhortations to repent constitute the main burden of all the prophets (cf. 2 Kgs 17:13).

433 Some consider the form of this imperative to be emphatic. Also, just a reminder that this particular Hebrew root occurs with various nuances in translation 22 times throughout Hosea.

upon as a recapitulation of all previous indictments: "for you have stumbled in (or because of) your iniquity" (cf. esp. 4:5; 5:5).

Hosea, in verses 2 and 3, even coaches the people as to what they should say when they approach the LORD. Respectively, the content of these two verses comes in the form of affirmation and denial. Concerning the prophet's instruction in verse 2, he says, "Take with you words and return to Yahweh; say to Him, 'Forgive all iniquity,[434] and take (or receive) (or accept) good,[435] and (or then) we will offer (or present) bulls (of) our lips.'" Lines 2, 3, and 4 of verse 2 stretch the translator and interpreter. Of these three, line 2 is the easiest, once it is admitted that this truly is one of those quite rare occurrences of a broken construct chain.[436] The third line most likely ties back into the covenant stipulation of Deuteronomy 6:18,[437] which the people had previously flouted, but now in true repentance would wish to evidence by backing up their words with their lives.

If God would graciously receive this as evidence of a genuine 180-degree return to Himself, then a further expression of gratitude

---

434 Literally, "all—may You lift up—iniquity" (most likely a rare, broken construct chain). A few however have taken the adjective "all" adverbially (e.g., "altogether forgive iniquity"), but this option is not very viable.

435 Although this is the same imperative which stood at the head of this verse, its meaning would be ambivalent in this small clause. Hosea's instructions might have continued herein by employing the statistically majority meaning of this Hebrew verb, "to take along with, take in hand," etc., and/or the minority meaning of "receive, accept," etc. and/or, as an aside, these observations could possibly contribute to the different views of Paul's utilization of Ps 68:18 in Eph 4:8.

436 Cf. note 434.

437 "You shall do what is right and good [i.e., the key word "good" in Hos 14:2c] in the sight of the LORD, that it may be well [i.e., the same key word] with you and that you may go in and possess the good [i.e., a third occurrence] land which the LORD swore to give your fathers" (Deut 6:18, NASB). Both sides of the coin are likely represented here also. Hosea is probably saying, 'Take along with you good (i.e., your hearts broken in genuine confession and repentance) and (or then) accept (or receive) the merciful forgiveness of God.'

would come through 'bulls of praise' from the people's lips.[438] The constituents of genuine confession, God's acceptance, and grateful praise evidenced in Hosea 14:2 can also be observed in penitent David's testimony in Psalm 51, esp. vv. 14-17.

A significant dimension of their repentant confession is the absolute denial of all they had previously trusted in outside of the one true God. The confession of verse 3 makes it clear that they would come to recognize that alliances, armies, and false gods were not only vain but that their confidence in them was an abominable affront to Yahweh, their God. The political and military feature of their confession is contained in the first two lines of verse 3: "Assyria will not save us,[439] we will not ride on horses"[440] (v. 3a,b, NASB). Something even more heinous from this track record follows, prompting them to affirm, "And we will say no more 'Our God,' to the work of our hands" (v. 3c, ESV).[441] The very last line of verse 3 provides an illustration of the ultimate ground of God's pardoning acceptance, "In You the orphan finds compassion."[442] Yahweh was ever and always known as exercising His tender loving care[443] toward the fatherless and widows (cf., e.g., Deut 10:18). Much like the prodigal son of Luke 15:11-32, the prodigal nation of Hosea's day had cut themselves off from their Father. Yet there is hope, so Hosea pours out his heart by pointing out the only pathway that would lead them Home.

Also, just as in the parable about the prodigal son, the Father will be waiting with open arms to pardon and restore His "son," the sinful

---

438 This line exhibits a well-known variant in the LXX, i.e., "fruit of lips" (cf. also the allusion to this phrase as found in Hebrews 13:15: "Through Him then, let us continually offer up a sacrifice of praise to God, that is, the fruit of lips that give thanks to His name" (NASB). God is ever and always pleased with this kind of sacrifice (cf. Pss 50:13-14; 69:30-31).

439 Contra 12:1e.

440 Remember again the words of Isa 31:1,3.

441 Contra 13:2, *et al.*

442 The Hebrew text begins with a relative pronoun that is best left untranslated.

443 This divine TLC captures the essence of this exceedingly important Hebrew root for mercy or compassion (remember 1:6-7 where it was denied because of sin).

nation (cf. 11:1). This is the nature of the final 'chapter' of this grand book. Yahweh Himself is speaking in verse 4 and following. He begins by declaring what He was going to do and what He would be like in response to true repentance: "I will heal[444] their defection (or apostasy);[445] I will love[446] them freely (or voluntarily),[447] because My anger has turned (or is turning[448]) away from him;[449] I will be like the dew to Israel" (vv. 4-5a). Indeed, their highly intentional apostasy (cf. 11:7) would be cured *only* by the initiation of a divine healing.[450] Truly, Yahweh's love for them would be unlike the love that they had historically endeavored to purchase (cf. 8:9); His would be freely bestowed from His heart. Also, unlike the loyalty of His people depicted as quickly evaporating dew (cf. 6:4; 13:3), Yahweh's would lavishly blanket this land, lending to great productivity[451] as will be evidenced in verses 5b-7. However, before commenting on those blessings of productivity, a word needs to be said about the reason undergirding the pledges of the LORD to heal, to love, and to be like dew. Does the assuaging of His anger mean that there would be no forthcoming judgment as promised and predicted? Once again, we must note that Assyria would come as God's disciplinary rod, and it

444 I.e., the normal Hebrew word for healing in its various dimensions (cf. in Hos 5:13; 6:1; 7:1; 11:3; also cf., e.g., Deut 32:39; 2 Kgs 20:8; 2 Chron 30:20; Isa 53:5; Jer 3:22; 17:14; 30:17; 33:6).

445 I.e., a noun introducing another word play based upon the Hebrew root related to turning to, turning away from (cf. esp. 11:7), returning, repentance, etc.

446 Cf. God's previously demonstrated love in the context of covenant commitment; e.g., in Deut 4:37; 7:13; 23:5 [v. 6, Hebrew].

447 This noun, functioning adverbially here, was often used for the free-will offerings of the OT. His love will be exercised without compulsion just like the Bible says about His grace and mercy.

448 The word play of vv. 1a and 4a *returns* (pun intended). Also, this verbal form of the Hebrew root could be taken as a perfect or a participle.

449 I.e., a singular pronoun likely bouncing back to the nation (cf. "Israel" in the next line); however, here it is most frequently rendered "them," i.e., representing the people who constitute the nation.

450 Assyria would turn out to be an ineffectual physician (cf. again, Hos 5:13).

451 Recall Isaac's blessing of Jacob/Israel in Gen 27:28.

did come against Hosea's generation. However, the actualization of the beneficent promises yet lies in the future, and it would coordinate with a true repentance on the part of the people. This mind-blowing reversal tension that has recurred several times throughout the book[452] probably stands behind the rendering of verse 4c in HCSB as "for My anger *will have turned* from him" (emphasis added).

At a future time of repentance, reconciliation and restoration of these sample blessings of an agrarian nature will become glorious realizations. The threefold reference to Lebanon in verses 5-7 illustrates the richness of these gracious, future blessings from Yahweh.[453] Verse 5b affirms that Israel "will bud (or sprout) (or blossom) like a lily." The verb of verse 5c is a little harder to handle. Literally it reads, "And he [i.e., Israel] will strike his roots[454] like Lebanon." This is probably appropriately understood and rendered, "And take root like [the cedars of] Lebanon" (v. 5c, HCSB). The next stages of growth are poetically designed to appeal to the senses of sight and smell.

First, it is said of Israel, being depicted as a maturing plant or tree, "His young shoots (or branches) shall spread" (v. 6a). Next comes an affirmation of its beauty, "And its [i.e., his = Israel] splendor (or majesty) shall be like the olive tree" (v. 6b). "Splendor" or "majesty" is a word used in other settings for the greatness of kings[455] and even for the King of kings, Yahweh Himself.[456] The simile of the olive tree is especially significant. Its agricultural importance in the ANE extended far beyond a food source; its oil was used for anointing and for the lamps that provided light. However, its symbolism conveyed great blessing. For example, when the nation was called by the LORD God, it was depicted

---

452 Cf., esp., 11:8-9 in its setting.

453 There are 71 references to Lebanon in the OT, and the overwhelming majority of them emphasize the abundance and beauty of the natural resources that that region was noted for.

454 Conceptually, cf. the shooting forth of roots in the tree imagery of Jer 17:8, and its consequent productivity.

455 Cf. 1 Chron 29:25.

456 Cf. 1 Chron 16:27; 29:11.

as "a green olive tree" (Jer 11:16a,17a); nevertheless, because of their subsequent rebellions, God would bring chastening judgments upon them
(cf. the rest of Jer 11:16-17 along with Hosea, *passim*). However, based
upon God's faithfulness to His promises, beyond severe discipline would
be a final time of great exaltation and blessing.[457] At that time Israel's
"fragrance" shall be like "Lebanon," i.e., "like [the forest of] Lebanon"
(v. 6c, HCSB).

In verse 7 the imagery shifts to the people who would dwell under
this restored tree-nation. The first line presents a bit of a textual and
translational challenge as reflected by the following renderings:

> "Those who live in his shadow will again raise grain" (v.
> 7a,b, NASB).

> "They shall return and dwell beneath my[458] shadow" (v.
> 7a, ESV).

> "Men will dwell again in his shade" (v. 7a, NIV).

> "The people will return and live beneath his shade" (v.
> 7a, HCSB).

Yet, the Hebrew text rendered literally[459] makes perfectly good sense:
"They will return dwelling in his [i.e., its = Israel's] shade." All the returning inhabitants will dwell safely in this divinely restored nation. In such a
protected state of existence, "They will cause grain to grow" (v. 7b).[460] In
verse 7c the people are pictured via another simile of productivity applied

---

457 The fulfillment of this promise is still awaiting the time when the "natural branches" will be
     grafted back in to "their own olive tree" (see Rom 11:17-24). This will come about at the
     second coming of Christ when in repentance they will confess Him as their Messiah-Savior
     (cf. Rom 11:25-29; Zech 12:10; *et al.*).

458 Assuming a variant of a first-person singular pronominal suffix instead of the third-person
     singular pronominal suffix of the printed text.

459 However, not taking the participle substantively but adverbially.

460 Another literal rendering of the Hebrew text.

directly to them: "And they will blossom like the vine" (v. 7c, NASB). Finally, returning to a panoramic portrayal of the blessed nation, v. 7d affirms that "his renown[461] will be like the wine of Lebanon."

The background of the probing question standing at the head of verse 8 is to be noted in Yahweh's multiple warnings against any and all forms of idolatry. It is especially fitting in the total context of Hosea in view of such exposures as chapter 4, verse 17a. Therefore, the LORD confronts the disloyal nation with this barb: "Ephraim, what have I ever[462] had to do with idols?"! Contrastingly, He affirms what should have been obvious to His people: "I[463] have answered and have regarded[464] him[465]" (v. 8b). Historically, God's faithfulness was incontestable, and that reality continues. Yahweh next depicts Himself as a stately tree, saying, "I am like a luxuriant cypress" (v. 8c, NASB). The picture is one of an exceedingly noble evergreen. The LORD also informs the nation that "from Me your fruit is found" (v. 8d), i.e., "your fruit comes from Me" (HCSB). Productivity was not attained from themselves but was generated by God Himself. This truth pervades the Scriptures and reaches a climax in Christ's parable of the vine and the branches (John 15:1-11).

The prophet having faithfully lived out (chs. 1-3), and having carefully delivered his oracles from God (chs. 4-14), now throws down before his wayward audience a gauntlet in the concluding verse of the book. It is

---

461 The noun most frequently means remembrance or memorial. It was employed for God's memorial name (Exod 3:15; cf. Hos 12:5 [v. 6, Hebrew]). Here in Hos 14:7 Israel, by implication, will experience an exalted reputation, having been reconciled with the only true God, whose memorial name is Yahweh.

462 In this immediate context, containing an idiom of non-association, this adverb, which sometimes carries with it an emphasis of continuance, seems to reinforce the LORD's point that He has *never* had any connection with idols. This would of course pertain to any form of syncretism.

463 An emphatic "I"; most versions read, "It is I who ...".

464 This verb could be rendered in context "to look out for," "to watch over," "to care for," etc. Possibly Hosea used this rarer verb instead of one that would explicitly carry with it a watch-care emphasis because it sounded like the word for Assyria (remember esp. the condemnatory statements in 7:11; 8:9).

465 Some versions emend the "him" to "you."

not one without weighty biblical precedent.[466] He begins his pointed challenge with probing solicitations for biblical wisdom: "Whoever is wise,[467] let him discern[468] these things; whoever is discerning let him know[469] them" (v. 9a,b). These responses are solidly grounded on theology proper (i.e., v. 9c). According to His perfect Person as revealed through His perfect operations,[470] Yahweh God will evaluate and differentiate between those who live righteously and those who live rebelliously.[471]

With these preliminary comments, it is time to allow the burdened Hosea to speak to his nation and to all of us in the 21st century. We need to hear, discern, and respond to what he says: "for the ways of the LORD are right, and the righteous walk in them, but the rebellious stumble[472] in them" (v. 9c,d,e, HCSB). This prophetic epitaph, like Psalm 1, verse 6, is an axiomatic truth that never loses historical relevance!

EXHORTATIONS

In this unforgettable concluding chapter, the LORD graciously initiates another call for Israel to return home to Himself. Through the prophet, the LORD even provides a clear explanation of the very thoughts and words that would lead to real and lasting reconciliation. This final plea

---

466   Cf. some various forms of it, e.g., in Ps 107:43; Jer 9:12; Matt 11:15; 13:9,14-16,43b; Luke 14:35b; James 3:13a; Rev 2:7,11,17,29; 3:6,13,22; 13:9.

467   Contra Ephraim as an unwise son in 13:13.

468   Contra this people without spiritual discernment in 4:14.

469   I.e., acknowledge them and appropriately respond to them in repentance.

470   We need to remember the transcendent nature of His ways (e.g. Isa 55:8-9), yet He is the perfect norm by which men will be judged (cf. Isa 55:7).

471   That His people had been stumbling was an incontestable fact (cf. Hos 14:1). This tendency on the part of the nation would heart-breakingly characterize the masses of Israel for millennia to come, esp. at the first arrival of their Messiah (cf. 1 Peter 2:7-8 with its sobering OT background). Yet there remains a future time guaranteed by God's gracious promises when masses of the ethnic and spiritual seed of Abraham would come to faith in Christ (1 Peter 2:6; Rom 11; etc.).

472   Cf. Hos 14:1b.

for repentance is followed by beautifully poetic descriptions of how the nation will thrive under the glorious blessings that the LORD will lavish on His penitent people. Reading the closing portion of Hosea brings a sense of relief and comfort. Relief comes from learning that stubborn Israel will eventually repent of their relentless disobedience and follow their God. Tremendous comfort is derived as the LORD willingly bestows grace, mercy, and forgiveness upon a people who have been so treacherously unfaithful to Him.

The first word of the chapter is "return," a verb used frequently by Hosea as a synonym for "repent." The same command is used in an almost identical context in chapter 12, "Therefore return to your God, observe kindness and justice, and wait for your God continually" (v. 6). Throughout the book, not only is Israel described as unwilling and unable to return to the LORD, they are also depicted as unwavering in their determination to turn *away* from Him (5:4; 7:10; 11:5,7). In many ways this last chapter functions as the corrective counterpart to chapter 6 in which Israel offered an insincere attempt at repentance which was rejected by the LORD (vv. 1-6). But here at the very culmination of the book, there is hope that the nation will finally heed the call for humble contrition, genuine confession, and submissive turning toward the LORD in the pattern of real repentance provided by Hosea.

(14:1–3) THE MARKS OF TRUE REPENTANCE

Sober Perception of Sin

Having urged God's people to repent, Hosea now provides them with an important motivation, "For you have stumbled because of your iniquity" (v. 1). The Hebrew concept of stumbling is not like the English idea of a clumsily tripping over a crack in the sidewalk and quickly recovering one's balance. Rather, Israel's iniquity has caused them to totter on the brink of destruction; their stumbling put them at risk of falling into utter ruin. Israel's perpetual iniquity had spiritually fatal consequences—real and present danger. Combining penitence with urgency, a truly repentant heart recognizes the mortal hazards in delayed obedience to the revealed will of God.

Contrite Admission of Sin

Motivated by the peril caused by their iniquity, Israel is now instructed to speak to the LORD in prayer about their need for the LORD to "take away all iniquity" (v. 2b). Integral to Israel coming home to God would be the recognition that they were sinful people who desperately needed the LORD to forgive (lit. take away or carry/lift off) their sin. The confession and renunciation of specific sins will follow, but Israel's contrition must begin with a comprehensive admission of their primary need of pardon for all their sins.

Humble Request for God's Grace

Hosea adds further content to Israel's long overdue penitential prayer with the words, "Receive us graciously" (v. 2c). The nation is instructed to approach the LORD with the humble admission that His gracious nature was their only hope that He would ever receive them back to Himself. While Israel's earlier feigned repentance *presumed* that the grace of God was something to which they were entitled (6:1-2), they now are instructed to *entreat* the LORD for His undeserved favor. All who truly repent are deeply convinced that they have no right to claim or demand that for which they have the greatest need, the grace of God.

Specific Renunciation of Sin

Having broadly acknowledged their guilt and need of grace, Israel is next urged to confess and renounce two specific sins, namely, their false trust in the surrounding pagan nations and the false worship of their self-made idols (v. 3). The exposure of these two sinful practices has dominated virtually every page of Hosea's oracles. Real repentance would require Israel to forsake their pattern of seeking refuge in Assyrian soldiers and Egyptian horses. Likewise the nation must abandon the perpetual creation of false gods to which they wrongly attributed the works of God.

The LORD had threatened that He would withdraw from them "until they acknowledge their guilt and seek My face" (5:15). Now Hosea recapitulates those same themes which are integral to Israel's return to the LORD: the absolute necessity of a thorough admission of personal guilt and an intense seeking of the face of God.

Grateful Confidence in God's Mercy

Hosea ends his instruction on the content of penitent prayer by encouraging Israel to express to the LORD their confidence in His mercy. Despite the depth and longevity of their sin, Israel is encouraged not to doubt God's tender love for them. As Israel in humble repentance perceives themselves to be as spiritually vulnerable and destitute as a pathetic orphan, they would receive the same deep pity which the LORD bestows. But Israel was not like the fatherless waif who suffered through no fault of his own. They had brought trouble on themselves through their continual spurning of the LORD's prophetic messages and longsuffering kindness. As John Newton once wrote, "The exceeding sinfulness of sin is manifested, not so much by its breaking through the restraint of threatenings and commands, as by its being capable of acting against light and against love" (The Works of John Newton, Vol. 1, p. 135). A vital part of Israel's repentance would be a deep conviction that the warm mercy of God is granted not because of any innate worth of the recipient. But rather, God generously bestows His mercy based purely upon His sovereign purposes: "I will show compassion on whom I will show compassion" (Exod 33:19). Genuine repentance possesses not only a deep conviction of God's *ability* to show mercy, but believes equally in His *willingness* to forgive those who repent!

(14:4–8) THE RECEPTION OF TRUE REPENTANCE

In contrast to the LORD's exasperated rejection of Israel's earlier quasi-repentance (6:1-6), in these closing verses of the book, God assures Israel that when they offer Him authentic repentance, it will indeed be fully accepted. With idyllic poetic imagery, the LORD describes Israel's flour-ishing in their future final restoration.

Gracious Assurances

The LORD begins these heartening verses with the assurance that when Israel follows the pattern of confession and repentance outlined by Hosea, their relationship with Him will be fully reconciled. First, the LORD offers the assurance that "I will heal their apostasy" (v. 4a). By God's curative power, Israel's chronic case of spiritual defection would be completely eradicated. Additionally, the LORD reassures, "I will love them freely" (v. 4b). The pledge of faithful love harkens back to the earliest chapters of the book in which Hosea is commanded to love an adulterous woman as a portrait of the LORD's faithful love for Israel even though they are guilty of flagrant spiritual harlotry (1:2; 3:1). The LORD's final consolation, "For My anger has turned away from them" (v. 4c), must have brought great comfort since Israel had heard Hosea's unambiguous forewarnings regarding the intensity of the LORD's wrath (5:10; 8:5; 13:11).

Magnificent Promises

In the concluding lines of the book, Israel's future prosperity is poetically described in terms of flourishing plant life. While elsewhere in Hosea agrarian imagery is at times used to depict Israel's sin or God's judgment (2:3,12; 9:10; 10:1), in this passage the lush images serve as a reversal of a previous negative picture. In the opening metaphor, Israel is a beautiful lily, and the LORD is the refreshing morning dew on her blooms. In an arid climate like Palestine, moisture is the key to survival. At one time Israel had arrogantly presumed on God's provision saying, "He will come to us like the rain, like the spring rain watering the earth" (6:3). Now the LORD pledges to attentively supply everything that His people will need to thrive and grow.

The next metaphor of a well-rooted cedar tree pictures Israel as estab-lished and stable. The cedars of Lebanon were as renowned in ancient

Israel for their monumental size as the giant redwoods and sequoias of California are today. The LORD promises Israel that one day they will be as permanent and unmovable as those mighty trees. The LORD will also ensure Israel's prosperity and fruitfulness, as "His shoots will sprout" (v. 6a). Further, the people of God will be blessed with the majestic splendor associated with the olive tree—highly prized because of the part it played in Israel's diet, medicinal anointing, and as fuel for household lamps. Israel will also possess the pleasing aroma of a forest of cedar trees (v. 6c). This may be a reference to Israel's acclaimed reputation or desirability among the nations, not unlike the prediction of Israel's renown in the following verse. With the LORD's promise to prosper Israel's fields and vineyards, the language has moved from metaphor to reality (v. 7).

Though these promises refer ultimately to a time of repentance, reconciliation, and restoration in Israel's future, they surely would have served to allay any lingering fears about whether or not the LORD would receive any Israelite who returned to Him in humble contrition. They also remind believers today that through Christ we may "draw near with confidence to the throne of grace, so that we may receive mercy and find grace to help in time of need" (Heb 4:16).

Final Appeal

Recognizing that Israel's wholesale repentance and restoration still lie in her future, the LORD makes a final plea for His people to exercise spiritual fidelity in the present. God's pathos-filled rhetorical question, "O Ephraim, what more have I to do with idols?" (v. 8a), functions more like a command for Israel to permanently renounce their adulterous syncretism. In essence the LORD demands, "Since I have never had anything to do with idols, you must never again have anything to do with them either!" The LORD's question echoes a similar previous promise, "For I will remove the names of the Baals from her mouth, so that they will be mentioned by their names no more" (2:17).

Knowing that the lure of idolatry was based on the bogus belief that false gods were the real source of the blessings that the worshipper sought, the LORD reminds His people that "It is I who answer and look after you, I am like a luxuriant cypress; from Me comes your fruit" (v. 8). The LORD had offered similar clarifications before: "It was I who gave her the grain, the new wine, and the oil, and lavished on her silver and gold" (2:8);"Yet it is I who taught Ephraim to walk, I took them in my arms; but they did not know that it was I who healed them" (v. 11:3). By likening Himself to an evergreen cypress, the LORD reminds Israel of His endless ability to supply the needs of His people. A deep faith in God's claim that He is the exclusive source of Israel's "fruit" would strengthen their resolve against the pursuit of all idolatry.

(14:9) EPILOGUE

With prophetic gravitas, Hosea's final words call the wise and discerning among Israel to diligently consider these oracles in order to clearly perceive their messages of warning and hope. The reason for Hosea's authoritative call to pore over the words of these prophecies is because "the ways of the LORD are right" (v. 9c). The central message of this book, and the heart of this brief epilogue, is that God is utterly righteous and just in all that He does. This particular context places an emphasis on the rightness of God's dealings with treacherous Israel. The LORD's longsuffering compassion, His severe chastisements, and His restoring love for His people are all perfectly righteous.

To conclude, the book Hosea draws a clear distinction between the way that the righteous man and the transgressor react to the declaration of God's flawless justice. Those whose hearts have been made righteous will submissively walk in the LORD's righteous path and seek to imitate His just dealings with others. But those whose hearts remain defiant and rebellious will fatally stumble into calamity over the LORD's perfectly righteous road. The reappearance of the word "stumble," which first appeared in the first verse of this chapter, "You have stumbled because of your iniquity," forms a bookend which brings this otherwise hopeful chapter to its sober conclusion. The idea of unbelievers stumbling over the LORD's holy character was also addressed by the prophet Isaiah (Isa 8:14-15). The apostle Peter took those words from Isaiah and used them to describe Christ as "a stone of stumbling and a rock of offense" (1 Peter

2:8). There remains today only two ways of responding to the message of Hosea. To remain a stubborn rebel is to choose to bear the eternal fury of God's wrath. But to humbly repent of your sins and trust Christ to absorb the wrath of God in your place is to know the astounding grace of God.